Practical System Programming for Rust Developers

Build fast and secure software for Linux/Unix systems with the help of practical examples

Prabhu Eshwarla

BIRMINGHAM—MUMBAI

Practical System Programming for Rust Developers

Copyright © 2020 Packt Publishing

Group Product Manager: Aaron Lazar
Publishing Product Manager: Richa Tripathi
Senior Editor: Nitee Shetty
Content Development Editor: Ruvika Rao
Technical Editor: Gaurav Gala
Copy Editor: Safis Editing
Project Coordinator: Francy Puthiry
Proofreader: Safis Editing
Indexer: Priyanka Dhadke
Production Designer: Nilesh Mohite

First published: December 2020

Production reference: 1231220

Published by Packt Publishing Ltd.
Livery Place
35 Livery Street
Birmingham
B3 2PB, UK.

ISBN 978-1-80056-096-3

www.packt.com

First and foremost, I'd like to thank my spiritual master, Sri Ganapathy Sachchidananda Swamiji, to whom I owe everything. He has instilled clear values in me and shown me the right attitude and purpose in life.

I wish to thank my parents for their unconditional love, the right guidance, and for standing by me at all times.

My source of strength comes from my loving wife and children—Parimala, Adithya, and Deekshita—without whose constant encouragement and support I would not have had the courage to write this book and persevere to complete it.

`Packt.com`

Subscribe to our online digital library for full access to over 7,000 books and videos, as well as industry leading tools to help you plan your personal development and advance your career. For more information, please visit our website.

Why subscribe?

- Spend less time learning and more time coding with practical eBooks and Videos from over 4,000 industry professionals
- Improve your learning with Skill Plans built especially for you
- Get a free eBook or video every month
- Fully searchable for easy access to vital information
- Copy and paste, print, and bookmark content

Did you know that Packt offers eBook versions of every book published, with PDF and ePub files available? You can upgrade to the eBook version at `packt.com` and as a print book customer, you are entitled to a discount on the eBook copy. Get in touch with us at `customercare@packtpub.com` for more details.

At `www.packt.com`, you can also read a collection of free technical articles, sign up for a range of free newsletters, and receive exclusive discounts and offers on Packt books and eBooks.

Contributors

About the author

Prabhu Eshwarla has been shipping high-quality, business-critical software to large enterprises and running IT operations for over 25 years. He is also a passionate teacher of complex technologies.

Prabhu has worked with Hewlett Packard and has deep experience in software engineering, engineering management, and IT operations.

Prabhu is passionate about Rust and blockchain and specializes in distributed systems. He considers coding to be a creative craft, and an excellent tool to create new digital worlds (and experiences) sustained through rigorous software engineering.

I'd like to thank the technical reviewer, Roman Krasiuk, whose meticulous reviews of the manuscript and code examples, and good understanding of the subject domain, have enhanced the technical quality of the book.

Last but not least, my sincere thanks to Packt for publishing this book, and specifically to the following people, without whom this book would not have been possible: Karan Gupta, for convincing me to write the book; Richa Tripathi, for providing market insights; Nitee Shetty, Ruvika Rao, and Prajakta Naik, for tirelessly working with me to improve the drafts; Francy Puthiry, for keeping me on schedule; Gaurav Gala, for the verification and packaging of code; and the others on the Packt team involved in copy editing, proofreading, publishing, and marketing the book.

About the reviewer

Roman Krasiuk is an R&D software engineer who has worked on industry-leading products in trading, blockchain, and energy markets. Having started his professional career at the age of 18, he loves to dispel the myth that young people cannot occupy lead roles.

His areas of expertise include large-scale infrastructure development, the automation of financial services, and big data engineering. Roman is a believer that coding is a form of art and his biggest desire is to create a masterpiece that will show people just how gorgeous code can be.

I would like to thank Daniel Durante for cultivating my love for Rust, Jonas Frost for teaching me code discipline, and Alex Do for showing that one person can have limitless knowledge. Special thanks to Alex Steiner for opening the door to the land of opportunities and unveiling the power of hard work.

Packt is searching for authors like you

If you're interested in becoming an author for Packt, please visit `authors.packtpub.com` and apply today. We have worked with thousands of developers and tech professionals, just like you, to help them share their insight with the global tech community. You can make a general application, apply for a specific hot topic that we are recruiting an author for, or submit your own idea.

Table of Contents

2

A Tour of the Rust Programming Language

3

Introduction to the Rust Standard Library

4

Managing Environment, Command Line, and Time

Section 2: Managing and Controlling System Resources in Rust

5

Memory Management in Rust

6

Working with Files and Directories in Rust

7

Implementing Terminal I/O in Rust

8
Working with Processes and Signals

9
Managing Concurrency

Section 3: Advanced Topics

10
Working with Device I/O

11
Learning Network Programming

12
Writing Unsafe Rust and FFI

Other Books You May Enjoy

Index

Preface

The modern software stack is evolving rapidly in size and complexity. Technology domains such as the cloud, the web, data science, machine learning, DevOps, containers, IoT, embedded systems, distributed ledgers, virtual and augmented reality, and artificial intelligence continue to evolve and specialize. This has resulted in a severe shortage of system software developers able to build out the system infrastructure components. Modern societies, businesses, and governments increasingly rely heavily on digital technologies, which puts greater emphasis on developing safe, reliable, and efficient systems software and software infrastructure that modern web and mobile applications are built on.

System programming languages such as C/C++ have proved their mettle for decades in this domain, and provide a high degree of control and performance, but it is at the cost of memory safety.

Higher-level languages such as Java, C#, Python, Ruby, and JavaScript provide memory safety but offer less control over memory layout, and suffer from garbage collection pauses.

Rust is a modern, open source system programming language that promises the best of three worlds: the type safety of Java; the speed, expressiveness, and efficiency of C++; and memory safety without a garbage collector.

This book adopts a unique three-step approach to teaching system programming in Rust. Each chapter in this book starts with an overview of the system programming fundamentals and kernel system calls for that topic in Unix-like operating systems (Unix/Linux/macOS). You will then learn how to perform common system calls using the Rust Standard Library, and in a few cases, external crates, using abundant code snippets. This knowledge is then reinforced through a practical example project that you will build. Lastly, there are questions in each chapter to embed learning.

By the end of this book, you will have a sound foundational understanding of how to use Rust to manage and control operating system resources such as memory, files, processes, threads, system environment, peripheral devices, networking interfaces, terminals, and shells, and you'll understand how to build cross-language bindings through FFI. Along the way, you will learn how to use the tools of the trade, and get a firm appreciation of the value Rust brings to build safe, performant, reliable, and efficient system-level software.

Who this book is for

This book is aimed at programmers with basic knowledge of Rust but little or no system programming or experience. This book is also for people who have a background in system programming and want to consider Rust as an alternative to C/C++.

The reader should have a basic understanding of programming concepts in any language, such as C, C++, Java, Python, Ruby, JavaScript, or Go.

What this book covers

Chapter 1, Tools of the Trade – Rust Toolchains and Project Structures, introduces the Rust toolchain for build and dependency management, automated testing, and documentation.

Chapter 2, A Tour of the Rust Programming Language, illustrates the key concepts of the Rust programming language including the type system, data structures, and memory management fundamentals through an example project.

Chapter 3, Introduction to the Rust Standard Library, introduces key modules of the Rust standard library that provide the building blocks and pre-defined functionality for system programming in Rust.

Chapter 4, Managing Environment, Command Line, and Time, covers a few foundational topics around how to programmatically deal with command-line parameters, set and manipulate the process environment, and work with system time.

Chapter 5, Memory Management in Rust, provides a comprehensive look at the memory management facilities provided by Rust. We will review Linux memory management basics, the traditional shortcomings of C/C++, and how Rust can be used to overcome many of these shortcomings.

Chapter 6, Working with Files and Directories in Rust, helps you understand how the Linux filesystem works, and how to master the Rust Standard Library for various scenarios in file and directory operations.

Chapter 7, Implementing Terminal I/O in Rust, helps you understand how a pseudo-terminal application works and how to create one. The result will be an interactive application that handles streams.

Chapter 8, Working with Processes and Signals, provides an explanation of what processes are, how to handle them in Rust, how to create and communicate with a child process, and how to handle signals and errors.

Chapter 9, Managing Concurrency, explains the basics of concurrency and various mechanisms for sharing data across threads in an idiomatic way in Rust, including channels, mutexes, and reference counters.

Chapter 10, Working with Device I/O, explains Linux I/O concepts such as buffering, standard inputs and outputs, and device I/O, and shows how to control I/O operations with Rust.

Chapter 11, Learning Network Programming, explains how to work with low-level network primitives and protocols in Rust, illustrated by building low-level TCP and UDP servers and clients, and a reverse proxy.

Chapter 12, Writing Unsafe Rust and FFI, describes the key motivations and risks associated with unsafe Rust, and shows how to use FFI to safely interface Rust with other programming languages.

To get the most out of this book

Rustup must be installed in your local development environment. Use this link for installation: https://github.com/rust-lang/rustup.

Refer to the following link for official installation instructions: https://www.rust-lang.org/tools/install.

After installation, check whether rustc, and cargo have been installed correctly with the following commands:

```
rustc --version
cargo -version
```

You can use Linux, macOS, or Windows.

While the Rust standard library largely is platform-independent, the general flavor of the book is oriented towards Linux/Unix-based systems. As a result, in a few chapters (or some sections within chapters) it is recommended to use a local Linux virtual machine, like Virtual box, (or if you have a cloud VM you may use it) for the code in the chapter to work. This may be because a command, or an external crate or a shared library used in example code and projects may be Linux/Unix specific.

> **Note for those using Windows for development**
> There are certain chapters that require a virtual machine or Docker image running Unix-like OSes (Unix/Linux/macOS).

There are two types of code in each chapter which are placed in the Packt GitHub repository for the book:

- The code corresponding to the example projects (which are referred to by named source files within the chapter),

- Independent code snippets, that are placed within the `miscellaneous` folder within each chapter (where applicable)

If you are using the digital version of this book, we advise you to type the code yourself or access the code via the GitHub repository (link available in the next section). Doing so will help you avoid any potential errors related to the copying and pasting of code.

While using `cargo run` command to build and run Rust programs, you may encounter 'permission denied' messages if the user ID with which the command is run does not have sufficient permissions to perform system-level operations (such as reading or writing to files). In such cases, one of the workarounds that can be used is to run the program with the following command:

```
sudo env "PATH=$PATH" cargo run
```

Download the example code files

You can download the example code files for this book from your account at www.packt.com. If you purchased this book elsewhere, you can visit www.packtpub.com/support and register to have the files emailed directly to you.

You can download the code files by following these steps:

1. Log in or register at www.packt.com.
2. Select the **Support** tab.
3. Click on **Code Downloads**.
4. Enter the name of the book in the **Search** box and follow the onscreen instructions.

Once the file is downloaded, please make sure that you unzip or extract the folder using the latest version of:

- WinRAR/7-Zip for Windows
- Zipeg/iZip/UnRarX for Mac
- 7-Zip/PeaZip for Linux

The code bundle for the book is also hosted on GitHub at `https://github.com/PacktPublishing/Practical-System-Programming-for-Rust-Developers`. In case there's an update to the code, it will be updated on the existing GitHub repository.

We also have other code bundles from our rich catalog of books and videos available at `https://github.com/PacktPublishing/`. Check them out!

> **Note**
>
> The code snippets in this book are designed for learning, and not intended to be of production quality. As a result, while the code examples are practical and use idiomatic Rust, they are not likely to be full-featured with robust error handling covering all types of edge cases. This is by design, so as not to impede the learning process.

Download the color images

We also provide a PDF file that has color images of the screenshots/diagrams used in this book. You can download it here: `https://static.packt-cdn.com/downloads/9781800560963_ColorImages.pdf`.

Conventions used

There are a number of text conventions used throughout this book.

`Code in text`: Indicates code words in text, database table names, folder names, filenames, file extensions, pathnames, dummy URLs, user input, and Twitter handles. Here is an example: "We can access the `now()` function from the `Utc` module to print out the current date and time."

A block of code is set as follows:

```
fn main() {
    println!("Hello, time now is {:?}", chrono::Utc::now());
}
```

When we wish to draw your attention to a particular part of a code block, the relevant lines or items are set in bold:

```
fn main() {
    println!("Hello, time now is {:?}", chrono::Utc::now());
}
```

Any command-line input or output is written as follows:

```
rustup toolchain install nightly
```

Bold: Indicates a new term, an important word, or words that you see onscreen. For example, words in menus or dialog boxes appear in the text like this. Here is an example: "You will see **Hello, world!** printed to your console."

> **Tips or important notes**
> Appear like this.

Get in touch

Feedback from our readers is always welcome.

General feedback: If you have questions about any aspect of this book, mention the book title in the subject of your message and email us at customercare@packtpub.com.

Errata: Although we have taken every care to ensure the accuracy of our content, mistakes do happen. If you have found a mistake in this book, we would be grateful if you would report this to us. Please visit www.packtpub.com/support/errata, selecting your book, clicking on the Errata Submission Form link, and entering the details.

Piracy: If you come across any illegal copies of our works in any form on the Internet, we would be grateful if you would provide us with the location address or website name. Please contact us at copyright@packt.com with a link to the material.

If you are interested in becoming an author: If there is a topic that you have expertise in and you are interested in either writing or contributing to a book, please visit authors.packtpub.com.

Reviews

Please leave a review. Once you have read and used this book, why not leave a review on the site that you purchased it from? Potential readers can then see and use your unbiased opinion to make purchase decisions, we at Packt can understand what you think about our products, and our authors can see your feedback on their book. Thank you!

For more information about Packt, please visit packt.com.

Section 1:
Getting Started with
System Programming
in Rust

This section covers the foundational concepts behind system programming in Rust. It includes a tour of Rust's features, Cargo tools, the Rust Standard Library, modules for managing environment variables, command-line parameters, and working with time. Example projects include a parser to evaluate arithmetic expressions, writing a feature of an HTML template engine, and building a command-line tool for image processing.

This section comprises the following chapters:

- *Chapter 1, Tools of the Trade – Rust Toolchains and Project Structures*
- *Chapter 2, A Tour of the Rust Programming Language*
- *Chapter 3, Introduction to the Rust Standard Library*
- *Chapter 4, Managing the Environment, Command Line, and Time*

1

Tools of the Trade – Rust Toolchains and Project Structures

Rust, as a modern systems programming language, has many inherent characteristics that make it easier to write safe, reliable, and performant code. Rust also has a compiler that enables a relatively fearless code refactoring experience as a project grows in size and complexity. But any programming language in itself is incomplete without the toolchains that support the software development life cycle. After all, where would software engineers be without their tools?

This chapter specifically discusses the Rust toolchain and its ecosystem, and techniques to structure code within Rust projects to write safe, testable, performant, documented, and maintainable code that is also optimized to run in the intended target environment.

The following are the key learning outcomes for this chapter:

- Choosing the right configuration of Rust for your project
- Cargo introduction and project structure
- Cargo build management
- Cargo dependencies

- Writing test scripts and doing automated unit and integration testing
- Automating the generation of technical documentation

By the end of this chapter, you will have learned how to select the right project type and toolchain; organize project code efficiently; add external and internal libraries as dependencies; build the project for development, test, and production environments; automate testing; and generate documentation for your Rust code.

Technical requirements

Rustup must be installed in the local development environment. Use this link for installation: https://github.com/rust-lang/rustup.

Refer to the following link for official installation instructions: https://www.rust-lang.org/tools/install.

After installation, check rustc, and cargo have been installed correctly with the following commands:

```
rustc --version
cargo --version
```

You must have access to any code editor of your choice.

Some of the code and commands in this chapter, especially those related to shared libraries and setting paths, require a Linux system environment. It is recommended to install a local virtual machine such as VirtualBox or equivalent with a Linux installation for working with the code in this chapter. Instructions to install VirtualBox can be found at https://www.virtualbox.org.

The Git repo for the examples in this chapter can be found at https://github.com/PacktPublishing/Practical-System-Programming-for-Rust-Developers/tree/master/Chapter01.

Choosing the right Rust configuration for your project

When you start with Rust programming, you have to first select a Rust release channel and a Rust project type.

This section discusses details of the Rust *release channels* and gives guidance on how to choose among them for your project.

Rust also allows you to build different types of binaries – standalone executables, static libraries, and dynamic libraries. If you know upfront what you will be building, you can create the right project type with the scaffolding code generated for you.

We will cover these in this section.

Choosing a Rust release channel

The Rust programming language is developed continually and there are three releases being developed simultaneously at any point in time, each called a **release channel**. Each channel has a purpose and has varying features and stability characteristics. The three release channels are *stable*, *beta*, and *nightly*. Unstable language features and libraries are developed in the **nightly** and **beta** channels, while stability guarantees are provided on the **stable** channel.

Rustup is the tool that installs the Rust compiler, the Rust Standard Library, the Cargo package manager, and other core tools for activities such as code formatting, testing, benchmarking, and documentation. All these tools are available in multiple flavors called *toolchains*. A *toolchain* is a combination of a *release channel* and a *host*, and optionally also has an associated archive date.

Rustup can install a toolchain from a *release channel*, or from other sources such as official archives and local builds. *Rustup* also determines the toolchain depending on the host platform. Rust is officially available on Linux, Windows, and macOS. Rustup thus is called a *tool multiplexer* as it installs and manages multiple toolchains, and in this sense is similar to *rbenv*, *pyenv*, or *nvm* in *Ruby*, *Python*, and *Node.js* respectively.

Rustup manages the complexity associated with toolchains but makes the installation process fairly straightforward as it provides sensible defaults. These can later be modified by the developer.

> **Note**
>
> Rust's stable version is released every 6 weeks; for example, Rust 1.42.0 was released on March 12, 2020, and 6 weeks later to the day, Rust 1.43 was released on April 23, 2020.
>
> A new nightly version of Rust is released every day. Once every 6 weeks, the latest master branch of nightly becomes the beta version.

Most Rust developers primarily use the *stable* channel. Beta channel releases are not used actively, but only to test for any regressions in the Rust language releases.

The *nightly* channel is for active language development and is published every night. The *nightly* channel lets Rust develop new and experimental features and allows early adopters to test them before they are stabilized. The price to be paid for early access is that there may be breaking changes to these features before they get into stable releases. Rust uses feature flags to determine what features are enabled in a given nightly release. A user who wants to use a cutting-edge feature in nightly version has to annotate the code with the appropriate *feature flag*.

An example of a feature flag is shown here:

```
#![feature(try_trait)]
```

Note that beta and stable releases cannot use feature flags.

Rustup is configured to use the stable channel by default. To work with other channels, here are a few commands. For a complete list, refer to the official link: https://github.com/rust-lang/rustup.

To install nightly Rust, use this command:

```
rustup toolchain install nightly
```

To activate nightly Rust globally, use this command:

```
rustup default nightly
```

To activate nightly at a directory level, use this command:

```
rustup override set nightly
```

To get the version of the compiler in nightly Rust, use this command:

```
rustup run nightly rustc --version
```

To reset rustup to use the stable channel, use this command:

```
rustup default stable
```

To show the installed toolchains and which is currently active, use this command:

```
rustup show
```

To update the installed toolchains to the latest versions, use this command:

```
rustup update
```

Note that once `rustup default <channel-name>` is set, other related tools, such as Cargo and Rustc, use the default channel set.

Which Rust channel should you use for your project? For any **production-bound** projects, it is advisable to use only the **stable** release channel. For any **experimental** projects, the **nightly** or **beta** channels may be used, with caution as there may be breaking changes needed for the code in future releases.

Selecting a Rust project type

There are two basic types of projects in Rust: **libraries** and **binaries** (or executables).

A *library* is a self-contained piece of code that is intended for use by other programs. The purpose of a library is to enable code reuse and speed up the development cycle by leveraging the hard work of other open source developers. Libraries, also called a **library crate** (or **lib crate**) in Rust, can be published to a public package repository (such as `crates.io`) that can be discovered and downloaded by other developers for use in their own programs. Program execution for a library crate begins in the `src/lib.rs` file.

A *binary* is a standalone executable that may download and link other libraries into a single binary. A binary project type is also called a **binary crate** (or **bin crate**). Program execution for a bin crate starts in the `main()` function that is present in the `src/main.rs` file.

It is important to determine whether you want to build a binary or a library program in Rust while initializing the project. We will see examples of these two types of projects later in this chapter. It's time to introduce the star tool and Swiss-Army knife in the Rust ecosystem, *Cargo*.

Introducing Cargo and project structures

Cargo is the official build and dependency management tool for Rust. It has many of the features of the other popular tools in this segment, such as Ant, Maven, Gradle, npm, CocoaPods, pip, and yarn, but provides a far more seamless and integrated developer experience for compiling code, downloading and compiling dependent libraries (called **crates** in Rust), linking libraries, and building development and release binaries. It also performs the incremental build of the code to reduce the compilation time as the programs evolve. In addition, it creates an idiomatic project structure while creating new Rust projects.

In short, Cargo as an integrated toolchain gives a seamless experience in the day-to-day tasks of creating a new project, building it, managing external dependencies, debugging, testing, generating documentation, and release management.

Cargo is the tool that can be used to set up the basic project scaffolding structure for a new Rust project. Before we create a new Rust project with Cargo, let's first understand the options for organizing code within Rust projects:

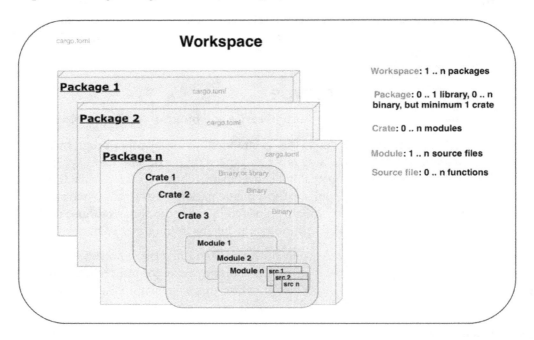

Figure 1.1 – Cargo project structure and hierarchy

Figure 1.1 shows how code can be organized within a Cargo-generated Rust project.

The smallest standalone unit of organization of code in a Rust project is a **function**. (Technically, the smallest unit of code organization is a block of code, but it is part of a function.) A function can accept zero or more input parameters, performs processing, and optionally, returns a value. A set of functions are organized as a **source file** with a specific name, for example, `main.rs` is a source file.

The next highest level of code organization is a **module**. Code within modules has its own unique namespace. A module can contain user-defined data types (such as structs, traits, and enums), constants, type aliases, other module imports, and function declarations. Modules can be nested within one another. Multiple module definitions can be defined within a single source file for smaller projects, or a module can contain code spread across multiple source files for larger projects. This type of organization is also referred to as a module system.

Multiple modules can be organized into **crates**. Crates also serve as the unit of code sharing across Rust projects. A crate is either a *library* or a *binary*. A crate developed by one developer and published to a public repository can be reused by another developer or team. The crate root is the source file that the Rust compiler starts from. For binary crates, the crate root is `main.rs` and for library crates it is `lib.rs`.

One or more crates can be combined into a **package**. A *package* contains a `Cargo.toml` file, which contains information on how to build the package, including downloading and linking the dependent crates. When Cargo is used to create a new Rust project, it creates a *package*. A *package* must contain at least one crate – either a library or a binary crate. A package may contain any number of binary crates, but it can contain either zero or only one library crate.

As Rust projects grow in size, there may be a need to split up a package into multiple units and manage them independently. A set of related packages can be organized as a **workspace**. A *workspace* is a set of packages that share the same `Cargo.lock` file (containing details of specific versions of dependencies that are shared across all packages in the workspace) and output directory.

Let's see a few examples to understand various types of project structures in Rust.

Automating build management with Cargo

When Rust code is compiled and built, the generated binary can either be a standalone executable binary or a library that can be used by other projects. In this section, we will look at how Cargo can be used to create Rust binaries and libraries, and how to configure metadata in `Cargo.toml` to provide build instructions.

Building a basic binary crate

In this section, we will build a basic binary crate. A binary crate when built, produces an executable binary file. This is the default crate type for the cargo tool. Let's now look at the command to create a binary crate.

1. The first step is to generate a Rust source package using the `cargo new` command.
2. Run the following command in a terminal session inside your working directory to create a new package:

```
cargo new --bin first-program && cd first-program
```

The `--bin` flag is to tell Cargo to generate a package that, when compiled, would produce a binary crate (executable).

`first-program` is the name of the package given. You can specify a name of your choice.

3. Once the command executes, you will see the following directory structure:

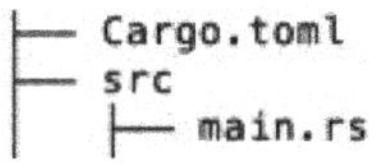

```
├── Cargo.toml
├── src
│   ├── main.rs
```

Figure 1.2 – Directory structure

The `Cargo.toml` file contains the metadata for the package:

```
[package]
name = "first-program"
version = "0.1.0"
authors = [<your email>]
edition = "2018"
```

And the `src` directory contains one file called `main.rs`:

```
fn main() {
    println!("Hello, world!");
}
```

4. To generate a binary crate (or executable) from this package, run the following command:

```
cargo build
```

This command creates a folder called `target` in the project root and creates a binary crate (executable) with the same name as the package name (`first-program`, in our case) in the location `target/debug`.

5. Execute the following from the command line:

```
cargo run
```

You will see the following printed to your console:

```
Hello, world!
```

> **Note on path setting to execute binaries**
>
> Note that LD_LIBRARY_PATH should be set to include the toolchain library in the path. Execute the following command for Unix-like platforms. If your executable fails with the error **Image not found**, for Windows, alter the syntax suitably:
>
> ```
> export LD_LIBRARY_PATH=$(rustc --print sysroot)/
> lib:$LD_LIBRARY_PATH
> ```
>
> Alternatively, you can build and run code with one command – cargo run, which is convenient for development purposes.

By default, the name of the binary crate (executable) generated is the same as the name of the source package. If you wish to change the name of the binary crate, add the following lines to Cargo.toml:

```
[[bin]]
name = "new-first-program"
path = "src/main.rs"
```

6. Run the following in the command line:

```
cargo run   --bin new-first-program
```

You will see a new executable with the name new-first-program in the target/debug folder. You will see **Hello, world!** printed to your console.

7. A cargo package can contain the source for multiple binaries. Let's learn how to add another binary to our project. In Cargo.toml, add a new [[bin]] target below the first one:

```
[[bin]]
name = "new-first-program"
path = "src/main.rs"
[[bin]]
name = "new-second-program"
path = "src/second.rs"
```

8. Next, create a new file, `src/second.rs`, and add the following code:

```
fn main() {
    println!("Hello, for the second time!");
}
```

9. Run the following:

```
cargo run --bin new-second-program
```

You will see the statement **Hello, for the second time!** printed to your console. You'll also find a new executable created in the `target/debug` directory with the name `new-second-program`.

Congratulations! You have learned how to do the following:

- Create your first Rust source package and compile it into an executable binary crate
- Give a new name to the binary, different from the package name
- Add a second binary to the same cargo package

Note that a `cargo` package can contain one or more binary crates.

Configuring Cargo

A cargo package has an associated `Cargo.toml` file, which is also called the **manifest**.

The manifest, at a minimum, contains the `[package]` section but can contain many other sections. A subset of the sections are listed here:

Specifying output targets for the package: Cargo packages can have five types of targets:

- `[[bin]]`: A binary target is an executable program that can be run after it is built.
- `[lib]`: A library target produces a library that can be used by other libraries and executables.
- `[[example]]`: This target is useful for libraries to demonstrate the use of external APIs to users through example code. The example source code located in the `example` directory can be built into executable binaries using this target.
- `[[test]]`: Files located in the `tests` directory represent integration tests and each of these can be compiled into a separate executable binary.
- `[[bench]]`: Benchmark functions defined in libraries and binaries are compiled into separate executables.

For each of these targets, the configuration can be specified, including parameters such as the name of the target, the source file of the target, and whether you want cargo to automatically run test scripts and generate documentation for the target. You may recall that in the previous section, we changed the name and set the source file for the generated binary executable.

Specifying dependencies for the package: The source files in a package may depend on other internal or external libraries, which are also called *dependencies*. Each of these in turn may depend on other libraries and so on. Cargo downloads the list of dependencies specified under this section and links them to the final output targets. The various types of dependencies include the following:

- `[dependencies]`: Package library or binary dependencies

- `[dev-dependencies]`: Dependencies for examples, tests, and benchmarks

- `[build-dependencies]`: Dependencies for build scripts (if any are specified)

- `[target]`: This is for the cross-compilation of code for various target architectures. Note that this is not to be confused with the output targets of the package, which can be lib, bin, and so on.

Specifying build profiles: There are four types of profiles that can be specified while building a cargo package:

- `dev`: The `cargo build` command uses the `dev` profile by default. Packages built with this option are optimized for compile-time speed.

- `release`: The `cargo build --release` command enables the release profile, which is suitable for production release, and is optimized for runtime speed.

- `test`: The `cargo test` command uses this profile. This is used to build test executables.

- `bench`: The `cargo bench` command creates the benchmark executable, which automatically runs all functions annotated with the `#[bench]` attribute.

Specifying the package as a workspace: A workspace is a unit of organization where multiple packages can be grouped together into a project and is useful to save disk space and compilation time when there are shared dependencies across a set of related packages. The `[workspace]` section can be used to define the list of packages that are part of the workspace.

Building a static library crate

We have seen how to create binary crates. Let's now learn how to create a library crate:

```
cargo new --lib my-first-lib
```

The default directory structure of a new cargo project is as follows:

```
├── Cargo.toml
├── src
│   └── lib.rs
```

Add the following code in `src/lib.rs`:

```
pub fn hello_from_lib(message: &str) {
    println!("Printing Hello {} from library",message);
}
```

Run the following:

```
cargo build
```

You will see the library built under `target/debug` and it will have the name `libmy_first_lib.rlib`.

To invoke the function in this library, let's build a small binary crate. Create a `bin` directory under `src`, and a new file, `src/bin/mymain.rs`.

Add the following code:

```
use my_first_lib::hello_from_lib;
fn main() {
    println!("Going to call library function");
    hello_from_lib("Rust system programmer");
}
```

The `use my_first_lib::hello_from_lib` statement tells the compiler to bring the library function into the scope of this program.

Run the following:

```
cargo run  --bin mymain
```

You will see the `print` statement in your console. Also, the binary `mymain` will be placed in the `target/debug` folder along with the library we wrote earlier. The binary crate looks for the library in the same folder, which it finds in this case. Hence it is able to invoke the function within the library.

If you want to place the `mymain.rs` file in another location (instead of within `src/bin`), then add a target in `Cargo.toml` and mention the name and path of the binary as shown in the following example, and move the `mymain.rs` file to the specified location:

```
[[bin]]
name = "mymain"
path = "src/mymain.rs"
```

Run `cargo run --bin mymain` and you will see the `println` output in your console.

Automating dependency management

You learned in the previous section how Cargo can be used to set up the base project directory structure and scaffolding for a new project, and how to build various types of binary and library crates. We will look at the dependency management features of Cargo in this section.

Rust comes with a built-in standard library consisting of language primitives and commonly used functions, but it is small by design (compared to other languages). Most real-world programs in Rust depend on additional external libraries to improve functionality and developer productivity. Any such external code that is used is a *dependency* for the program. Cargo makes it easy to specify and manage dependencies.

In the Rust ecosystem, *crates.io* is the central public package registry for discovering and downloading libraries (called **packages** or **crates** in Rust). It is similar to *npm* in the JavaScript world. Cargo uses `crates.io` as the default package registry.

Dependencies are specified in the `[dependencies]` section of `Cargo.toml`. Let's see an example.

Start a new project with this command:

```
cargo new deps-example && cd deps-example
```

In `Cargo.toml`, make the following entry to include an external library:

```
[dependencies]
chrono = "0.4.0"
```

Chrono is a datetime library. This is called a dependency because our deps-example crate depends on this external library for its functionality.

When you run cargo build, cargo looks for a crate on crates.io with this name and version. If found, it downloads this crate along with all of its dependencies, compiles them all, and updates a file called Cargo.lock with the exact versions of packages downloaded. The Cargo.lock file is a generated file and not meant for editing.

Each dependency in Cargo.toml is specified in a new line and takes the format <crate-name> = "<semantic-version-number>". **Semantic versioning or Semver** has the form X.Y.Z, where X is the major version number, Y is the minor version, and Z is the patch version.

Specifying the location of a dependency

There are many ways to specify the location and version of dependencies in Cargo.toml, some of which are summarized here:

- **Crates.io registry**: This is the default option and all that is needed is to specify the package name and version string as we did earlier in this section.

- **Alternative registry**: While crates.io is the default registry, Cargo provides the option to use an alternate registry. The registry name has to be configured in the .cargo/config file, and in Cargo.toml, an entry is to be made with the registry name, as shown in the example here:

```
[dependencies]
cratename = { version = "2.1", registry = "alternate-
    registry-name" }
```

- **Git repository**: A Git repo can be specified as the dependency. Here is how to do it:

```
[dependencies]
chrono = { git = "https://github.com/chronotope/chrono" ,
    branch = "master" }
```

Cargo will get the repo at the branch and location specified, and look for its Cargo.toml file in order to fetch its dependencies.

- **Specify a local path**: Cargo supports path dependencies, which means the library can be a sub-crate within the main cargo package. While building the main cargo package, the sub-crates that have also been specified as dependencies will be built. But dependencies with only a path dependency cannot be uploaded to the *crates.io* public registry.

- **Multiple locations**: Cargo supports the option to specify both a registry version *and* either a Git or path location. For local builds, the Git or path version is used, and the registry version will be used when the package is published to *crates.io*.

Using dependent packages in source code

Once the dependencies are specified in the `Cargo.toml` file in any of the preceding formats, we can use the external library in the package code as shown in the following example. Add the following code to `src/main.rs`:

```
use chrono::Utc;
fn main() {
    println!("Hello, time now is {:?}", Utc::now());
}
```

The `use` statement tells the compiler to bring the `chrono` package `Utc` module into the scope of this program. We can then access the function `now()` from the `Utc` module to print out the current date and time. The `use` statement is not mandatory. An alternative way to print datetime would be as follows:

```
fn main() {
    println!("Hello, time now is {:?}", chrono::Utc::now());
}
```

This would give the same result. But if you have to use functions from the `chrono` package multiple times in code, it is more convenient to bring `chrono` and required modules into scope once using the `use` statement, and it becomes easier to type.

It is also possible to rename the imported package with the `as` keyword:

```
use chrono as time;
fn main() {
    println!("Hello, time now is {:?}", time::Utc::now());
}
```

For more details on managing dependencies, refer to the Cargo docs: `https://doc.rust-lang.org/cargo/reference/specifying-dependencies.html`.

In this section, we have seen how to add dependencies to a package. Any number of dependencies can be added to `Cargo.toml` and used within the program. Cargo makes the dependency management process quite a pleasant experience.

Let's now look at another useful feature of Cargo – running automated tests.

Writing and running automated tests

The Rust programming language has built-in support for writing automated tests.

Rust tests are basically Rust functions that verify whether the other non-test functions written in the package work as intended. They basically invoke the other functions with the specified data and assert that the return values are as expected.

Rust has two types of tests – unit tests and integration tests.

Writing unit tests in Rust

Create a new Rust package with the following command:

```
cargo new test-example && cd test-example
```

Write a new function that returns the process ID of the currently running process. We will look at the details of process handling in a later chapter, so you may just type in the following code, as the focus here is on writing unit tests:

```
use std::process;
fn main() {
    println!("{}", get_process_id());
}
fn get_process_id() -> u32 {
    process::id()
}
```

We have written a simple (silly) function to use the standard library process module and retrieve the process ID of the currently running process.

Run the code using cargo check to confirm there are no syntax errors.

Let's now write a unit test. Note that we cannot know upfront what the process ID is going to be, so all we can test is whether a number is being returned:

```
#[test]
fn test_if_process_id_is_returned() {
    assert!(get_process_id() > 0);
}
```

Run `cargo test`. You will see that the test has passed successfully, as the function returns a non-zero positive integer.

Note that we have written the unit tests in the same source file as the rest of the code. In order to tell the compiler that this is a test function, we use the `#[test]` annotation. The `assert!` macro (available in standard Rust library) is used to check whether a condition evaluates to true. There are two other macros available, `assert_eq!` and `assert_ne!`, which are used to test whether the two arguments passed to these macros are equal or not.

A custom error message can also be specified:

```
#[test]
fn test_if_process_id_is_returned() {
    assert_ne!(get_process_id(), 0, "There is error in code");
}
```

To compile but not run the tests, use the `--no-run` option with the `cargo test` command.

The preceding example has only one simple `test` function, but as the number of tests increases, the following problems arise:

- How do we write any helper functions needed for test code and differentiate it from the rest of the package code?

- How can we prevent the compiler from compiling tests as part of each build (to save time) and not include test code as part of the normal build (saving disk/ memory space)?

In order to provide more modularity and to address the preceding questions, it is idiomatic in Rust to group test functions in a `test` module:

```
#[cfg(test)]
mod tests {
    use super::get_process_id;
    #[test]
    fn test_if_process_id_is_returned() {
        assert_ne!(get_process_id(), 0, "There is
            error in code");
    }
}
```

Here are the changes made to the code:

- We have moved the `test` function under the `tests` module.
- We have added the `cfg` attribute, which tells the compiler to compile test code only if we are trying to run tests (that is, only for `cargo test`, not for `cargo build`).
- There is a `use` statement, which brings the `get_process_id` function into the scope of the `tests` module. Note that `tests` is an inner module and so we use `super::` prefix to bring the function that is being tested into the scope of the `tests` module.

`cargo test` will now give the same results. But what we have achieved is greater modularity, and we've also allowed for the conditional compilation of test code.

Writing integration tests in Rust

In the *Writing unit tests in Rust* section, we saw how to define a `tests` module to hold the unit tests. This is used to test fine-grained pieces of code such as an individual function call. Unit tests are small and have a narrow focus.

For testing broader test scenarios involving a larger scope of code such as a workflow, integration tests are needed. It is important to write both types of tests to fully ensure that the library works as expected.

To write integration tests, the convention in Rust is to create a `tests` directory in the package root and create one or more files under this folder, each containing one integration test. Each file under the `tests` directory is treated as an individual crate.

But there is a catch. Integration tests in Rust are not available for binary crates, only library crates. So, let's create a new library crate:

```
cargo new --lib integ-test-example && cd integ-test-example
```

In `src/lib.rs`, replace the existing code with the following. This is the same code we wrote earlier, but this time it is in `lib.rs`:

```
use std::process;
pub fn get_process_id() -> u32 {
    process::id()
}
```

Let's create a `tests` folder and create a file, `tests/integration_test1.rs`. Add the following code in this file:

```
use integ_test_example;
#[test]
fn test1() {
    assert_ne!(integ_test_example::get_process_id(), 0, "Error
        in code");
}
```

Note the following changes to the test code compared to unit tests:

- Integration tests are external to the library, so we have to bring the library into the scope of the integration test. This is simulating how an external user of our library would call a function from the public interface of our library. This is in place of `super::` prefix used in unit tests to bring the tested function into scope.

- We did not have to specify the `#[cfg(test)]` annotation with integration tests, because these are stored in a separate folder and cargo compiles files in this directory only when we run `cargo test`.

- We still have to specify the `#[test]` attribute for each `test` function to tell the compiler these are the test functions (and not helper/utility code) to be executed.

Run `cargo test`. You will see that this integration test has been run successfully.

Controlling test execution

The `cargo test` command compiles the source code in test mode and runs the resultant binary. `cargo test` can be run in various modes by specifying command-line options. The following is a summary of the key options.

Running a subset of tests by name

If there are a large number of tests in a package, `cargo test` runs all tests by default each time. To run any particular test cases by name, the following option can be used:

```
cargo test -- testfunction1, testfunction2
```

To verify this, let's replace the code in the `integration_test1.rs` file with the following:

```
use integ_test_example;
#[test]
fn files_test1() {
    assert_ne!(integ_test_example::get_process_id(),0,"Error
        in code");
}


#[test]
fn files_test2() {
    assert_eq!(1+1, 2);
}


#[test]
fn process_test1() {
    assert!(true);
}
```

This last dummy `test` function is for purposes of the demonstration of running selective cases.

Run `cargo test` and you can see both tests executed.

Run `cargo test files_test1` and you can see `files_test1` executed.

Run `cargo test files_test2` and you can see `files_test2` executed.

Run `cargo test files` and you will see both `files_test1` and `files_test2` tests executed, but `process_test1` is not executed. This is because cargo looks for all test cases containing the term `'files'` and executes them.

Ignoring some tests

In some cases, you want to execute most of the tests every time but exclude a few. This can be achieved by annotating the `test` function with the `#[ignore]` attribute.

In the previous example, let's say we want to exclude `process_test1` from regular execution because it is computationally intensive and takes a lot of time to execute. The following snippet shows how it's done:

```
#[test]
#[ignore]
fn process_test1() {
    assert!(true);
}
```

Run `cargo test`, and you will see that `process_test1` is marked as ignored, and hence not executed.

To run only the ignored tests in a separate iteration, use the following option:

```
cargo test -- --ignored
```

The first `- -` is a separator between the command-line options for the `cargo` command and those for the `test` binary. In this case, we are passing the `--ignored` flag for the test binary, hence the need for this seemingly confusing syntax.

Running tests sequentially or in parallel

By default, `cargo test` runs the various tests in parallel in separate threads. To support this mode of execution, the `test` functions must be written in a way that there is no common data sharing across test cases. However if there is indeed such a need (for example, one test case writes some data to a location and another test case reads it), then we can run the tests in sequence as follows:

```
cargo test -- --test-threads=1
```

This command tells cargo to use only one thread for executing tests, which indirectly means that tests have to be executed in sequence.

In summary, Rust's strong built-in type system and strict ownership rules enforced by the compiler, coupled with the ability to script and execute unit and integration test cases as an integral part of the language and tooling, makes it very appealing to write robust, reliable systems.

Documenting your project

Rust ships with a tool called `Rustdoc`, which can generate documentation for Rust projects. Cargo has integration with `Rustdoc`, so you can use either tool to generate documentation.

To get an idea of what it means to have documentation generated for Rust projects, go to `http://docs.rs`.

This is a documentation repository for all the crates in *crates.io*. To see a sample of the generated documentation, select a crate and view the docs. For example, you can go to `docs.rs/serde` to see docs for the popular serialization/deserialization library in Rust.

To generate similar documentation for your Rust projects, it is important to think through what to document, and how to document it.

But what can you document? The following are some of the aspects of a crate that it would be useful to document:

- An overall short description of what your Rust library does
- A list of modules and public functions in the library
- A list of other items, such as `traits`, `macros`, `structs`, enums, and `typedefs`, that a public user of the library needs to be familiar with to use various features
- For binary crates, installation instructions and command-line parameters.
- Examples that demonstrate to users how to use the crate
- Optionally, design details for the crate

Now that we know **what** to document, we have to learn **how** to document it. There are two ways to document your crate:

- Inline documentation comments within the crate
- Separate markdown files

You can use either approach, and the `rustdoc` tool will convert them into HTML, CSS, and `JavaScript` code that can be viewed from a browser.

Writing inline documentation comments within crate

Rust has two types of comments: **code comments** (aimed at developers) and **documentation comments** (aimed at users of the library/crate).

Code comments are written using:

- `//` for single-line comments and writing inline documentation comments within crate
- `/* */` for multi-line comments

Documentation comments are written using two styles:

The first style is to use three slashes `///` for commenting on individual items that follow the comments. Markdown notation can be used to style the comments (for example, bold or italic). *This is typically used for item-level documentation.*

The second style is to use `//!`. This is used to add documentation for the item that contains these comments (as opposed to the first style, which is used to comment items that follow the comments). *This is typically used for crate-level documentation.*

In both cases, `rustdoc` extracts documentation from the crate's documentation comments.

Add the following comments to the `integ-test-example` project, in `src/lib.rs`:

```
//! This is a library that contains functions related to
//! dealing with processes,
//! and makes these tasks more convenient.

use std::process;

/// This function gets the process ID of the current
/// executable. It returns a non-zero  number
pub fn get_process_id() -> u32 {
    process::id()
}
```

Run `cargo doc -open` to see the generated HTML documentation corresponding to the documentation comments.

Writing documentation in markdown files

Create a new folder, doc, under the crate root, and add a new file, itest.md, with the following markdown content:

```
# Docs for integ-test-example crate

This is a project to test `rustdoc`.

[Here is a link!](https://www.rust-lang.org)

// Function signature

pub fn get_process_id() -> u32 {}
```

This function returns the process ID of the currently running executable:

```
// Example

```rust

use integ_test_example;

fn get_id() -> i32 {
  let my_pid = get_process_id();
  println!("Process id for current process is: {}", my_pid);
}
```
```

Note that the preceding code example is only representational.

Unfortunately, cargo does not directly support generating HTML from standalone markdown files (at the time of this writing), so we have to use rustdoc as follows:

```
rustdoc doc/itest.md
```

You will find the generated HTML document itest.html in the same folder. View it in your browser.

Running documentation tests

If there are any code examples written as part of the documentation, `rustdoc` can execute the code examples as tests.

Let's write a code example for our library. Open `src/lib.rs` and add the following code example to existing code:

```
//! Integration-test-example crate
//!
//! This is a library that contains functions related to
//! dealing with processes
//! , and makes these tasks more convenient.

use std::process;
/// This function gets the process id of the current
/// executable. It returns a non-zero number
/// ```
/// fn get_id() {
/// let x = integ_test_example::get_process_id();
/// println!("{}",x);
/// }
/// ```
pub fn get_process_id() -> u32 {
    process::id()
}
```

If you run `cargo test --doc`, it will run this example code and provide the status of the execution.

Alternatively, running `cargo test` will run all the test cases from the `tests` directory (except those that are marked as ignored), and then run the documentation tests (that is, code samples provided as part of the documentation).

Summary

Understanding the Cargo ecosystem of toolchains is very important to be effective as a Rust programmer, and this chapter has provided the foundational knowledge that will be used in future chapters.

We learned that there are three release channels in Rust – stable, beta, and nightly. Stable is recommended for production use, nightly is for experimental features, and beta is an interim stage to verify that there isn't any regression in Rust language releases before they are marked `stable`. We also learned how to use rustup to configure the toolchain to use for the project.

We saw different ways to organize code in Rust projects. We also learned how to build executable binaries and shared libraries. We also looked at how to use Cargo to specify and manage dependencies.

We covered how to write unit tests and integration tests for a Rust package using Rust's built-in test framework, how to invoke automated tests using cargo, and how to control test execution. We learned how to document packages both through inline documentation comments and using standalone markdown files.

In the next chapter, we will take a quick tour of the Rust programming language, through a hands-on project.

Further reading

- The Cargo Book (https://doc.rust-lang.org/cargo)
- The Rust Book (https://doc.rust-lang.org/book/)
- Rust Forge (https://forge.rust-lang.org/)
- The Rustup book (https://rust-lang.github.io/rustup/index.html)
- The Rust style guide – the Rust style guide contains conventions, guidelines, and best practices to write idiomatic Rust code, and can be found at the following link: https://github.com/rust-dev-tools/fmt-rfcs/blob/master/guide/guide.md

2

A Tour of the Rust Programming Language

In the previous chapter, we looked at the Rust tooling ecosystem for build and dependency management, testing, and documentation. These are critical and highly developer-friendly tools that give us a strong foundation for starting to work on Rust projects. In this chapter, we will build a working example that will serve to act as a refresher, and also strengthen key Rust programming concepts.

The goal of this chapter is to get more proficient in core Rust concepts. This is essential before diving into the specifics of systems programming in Rust. We will achieve this by designing and developing a **command-line interface (CLI)** in Rust.

The application we will be building is an **arithmetic expression evaluator**. Since this is a mouthful, let's see an example.

Let's assume the user enters the following arithmetic expression on the command line:

```
1+2*3.2+(4/2-3/2)-2.11+2^4
```

The tool will print out the result **21.79**.

For the user, it appears to be a calculator, but there is a lot involved to implement this. This example project will introduce you to the core computer science concepts used in parsers and compiler design. It is a non-trivial project that allows us to test the depths of core Rust programming, but is not so overly complex that it will intimidate you.

Before you continue reading, I would recommend that you clone the code repository, navigate to the `chapter2` folder, and execute the `cargo run` command. At the command-line prompt, enter a few arithmetic expressions and see the results returned by the tool. You can exit the tool with *Ctrl + C*. This would give you a better appreciation for what you are going to build in this chapter.

The following are the key learning steps for this chapter, which correspond to the various stages of building our project:

- Analyzing the problem domain
- Modeling system behavior
- Building the tokenizer
- Building the parser
- Building the evaluator
- Dealing with errors
- Building a command-line application

Technical requirements

You should have Rustup and Cargo installed in your local development environment.

The GitHub repository for the code in this chapter can be found at `https://github.com/PacktPublishing/Practical-System-Programming-for-Rust-Developers/tree/master/Chapter02`.

Analyzing the problem domain

In this section, we will define the scope of the project and the technical challenges that we need to address.

Understanding and analyzing the problem domain is the first step in building any system. It is important to unambiguously articulate the problem we are trying to solve, and the boundaries of the system. These can be captured in the form of system requirements.

Let's look at the requirements for the CLI tool we are going to build.

The tool should accept an arithmetic expression as input, evaluate it, and provide the numerical output as a floating-point number. For example, the expression *1+2*3.2+ (4/2-3/2)-2.11+2^4* should evaluate to *21.79*.

The arithmetic operations in scope are **addition** (+), **subtraction** (-), **multiplication** (*), **division** (/), **power** (^), the **negative prefix** (-), and expressions enclosed in **parentheses** ().

Mathematical functions such as trigonometric and logarithmic functions, absolute, square roots, and so on are *not* in scope.

With such an expression, the challenges that need to be resolved are as follows:

- The user should be able to input an arithmetic expression as *free text* on the command line. Numbers, arithmetic operators, and parentheses (if any) should be segregated and processed with different sets of rules.

- The rules of *operator precedence* must be taken into account (for example, multiplication takes precedence over addition).

- Expressions enclosed within *parentheses ()* must be given *higher precedence.*

- The user may not give spaces between the number and operator, but still the program must be capable of *parsing inputs with or without spaces* between the characters.

- If numbers contain a *decimal point*, continue reading the rest of the number until an operator or parenthesis is encountered.

- *Invalid inputs* should be dealt with and the program should abort with a suitable error message. Here are some examples of invalid input:

   Invalid input 1: Since we don't deal with variables in this program, if a character is entered, the program should exit with a suitable error message (for example, *2 * a* is invalid input).

   Invalid input 2: If only a single parenthesis is encountered (without a matching closing parenthesis), the program should exit with an error message.

   Invalid input 3: If the arithmetic operator is not recognized, the program should exit with an error message.

There are clearly other types of edge cases that can cause errors. But we will focus only on these. The reader is encouraged to implement other error conditions as a further exercise.

Now that we know the scope of what we are going to build, let's design the system.

Modeling the system behavior

In the last section, we confirmed the system requirements. Let's now design the logic for processing the arithmetic expression. The components of the system are shown in *Figure 2.1*:

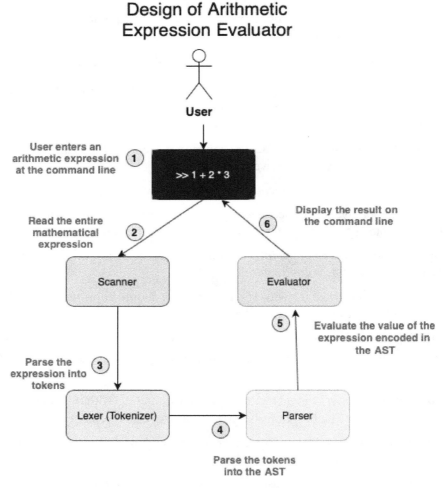

Figure 2.1 – Design of an arithmetic expression evaluator

The components shown in the preceding figure work together as follows:

1. The user enters an arithmetic expression at the command-line input and presses the *Enter* key.

2. The user input is scanned in its entirety and stored in a local variable.

3. The arithmetic expression (from the user) is scanned. The numbers are stored as tokens of the `Numeric` type. Each arithmetic operator is stored as a token of that appropriate type. For example, the + symbol will be represented as a token of type `Add`, and the number 1 will be stored as a token of type `Num` with a value of 1. This is done by the `Lexer` (or `Tokenizer`) module.

4. An **Abstract Syntax Tree (AST)** is constructed from the tokens in the previous step, taking into account the sequence in which the tokens have to be evaluated. For example, in the expression 1+2*3, the product of 2 and 3 must be evaluated before the addition operator. Also, any sub-expressions enclosed within parentheses must be evaluated on a higher priority. The final AST will reflect all such processing rules. This is done by the `Parser` module.

5. From the constructed AST, the last step is to evaluate each node of the AST in the right sequence, and aggregate them to arrive at the final value of the complete expression. This is done by the `Evaluator` module.

6. The final computed value of the expression is displayed on the command line as a program output to the user. Alternatively, any error in processing is displayed as an error message.

This is the broad sequence of steps for processing. We will now take a look at translating this design into Rust code.

Differences between lexers, parsers, and ASTs

Lexers and *parsers* are concepts used in computer science to build *compilers* and *interpreters*. A *lexer* (also called a *tokenizer*) splits text (source code) into words and assigns a *lexical* meaning to it such as *keyword, expression, operator, function call*, and so on. *Lexers* generate tokens (hence the name *tokenizer*).

A *parser* takes the output of the *lexer* and arranges the tokens into a tree structure (a tree is a type of data structure). Such a tree structure is also called an *AST*. With the *AST*, the compiler can generate machine code and the interpreter can evaluate an instruction. *Figure 2.7* of this chapter shows an illustration of an *AST*.

The lexing and parsing phases are two different steps in the compilation process, but in some cases they are combined. Note that concepts such as *lexers, parsers*, and *ASTs* have a broader range of applications beyond just compilers or interpreters, such as to render HTML web pages or SVG images.

We've so far seen the high-level design of the system. Let's now understand how the code will be organized. A visual representation of the project structure is shown here:

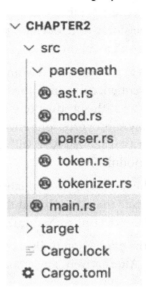

Figure 2.2 – Code structure for the project

Let's check each one of those paths:

- `src/parsemath`: The module containing the core processing logic
- `src/parsemath/ast.rs`: Contains the AST code
- `src/parsemath/parser.rs`: Contains code for the parser
- `src/parsemath/tokenizer.rs`: Contains code for the tokenizer
- `src/parsemath/token.rs`: Contains the data structures for token and operator precedence
- `src/main.rs`: The main command-line application

Let's now set up the project as follows:

1. Create a new project with `cargo new chapter2 && cd chapter2`.
2. Create a folder named `parsemath` under the `src` folder.

3. Create the following files within the `src/parsemath` folder: `ast.rs`, `token.rs`, `tokenizer.rs`, `parser.rs`, and `mod.rs`.

4. Add the following to `src/parsemath/mod.rs`:

```
pub mod ast;
pub mod parser;
pub mod token;
pub mod tokenizer;
```

Note that the Rust module system was used to structure this project. All functionality related to parsing is in the `parsemath` folder. The `mod.rs` file in this folder indicates this is a Rust module. The `mod.rs` file exports the functions in the various files contained in this folder and makes it available to the `main()` function. In the `main()` function, we then register the `parsemath` module so that the module tree is constructed by the Rust compiler. Overall, the Rust module structure helps us organize code in different files in a way that is flexible and maintainable.

Important note on code snippets in this chapter

This chapter goes through the design of the command-line tool in detail, supplemented by illustrations with diagrams. The code snippets for all the key methods are also provided with explanations. However, in some places, a few elements to complete the code, such as module imports, test scripts, and definitions of `impl` blocks, are not included here but can be directly found in the GitHub repo. Please keep this in mind if you choose to code along. Otherwise, you can follow the explanations in this chapter in conjunction with the completed code in the code repository.

Also a heads-up that you will see usage of the `?` operator in the upcoming sections on building the tokenizer, parser, and evaluator. Just bear in mind that `?` is a shortcut for error handling, in order to propagate errors automatically from a given function to its calling function. This will be explained in the later *Dealing with errors* section.

We're set now. Let's get started.

Building the tokenizer

The **tokenizer** is the module in our system design that reads one or more characters from an arithmetic expression and translates it into a *token*. In other words, *input* is a set of characters and *output* is a set of tokens. In case you are wondering, examples of tokens are *Add*, *Subtract*, and *Num(2.0)*.

We have to first create a data structure for two things:

- To store the *input* arithmetic expression from the user
- To represent the *output* tokens

In the following section, we will delve into how to determine the right data structures for the `tokenizer` module.

Tokenizer data structure

To store the input arithmetic expression, we can choose among the following data types:

- String slice
- String

We will choose the `&str` type, as we do not need to own the value or dynamically increase the size of the expression. This is because the user will provide the arithmetic expression once, and then the expression won't change for the duration of processing.

Here is one possible representation of the `Tokenizer` data structure:

src/parsemath/tokenizer.rs

```
pub struct Tokenizer {
expr: &str
}
```

If we took this approach, we may run into a problem. To understand the problem, let's understand how tokenization takes place.

For the expression *1+21*3.2*, the individual characters scanned will appear as eight separate values, *1, +, 2, 1, *, 3, ., 2*.

From this, we will have to extract the following five tokens:

Num(1.0), Add, Num(21.0), Multiply, Num(3.2)

In order to accomplish this, we not only need to read a character to convert it into a token, but also take a look at the character beyond the next one. For example, given the input expression *1+21*3.2*, to tokenize number *21* into *Num(21)*, we need to read character *2*, followed by *1*, followed by *** in order to conclude that the second operand for the first addition operation has a value of *21*.

In order to accomplish this, we have to convert the string slice into an iterator, which not only allows us to iterate through the string slice to read each character, but also allows us to *peek* ahead and see value of the character following that.

Let's see how to implement an iterator over the string slice. Rust incidentally has a built-in type for this. It's a part of the `str` module in the standard library and the struct is called `Chars`.

So, the definition of our `Tokenizer` struct could look as follows:

src/parsemath/tokenizer.rs

```
pub struct Tokenizer {
expr: std::str::Chars
}
```

Note that we have changed the type of the `expr` field from a string slice (`&str`) to an iterator type (`Chars`). `Chars` is an iterator over the characters of a string slice. This will allow us to do iterations on `expr` such as `expr.next()`, which will give the value of the next character in the expression. But we also need to take a peek at the character following the next character in the input expression, for reasons we mentioned earlier.

For this, the Rust standard library has a struct called `Peekable`, which has a `peek()` method. The usage of `peek()` can be illustrated with an example. Let's take the arithmetic expression `1+2`:

```
let expression = '1+2';
```

Because we will store this expression in the expr field of Tokenizer, which is of the peekable iterator type, we can perform next() and peek() methods on it in sequence, as shown here:

1. expression.next() returns 1. The iterator now points to character 1.

2. Then, expression.peek() returns + but does not consume it, and the iterator still points to character 1.

3. Then, expression.next() returns +, and the iterator now points to character +.

4. Then, expression.next() returns 2, and the iterator now points to character 2.

To enable such an iteration operation, we will define our Tokenizer struct as follows:

src/parsemath/tokenizer.rs

```
use std::iter::Peekable;
use std::str::Chars;
pub struct Tokenizer {
expr: Peekable<Chars>
}
```

We are still not done with the Tokenizer struct. The earlier definition would throw a compiler error asking to add a lifetime parameter. *Why is this?*, you may ask.

Structs in Rust can hold references. But Rust needs explicit lifetimes to be specified when working with structs that contain references. That is the reason we get the compiler error on the Tokenizer struct. To fix this, let's add lifetime annotation:

src/parsemath/tokenizer.rs

```
pub struct Tokenizer<'a> {
expr: Peekable<Chars<'a>>
}
```

You can see that the Tokenizer struct has been given a lifetime annotation of 'a. We have done this by declaring the name of the generic lifetime parameter 'a inside angle brackets after the name of the struct. This tells the Rust compiler that any reference to the Tokenizer struct cannot outlive the reference to the characters it contains.

> **Lifetimes in Rust**
>
> In system languages such as C/C++, operations on references can lead to unpredictable results or failures, if the value associated with the reference has been freed in memory.
>
> In Rust, every reference has a lifetime, which is the scope for which the lifetime is valid. The Rust compiler (specifically, the borrow checker) verifies that the lifetime of the reference is not longer than the lifetime of the underlying value pointed to by the reference.
>
> How does the compiler know the lifetime of references? Most of the time, the compiler tries to infer the lifetime of references (called **elision**). But where this is not possible, the compiler expects the programmer to annotate the lifetime of the reference explicitly. Common situations where the compiler expects explicit lifetime annotations are in *function signatures* where two or more arguments are references, and in *structs* where one or more members of the struct are reference types.
>
> More details can be found in the Rust documentation, at `https://doc.rust-lang.org/1.9.0/book/lifetimes.html`.

As explained, the **lifetime** annotation is to prevent the possibility of dangling references. When we instantiate the `Tokenizer` struct, we pass the string reference to it, which contains the arithmetic expression. As per the conventional rules of variable scoping (common to most programming languages), the `expr` variable needs to be valid for the duration that the `Tokenizer` object is in existence. If the value corresponding to the `expr` reference is deallocated while the `Tokenizer` object is in existence, then it constitutes a dangling (invalid) reference scenario. To prevent this, we tell the compiler through the lifetime annotation of `<'a>` that the `Tokenizer` object cannot outlive the reference it holds in the `expr` field.

The following screenshot shows the `Tokenizer` data struct:

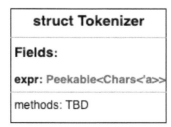

Figure 2.3 – The Tokenizer struct

We've seen so far how to define the `Tokenizer` struct, which contains the reference to input arithmetic expression. We will next take a look at how to represent the tokens generated as output from the `Tokenizer`.

To be able to represent the list of tokens that can be generated, we have to first consider the data type of these tokens. Since the tokens can be of the `Num` type or one of the operator types, we have to pick a data structure that can accommodate multiple data types. The data type options are tuples, HashMaps, structs, and enums. If we add the constraint that the type of data in a token can be one of many predefined *variants* (allowed values), that leaves us with just one option—*enums*. We will define the tokens using the `enum` data structure.

The representation of tokens in the `enum` data structure is shown in the following screenshot:

Figure 2.4 – Token enum

Here is the explanation for what value gets stored in the `Token` enum:

- If the + character is encountered, the `Add` token is generated.
- If the - character is encountered, the `Subtract` token is generated.
- If the * character is encountered, the `Multiply` token is generated.
- If the / character is encountered, the `Divide` token is generated.
- If the ^ character is encountered, the `Caret` token is generated.

- If the (character is encountered, the LeftParen token is generated.

- If the) character is encountered, the RightParen token is generated.

- If any number x is encountered, the Num(x) token is generated.

- If EOF is encountered (at the end of scanning the entire expression), the EOF token is generated.

Now that we have defined the data structures to capture the *input* (arithmetic expression) and *outputs* (tokens) for the Tokenizer module, we now can write the code to do the actual processing.

Tokenizer data processing

The following screenshot shows the Tokenizer with its data elements and methods:

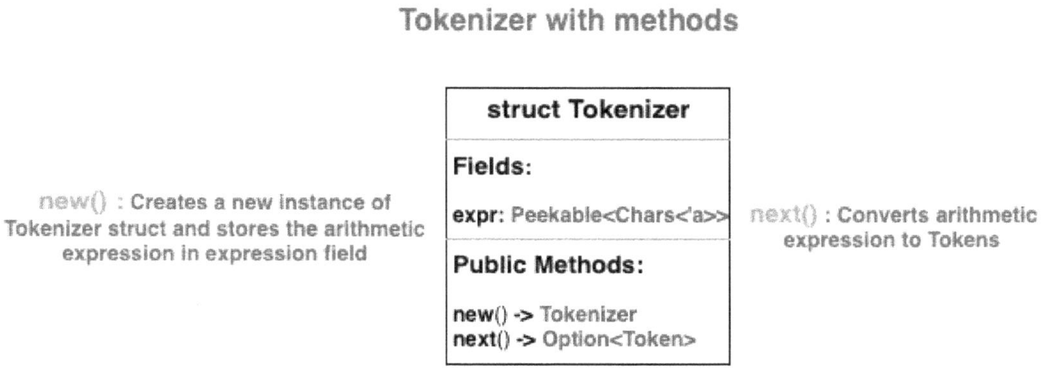

Figure 2.5 – The Tokenizer with its methods

The Tokenizer has two public methods:

- new(): Creates a new tokenizer using the arithmetic expression provided by the user

- next(): Reads the characters in the expression and return the next token

The following screenshot shows the full design of the Tokenizer module:

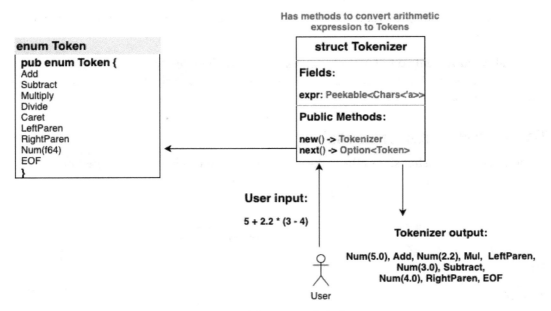

Figure 2.6 – Tokenizer module design

The code for the new() method is as follows:

src/parsemath/tokenizer.rs

```
impl<'a> Tokenizer<'a> {
    pub fn new(new_expr: &'a str) -> Self {
        Tokenizer {
            expr: new_expr.chars().peekable(),
        }
    }
}
```

You'll notice that we are declaring a lifetime for Tokenizer in the impl line. We are repeating 'a twice. Impl<'a> declares the lifetime 'a, and Tokenizer<'a> uses it.

> **Observations on lifetimes**
>
> You've seen that for `Tokenizer`, we declare its lifetime in three places:
>
> 1) The declaration of the `Tokenizer` struct
>
> 2) The declaration of the `impl` block for the `Tokenizer` struct
>
> 3) The method signature within the `impl` block
>
> This may seem verbose, but Rust expects us to be specific about lifetimes because that's how we can avoid memory-safety issues such as *dangling pointers* or *use-after-free* errors.

The `impl` keyword allows us to add functionality to the `Tokenizer` struct. The `new()` method accepts a string slice as a parameter that contains a reference to the arithmetic expression input by the user. It constructs a new `Tokenizer` struct initialized with the supplied arithmetic expression, and returns it from the function.

Note that the arithmetic expression is not stored in the struct as a string slice, but as a peekable iterator over the string slice.

In this code, `new_expr` represents the string slice, `new_expr.chars()` represents an iterator over the string slice, and `new_expr.chars().peekable()` creates a peekable iterator over the string slice.

The difference between a regular iterator and peekable iterator is that in the former, we can consume the next character in the string slice using the `next()` method, while in the latter we can also optionally peek into the next character in the slice *without consuming it*. You will see how this works as we write the code for the `next()` method of the `Tokenizer`.

We will write the code for the `next()` method on the `Tokenizer` by implementing the `Iterator` trait on the `Tokenizer` struct. Traits enable us to add behaviors to structs (and enums). The `Iterator` trait in the standard library (`std::iter::Iterator`) has a method that is required to be implemented with the following signature:

```
fn next(&mut self) -> Option<Self::Item>
```

The method signature specifies that this method can be called on an instance of the `Tokenizer` struct and it returns `Option<Token>`. This means that it either returns `Some(Token)` or `None`.

Here is the code to implement the Iterator trait on the Tokenizer struct:

src/parsemath/tokenizer.rs

```rust
impl<'a> Iterator for Tokenizer<'a> {
    type Item = Token;

    fn next(&mut self) -> Option<Token> {
        let next_char = self.expr.next();

        match next_char {
            Some('0'..='9') => {
                let mut number = next_char?.to_string();

                while let Some(next_char) = self.expr.peek() {
                    if next_char.is_numeric() || next_char ==
                        &'.' {
                        number.push(self.expr.next()?);
                    } else if next_char == &'(' {
                        return None;
                    } else {
                        break;
                    }
                }

                Some(Token::Num(number.parse::<f64>().
                    unwrap()))
            },
            Some('+') => Some(Token::Add),
            Some('-') => Some(Token::Subtract),
            Some('*') => Some(Token::Multiply),
            Some('/') => Some(Token::Divide),
            Some('^') => Some(Token::Caret),
            Some('(') => Some(Token::LeftParen),
            Some(')') => Some(Token::RightParen),
            None => Some(Token::EOF),
```

```
            Some(_) => None,
        }
    }
}
```

Notice how there are two iterators at play here:

- The next() method on expr (which is a field within the Tokenizer struct) returns the next character (we achieved this by assigning a type of Peekable<Chars> to the expr field).

- The next() method on the Tokenizer struct returns a token (we achieved this by implementing the Iterator trait on the Tokenizer struct).

Let's understand stepwise what happens when the next() method is called on Tokenizer:

- The calling program instantiates the Tokenizer struct first by calling the new() method, and then invokes the next() method on it. The next() method on the Tokenizer struct reads the next character in the stored arithmetic expression by calling next() on the expr field, which returns the next character in the expression.

- The returned character is then evaluated using a match statement. Pattern matching is used to determine what token to return, depending on what character is read from the string slice reference in the expr field.

- If the character returned from string slice is an arithmetic operator (+, -, *, /, ^) or if it is a parenthesis, the appropriate Token from the Token enum is returned. There is a one-to-one correspondence between the *character* and Token here.

- If the character returned is a number, then there is some additional processing needed. The reason is, a number may have multiple digits. Also, a number may be decimal, in which case it could be of the form *xxx.xxx,* where the amounts of digits before and after the decimal are completely unpredictable. So, for numbers, we should use the peekable iterator on the arithmetic expression to consume the next character and *peek* into the character after that to determine whether to continue reading the number.

The complete code for the Tokenizer can be found in the tokenizer.rs file in the code folder on GitHub.

Building the parser

The **parser** is the module in our project that constructs the AST, which is a tree of nodes with each node representing a token (a number or an arithmetic operator). The AST is a recursive tree structure of token nodes, that is, the root node is a token, which contains child nodes that are also tokens.

Parser data structure

The parser is a higher-level entity compared to the Tokenizer. While the Tokenizer converts user input into fine-grained tokens (for example, various arithmetic operators), the parser uses the Tokenizer outputs to construct an overall AST, which is a hierarchy of nodes. The structure of the AST constructed from the parser is illustrated in the following diagram:

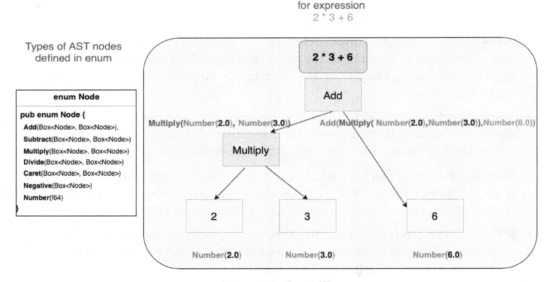

Figure 2.7 – Our AST

In the preceding figure, each of the following are nodes:

- *Number(2.0)*

- *Number(3.0)*

- *Multiply(Number(2.0),Number(3.0))*

- *Number(6.0)*

- *Add(Multiply(Number(2.0),Number(3.0)),Number(6.0))*

Each of these nodes is stored in a **boxed** data structure, which means the actual data value for each node is stored in the heap memory, while the pointer to each of the nodes is stored in a `Box` variable as part of the `Node` enum.

The overall design of the `Parser` struct is as follows:

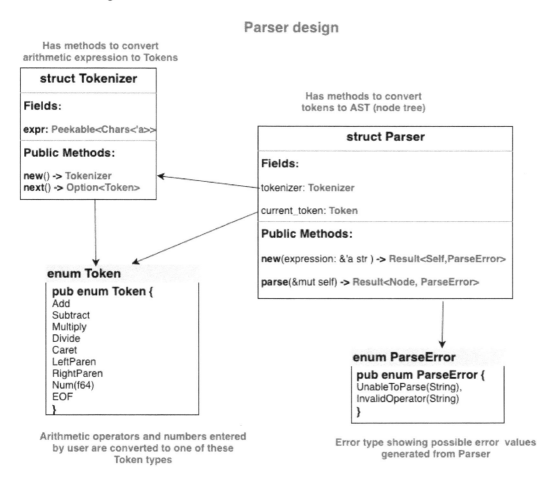

Figure 2.8 – Design of the Parser struct

As shown in the preceding figure, `Parser` will have two data elements: an instance of `Tokenizer` (that we built in the previous section), and the current token to indicate up to which point we have evaluated the arithmetic expression.

Parser methods

The `Parser` struct will have two public methods:

- `new()`: To create a new instance of the parser. This `new()` method will create a tokenizer instance passing in the arithmetic expression, and then stores the first token (returned from `Tokenizer`) in its `current_token` field.

- `parse()`: To generate the AST (the node tree) from the tokens, which is the main output of the parser.

Here is the code for the `new()` method. The code is self-explanatory, it creates a new instance of `Tokenizer`, initializing it with the arithmetic expression, and then tries to retrieve the first token from the expression. If successful, the token is stored in the `current_token` field. If not, `ParseError` is returned:

src/parsemath/parser.rs

```
// Create a new instance of Parserpub fn new(expr: &'a str) ->
Result<Self, ParseError> {
    let mut lexer = Tokenizer::new(expr);
    let cur_token = match lexer.next() {
        Some(token) => token,
        None => return Err(ParseError::InvalidOperator
            ("Invalid character".into())),
    };
    Ok(Parser {
        tokenizer: lexer,
        current_token: cur_token,
    })
}
```

The following is the code for the public `parse()` method. It invokes a private `generate_ast()` method that does the processing recursively and returns an AST (a tree of nodes). If successful, it returns the Node tree; if not, it propagates the error received:

src/parsemath/parser.rs

```
// Take an arithmetic expression as input and return an AST
pub fn parse(&mut self) -> Result<Node, ParseError> {
    let ast = self.generate_ast(OperPrec::DefaultZero);
    match ast {
```

```
        Ok(ast) => Ok(ast),
        Err(e) => Err(e),
    }
}
```

The following image lists all the private and public methods in the `Parser` struct:

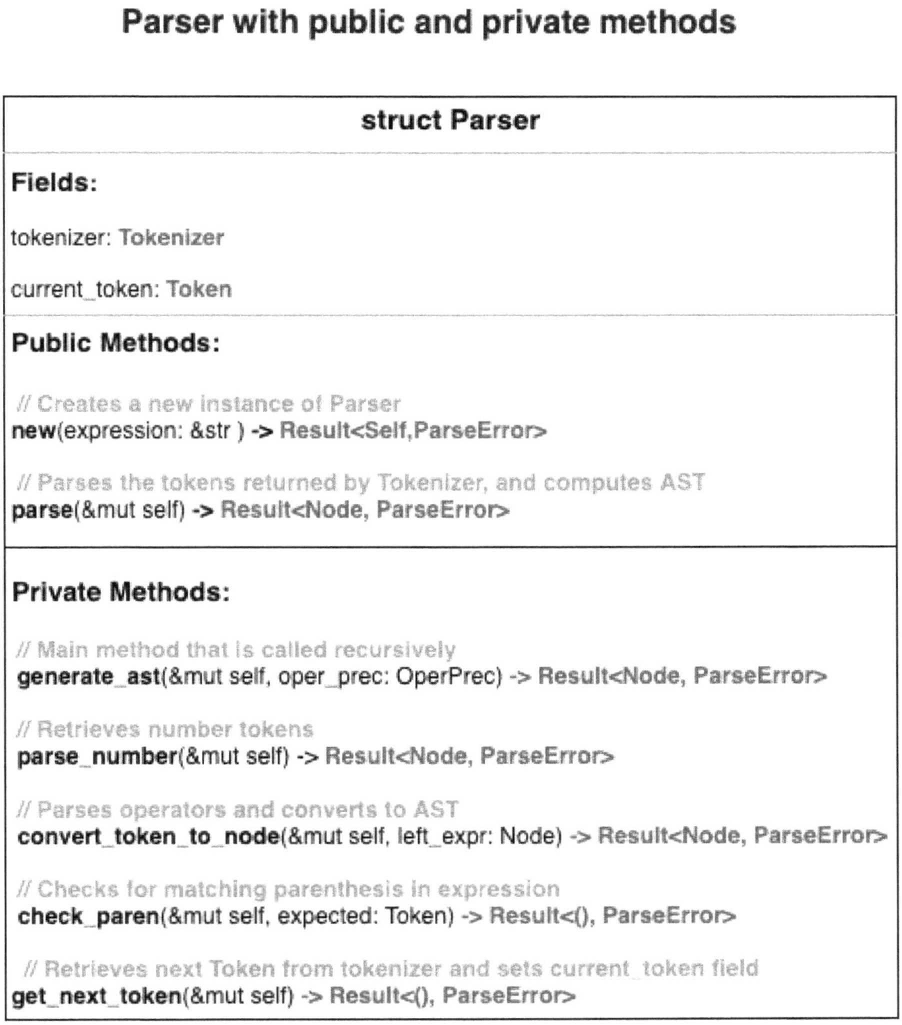

Parser with public and private methods

struct Parser
Fields:
tokenizer: Tokenizer
current_token: Token

Public Methods:
 	
// Creates a new instance of Parser
new(expression: &str) -> Result<Self,ParseError>
 	
// Parses the tokens returned by Tokenizer, and computes AST
parse(&mut self) -> Result<Node, ParseError>

Private Methods:
 	
// Main method that is called recursively
generate_ast(&mut self, oper_prec: OperPrec) -> Result<Node, ParseError>
 	
// Retrieves number tokens
parse_number(&mut self) -> Result<Node, ParseError>
 	
// Parses operators and converts to AST
convert_token_to_node(&mut self, left_expr: Node) -> Result<Node, ParseError>
 	
// Checks for matching parenthesis in expression
check_paren(&mut self, expected: Token) -> Result<(), ParseError>
 	
// Retrieves next Token from tokenizer and sets current_token field
get_next_token(&mut self) -> Result<(), ParseError>

Figure 2.9 – Parser methods overview

Let's now look at the code for the get_next_token() method. This method retrieves the next token from the arithmetic expression using the Tokenizer struct and updates the current_token field of the Parser struct. If unsuccessful, it returns ParseError:

src/parsemath/parser.rs

```
fn get_next_token(&mut self) -> Result<(), ParseError> {
    let next_token = match self.tokenizer.next() {
        Some(token) => token,
        None => return Err(ParseError::InvalidOperator
            ("Invalid character".into())),
    };
    self.current_token = next_token;
    Ok(())
}
```

Note the empty tuple () returned in Result<(), ParseError>. This means if nothing goes wrong, no concrete value is returned.

Here's the code for the check_paren() method. This is a helper method used to check whether there are matching pairs of parentheses in the expression. Otherwise, an error is returned:

src/parsemath/parser.rs

```
fn check_paren(&mut self, expected: Token) -> Result<(),
ParseError> {
    if expected == self.current_token {
        self.get_next_token()?;
        Ok(())
    } else {
        Err(ParseError::InvalidOperator(format!(
            "Expected {:?}, got {:?}",
            expected, self.current_token
        )))
    }
}
```

Let's now look at the remaining three private methods that do the bulk of the parser processing.

The `parse_number()` method takes the current token, and checks for three things:

- Whether the token is a number of the form *Num(i)*.

- Whether the token has a sign, in case it is a negative number. For example, the expression *-2.2 + 3.4* is parsed into AST as *Add(Negative(Number(2.2)), Number(3.4))*.

- Pairs of parenthesis: If an expression is found within pairs of parenthesis, it treats it as a multiplication operation. For example, *1*(2+3)* is parsed as *Multiply(Number(1.0), Add(Number(2.0), Number(3.0)))*.

In case of errors in any of the preceding operations, `ParseError` is returned.

Here is the code for the `parse_number()` method:

src/parsemath/parser.rs

```
// Construct AST node for numbers, taking into account
// negative prefixes while handling parenthesis
fn parse_number(&mut self) -> Result<Node, ParseError> {
    let token = self.current_token.clone();
    match token {
        Token::Subtract => {
            self.get_next_token()?;
            let expr = self.generate_ast(OperPrec::Negative)?;
            Ok(Node::Negative(Box::new(expr)))
        }
        Token::Num(i) => {
            self.get_next_token()?;
            Ok(Node::Number(i))
        }
        Token::LeftParen => {
            self.get_next_token()?;
            let expr = self.generate_ast
                (OperPrec::DefaultZero)?;
            self.check_paren(Token::RightParen)?;
            if self.current_token == Token::LeftParen {
                let right = self.generate_ast
                    (OperPrec::MulDiv)?;
```

```
            return Ok(Node::Multiply(Box::new(expr),
                Box::new(right)));
        }

        Ok(expr)
    }
    _ => Err(ParseError::UnableToParse("Unable to
        parse".to_string())),
    }
}
```

The `generate_ast()` method is the main workhorse of the module and is invoked recursively. It does its processing in the following sequence:

1. It processes numeric tokens, negative number tokens, and expressions in parentheses using the `parse_number()` method.

2. It parses each token from the arithmetic expression in a sequence within a loop to check if the precedence of the next two operators encountered, and constructs AST by calling the `convert_token_to_node()` method in such a way that the expression containing an operator with higher precedence is executed before an expression containing an operator with lower precedence. For example, the expression *1+2*3* is evaluated as *Add(Number(1.0), Multiply(Number(2.0), Number(3.0)))*, whereas the expression *1*2+3* is evaluated as *Add(Multiply(Number(1.0), Number(2.0)), Number(3.0))*.

Let's now look at the code for the `generate_ast()` method:

src/parsemath/parser.rs

```
fn generate_ast(&mut self, oper_prec: OperPrec) -> Result<Node,
ParseError> {
    let mut left_expr = self.parse_number()?;

    while oper_prec < self.current_token.get_oper_prec() {
        if self.current_token == Token::EOF {
            break;
        }
        let right_expr = self.convert_token_to_node
            (left_expr.clone())?;
```

```
        left_expr = right_expr;
    }
    Ok(left_expr)
}
```

We have seen the various methods associated with the parser. Let's now look at another key aspect when dealing with arithmetic operators—*operator precedence.*

Operator precedence

Operator precedence rules determine the order in which the arithmetic expression is processed. Without defining this correctly, we will not be able to calculate the right computed value of the arithmetic expression. The enum for operator precedence is as follows:

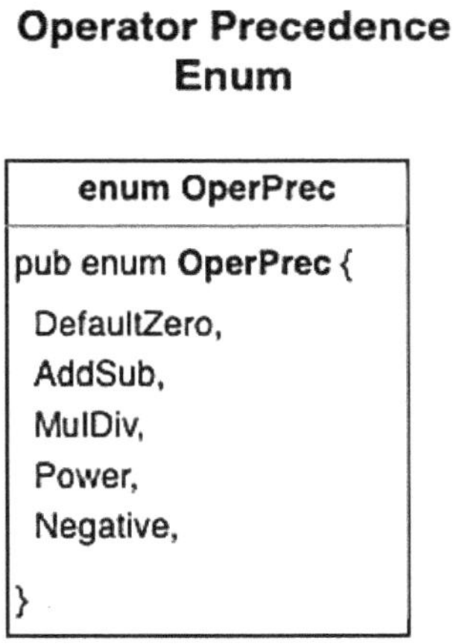

Operator Precedence Enum

enum OperPrec

pub enum **OperPrec** {
 	
  DefaultZero,
  AddSub,
  MulDiv,
  Power,
  Negative,
 	
}

Figure 2.10 – Operator precedence enum

The operator precedence enum has the following values:

- DefaultZero: The default precedence (lowest priority)
- AddSub: The precedence applied if the arithmetic operation is addition or subtraction
- MulDiv: The precedence applied if the arithmetic operation is multiplication or division
- Power: The precedence applied if the caret (^) operator is encountered
- Negative: The precedence applied for the negative (-) prefix before a number

The precedence order increases from top to bottom, that is, DefaultZero < AddSub < MulDiv < Power < Negative.

Define the operator precedence enum as shown:

src/parsemath/token.rs

```
#[derive(Debug, PartialEq, PartialOrd)]
/// Defines all the OperPrec levels, from lowest to highest.
pub enum OperPrec {
    DefaultZero,
    AddSub,
    MulDiv,
    Power,
    Negative,
}
```

The get_oper_prec() method is used to get the operator precedence given an operator. The following is the code that shows this method in action. Define this method in the impl block of the Token struct:

src/parsemath/token.rs

```
impl Token {
    pub fn get_oper_prec(&self) -> OperPrec {
        use self::OperPrec::*;
        use self::Token::*;
        match *self {
            Add | Subtract => AddSub,
            Multiply | Divide => MulDiv,
            Caret => Power,

            _ => DefaultZero,
        }
    }
}
```

Now, let's look at the code for convert_token_to_node(). This method basically constructs the operator-type AST nodes by checking whether the token is Add, Subtract, Multiply, Divide, or Caret. In the case of an error, ParseError is returned:

src/parsemath/parser.rs

```
fn convert_token_to_node(&mut self, left_expr: Node) ->
Result<Node, ParseError> {
    match self.current_token {
        Token::Add => {
            self.get_next_token()?;
            //Get right-side expression
            let right_expr = self.generate_ast
                (OperPrec::AddSub)?;
            Ok(Node::Add(Box::new(left_expr),
                Box::new(right_expr)))
        }
        Token::Subtract => {
            self.get_next_token()?;
            //Get right-side expression
            let right_expr = self.generate_ast
                (OperPrec::AddSub)?;
            Ok(Node::Subtract(Box::new(left_expr),
                Box::new(right_expr)))
        }
        Token::Multiply => {
            self.get_next_token()?;
            //Get right-side expression
            let right_expr = self.generate_ast
                (OperPrec::MulDiv)?;
            Ok(Node::Multiply(Box::new(left_expr),
                Box::new(right_expr)))
        }
        Token::Divide => {
            self.get_next_token()?;
            //Get right-side expression
            let right_expr = self.generate_ast
                (OperPrec::MulDiv)?;
            Ok(Node::Divide(Box::new(left_expr),
                Box::new(right_expr)))
        }
```

```
        Token::Caret => {
            self.get_next_token()?;
            //Get right-side expression
            let right_expr = self.generate_ast
                (OperPrec::Power)?;
            Ok(Node::Caret(Box::new(left_expr),
                Box::new(right_expr)))
        }
        _ => Err(ParseError::InvalidOperator(format!(
            "Please enter valid operator {:?}",
            self.current_token
        ))),
    }
}
```

We will look in detail at error handling later in the chapter in the *Dealing with errors* section. The complete code for `Parser` can be found in the `parser.rs` file in the GitHub folder for the chapter.

Building the evaluator

Once the `AST` (node tree) is constructed in the parser, evaluating the numeric value from `AST` is a straightforward operation. The evaluator function parses each node in the `AST` tree recursively and arrives at the final value.

For example, if the `AST` node is *Add(Number(1.0),Number(2.0))*, it evaluates to *3.0*.

If the `AST` node is *Add(Number(1.0),Multiply(Number(2.0),Number(3.0)))*:

- It evaluates value of *Number(1.0)* to *1.0*.

- Then it evaluates *Multiply(Number(2.0), Number(3.0))* to *6.0*.

- It then adds *1.0* and *6.0* to get the final value of *7.0*.

Let's now look at the code for the `eval()` function:

src/parsemath/ast.rs

```
pub fn eval(expr: Node) -> Result<f64, Box<dyn error::Error>> {
    use self::Node::*;
    match expr {
        Number(i) => Ok(i),
        Add(expr1, expr2) => Ok(eval(*expr1)? +
```

```
            eval(*expr2)?),
    Subtract(expr1, expr2) => Ok(eval(*expr1)? -
            eval(*expr2)?),
    Multiply(expr1, expr2) => Ok(eval(*expr1)? *
            eval(*expr2)?),
    Divide(expr1, expr2) => Ok(eval(*expr1)? /
            eval(*expr2)?),
    Negative(expr1) => Ok(-(eval(*expr1)?)),
    Caret(expr1, expr2) => Ok(eval(*expr1)?
            .powf(eval(*expr2)?)),
    }
}
```

Trait objects

In the `eval()` method, you will notice that the method returns `Box<dyn error::Error>` in case of errors. This is an example of a **trait object**. We will explain this now.

In the Rust standard library, `error::Error` is a trait. Here, we are telling the compiler that the `eval()` method should return something that implements the `Error` trait. We don't know at compile time what the exact type being returned is; we just know that whatever is returned will implement the `Error` trait. The underlying error type is only known at runtime and is not statically determined. Here, `dyn error::Error` is a trait object. The use of the `dyn` keyword indicates it is a trait object.

When we use trait objects, the compiler does not know at compile time which method to call on which types. This is only known at runtime, hence it is called *dynamic-dispatch* (when the compiler knows what method to call at compile time, it is called *static dispatch*).

Note also that we are boxing the error with `Box<dyn error::Error>`. This is because we don't know the size of the error type at runtime, so boxing is a way to get around this problem (`Box` is a reference type that has a known size at compile time). The Rust standard library helps in boxing our errors by having `Box` implement conversion from any type that implements the `Error` trait into the trait object `Box<Error>`.

More details can be found in the Rust documentation, at `https://doc.rust-lang.org/book/ch17-02-trait-objects.html`.

Dealing with errors

Error handling deals with the question: *how do we communicate program errors to users?*

In our project, errors can occur due to two main reasons—there could be a programming error, or an error could occur due to invalid inputs. Let's first discuss the Rust approach to error handling.

In Rust, errors are first-class citizens in that an error is a data type in itself, just like an `integer`, `string`, or `vector`. Because `error` is a data type, type checking can happen at compile time. The Rust standard library has a `std::error::Error` trait implemented by all errors in the Rust standard library. Rust does not use exception handling, but a unique approach where a computation can return a `Result` type:

```
enum Result<T, E> {   Ok(T),   Err(E),}
```

`Result<T, E>` is an enum with two variants, where `Ok(T)` represents *success* and `Err(E)` represents the *error* returned. Pattern matching is used to handle the two types of return values from a function.

To gain greater control over error handling and to provide more user-friendly errors for application users, it is recommended to use a custom error type that implements the `std::error::Error` trait. All types of errors from different modules in the program can then be converted to this custom error type for uniform error handling. This is a very effective way to deal with errors in Rust.

A lightweight approach to error handling could be to use `Option<T>` as the return value from a function, where `T` is any generic type:

```
pub enum Option<T> {   None,   Some(T),}
```

The `Option` type is an enum with two variants, `Some(T)` and `None`. If processing is successful, a `Some(T)` value is returned, otherwise, `None` is returned from the function.

We will use both the `Result` and `Option` types for error handling in our project.

The error handling approach chosen for our project is as follows:

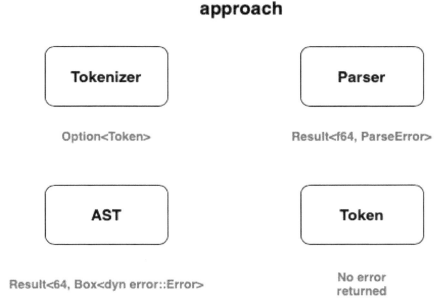

Figure 2.11 – Error handling approach

For our project, the approach for the four modules that contain the core processing is as follows:

- **Tokenizer module**: This has two public methods—new() and next(). The new() method is fairly simple and just creates a new instance of the Tokenizer struct and initializes it. No error will be returned in this method. However, the next() method returns a Token, and if there is any invalid character in the arithmetic expression, we need to deal with this situation and communicate it to the calling code. We will use a lightweight error handling approach here, with Option<Token> as the return value from the next() method. If a valid Token can be constructed from the arithmetic expression, Some(Token) will be returned. In the case of invalid input, None will be returned. The calling function can then interpret None as an error condition and take care of the necessary handling.

- **AST module**: This has one main `eval()` function that computes a numeric value given a node tree. We will return a vanilla `std::error::Error` in case of an error during processing, but it will be a `Boxed` value because otherwise, the Rust compiler will not know the size of the error value at compile time. The return type from this method is `Result<f64, Box<dyn error::Error>>`. If processing is successful, a numeric value (`f64`) is returned, else a `Boxed` error is returned. We could have defined a custom error type for this module to avoid the complex `Boxed` error signature, but this approach has been chosen to showcase the various ways to do error handling in Rust.

- **Token module**: This has one function, `get_oper_prec()`, which returns the operator precedence given an arithmetic operator as input. Since we do not see any possibility of errors in this simple method, there will be no error type defined in the return value of the method.

- **Parser module**: The `Parser` module contains the bulk of the processing logic. Here, a custom error type, `ParseError,` will be defined, which has the following structure:

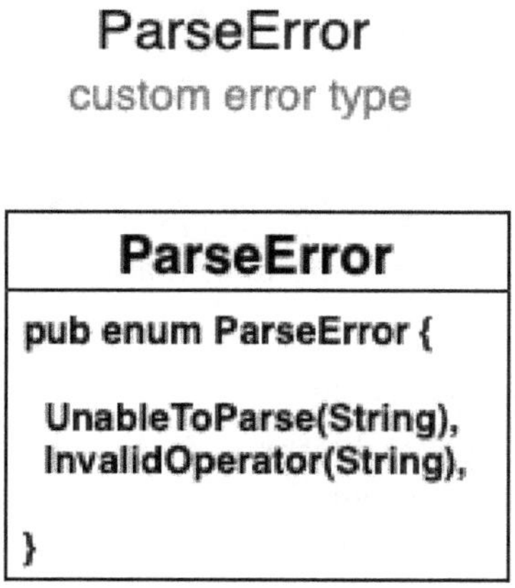

Figure 2.12 – Custom error type

Our custom error type has two variants, `UnableToParse(String)` and `InvalidOperator(String)`.

The first variant will be a generic error for any type of error during processing, and the second variant will be used specifically if there is an invalid arithmetic operator provided by the user; for example, *2=3*.

Let's define a custom error type for the parser:

src/parsemath/parser.rs

```
#[derive(Debug)]
pub enum ParseError {
    UnableToParse(String),
    InvalidOperator(String),
}
```

To print errors, we also need to implement the Display trait:

src/parsemath/parser.rs

```
impl fmt::Display for ParseError {
    fn fmt(&self, f: &mut fmt::Formatter) -> fmt::Result {
        match &self {
            self::ParseError::UnableToParse(e) => write!(f,
                "Error in evaluating {}", e),
            self::ParseError::InvalidOperator(e) => write!(f,
                "Error in evaluating {}", e),
        }
    }
}
```

Since ParseError will be the main error type returned from processing, and because the AST module returns a Boxed error, we can write code to automatically convert any Boxed error from the AST module into ParseError that gets returned by Parser. The code is as follows:

src/parsemath/parser.rs

```
impl std::convert::From<std::boxed::Box<dyn std::error::Error>>
for ParseError {
    fn from(_evalerr: std::boxed::Box<dyn std::error::Error>)
        -> Self {
        return ParseError::UnableToParse("Unable to
            parse".into());
    }
}
```

This code allows us to write code such as the following:

```
let num_value = eval(ast)?
```

Note in particular the ? operator. It is a shortcut for the following: ·

- If eval() processing is successful, store the returned value in the num_value field.

- If processing fails, convert the Boxed error returned by the eval() method into ParseError and propagate it further to the caller.

This concludes the discussion on the arithmetic expression evaluator modules. In the next section, we will take a look at how to call this module from a main() function.

Putting it all together

We have seen in previous sections how to design and write code for the various processing modules of our project. We will now tie all of them together in a main() function that serves as the command-line application. This main() function will do the following:

1. Display prompts with instructions for the user to enter an arithmetic expression.

2. Accept an arithmetic expression in the command-line input from the user.

3. Instantiate Parser (returns a Parser object instance).

4. Parse the expression (returns the AST representation of the expression).

5. Evaluate the expression (computes the mathematical value of the expression).

6. Display the result to the user in the command-line output.

7. Invoke Parser and evaluate the mathematical expression.

The code for the main() function is as follows:

src/main.rs

```
fn main() {
    println!("Hello! Welcome to Arithmetic expression
        evaluator.");
    println!("You can calculate value for expression such as
        2*3+(4-5)+2^3/4. ");
    println!("Allowed numbers: positive, negative and
        decimals.");
    println!("Supported operations: Add, Subtract, Multiply,
```

```
        Divide, PowerOf(^). ");
println!("Enter your arithmetic expression below:");
loop {
    let mut input = String::new();
    match io::stdin().read_line(&mut input) {
        Ok(_) => {
            match evaluate(input) {
                Ok(val) => println!("The computed number
                    is {}\n", val),
                Err(_) => {
                    println!("Error in evaluating
                        expression. Please enter valid
                        expression\n");
                }
            };
        }

        Err(error) => println!("error: {}", error),
    }
}
}
```

The main() function displays a prompt to the user, reads a line from stdin (the command line), and invokes the evaluate() function. If the computation is successful, it displays the computed AST and the numerical value. If unsuccessful, it prints an error message.

The code for the evaluate() function is as follows:

src/main.rs

```
fn evaluate(expr: String) -> Result<f64, ParseError> {
    let expr = expr.split_whitespace().collect::<String>();
    // remove whitespace chars
    let mut math_parser = Parser::new(&expr)?;
    let ast = math_parser.parse()?;
    println!("The generated AST is {:?}", ast);

    Ok(ast::eval(ast)?)
}
```

The `evaluate()` function instantiates a new `Parser` with the provided arithmetic expression, parses it, and then invokes the `eval()` method on the `AST` module. Note the use of the `?` operator for automated propagation of any processing errors to the `main()` function, where they are handled with a `println!` statement.

Run the following command to compile and run the program:

```
cargo run
```

You can try out various combinations of positive and negative numbers, decimals, arithmetic operators, and optional sub-expressions in parentheses. You can also check how an invalid input expression will produce an error message.

You can expand this project to add support for mathematical functions such as square roots, trigonometric functions, logarithmic functions, and so on. You can also add edge cases.

With this, we conclude the first full-length project in this book. I hope this project has given you an idea not just of how idiomatic Rust code is written, but also of how to think in Rust terms while designing a program.

The complete code for the `main()` function can be found in the `main.rs` file in the GitHub folder for this chapter.

Summary

In this chapter, we built a command-line application from scratch in Rust, without using any third-party libraries, to compute the value of the arithmetic expressions. We covered many basic concepts in Rust, including data types, how to model and design an application domain with Rust data structures, how to split code across modules and integrate them, how to structure code within a module as functions, how to expose module functions to other modules, how to do pattern matching for elegant and safe code, how to add functionality to structs and enums, how to implement traits and annotate lifetimes, how to design and propagate custom error types, how to box types to make data sizes predictable for the compiler, how to construct a recursive node tree and navigate it, how to write code that recursively evaluates an expression, and how to specify lifetime parameters for structs.

Congratulations if you successfully followed along and got some working code! If you had any difficulties, you can refer to the final code in the GitHub repository.

This example project establishes a strong foundation from which to dig into the details of system programming in the upcoming chapters. If you haven't fully understood every detail of the code, there is no reason to fret. We will be writing a lot more code and reinforcing the concepts of idiomatic Rust code as we go along in the coming chapters.

In the next chapter, we will cover the Rust standard library, and see how it supports a rich set of built-in modules, types, traits, and functions to perform systems programming.

3

Introduction to the Rust Standard Library

In the previous chapter, we built a command-line tool using various Rust language primitives and modules from the Rust Standard Library. However, in order to fully exploit the power of Rust, it is imperative to understand the breadth of what features are available within the standard library for system programming tasks, without having to reach out to third-party crates.

In this chapter, we'll deep-dive into the structure of the Rust Standard Library. You'll get an introduction to the standard modules for accessing system resources and learn how to manage them programmatically. With the knowledge gained, we will implement a tiny portion of a template engine in Rust. By the end of this chapter, you will be able to confidently navigate the Rust Standard Library and make use of it in your projects.

The following are the key learning outcomes for this chapter:

- Introducing the Rust Standard Library
- Writing one feature of a template engine using the standard library modules

Technical requirements

Rustup and Cargo must be installed in your local development environment. The GitHub repository for the examples in this chapter can be found at `https://github.com/PacktPublishing/Practical-System-Programming-for-Rust-Developers/tree/master/Chapter03`.

The Rust Standard Library and systems programming

Before we dive into the standard library, let's understand the context of how it fits into systems programming.

In systems programming, one of the cardinal requirements is to manage system resources such as memory, files, network I/O, devices, and processes. Every operating system has a kernel (or equivalent), which is the central software module that is loaded in memory and connects the system hardware with the application processes. You may think, where does the Rust Standard Library fit in then? Are we going to write a kernel in Rust? No, that's not the purpose of this book. The most popular operating systems, which are basically the Unix, Linux, and Windows variants, all have kernels written mostly in **C** with a mix of assembly. It is still early days for Rust to augment C as the kernel development language, though there are several experimental efforts in that direction. However, what the Rust Standard Library offers is an API interface to make system calls from Rust programs, in order to manage and manipulate various system resources. The following figure shows this context:

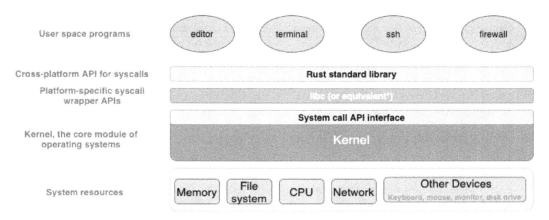

Figure 3.1 – Rust Standard Library

Let's walk through this figure to understand each of the components better:

- **Kernel**: The kernel is the central component of an operating system that manages system resources such as memory, disk and file systems, CPU, network, and other devices such as the mouse, keyboard, and monitors. User programs (for example, a *command-line tool* or *text editor*) cannot manage system resources directly. They have to rely on the kernel to perform operations. If a text editor program wants to read a file, it will have to make a corresponding system call, `read()`, which the kernel will then execute on behalf of the editor program. The reason for this restriction is that modern processor architectures (such as x86-64) allow the CPU to operate at two different privilege levels—*kernel mode* and *user mode*. The user mode has a lower level of privilege than the kernel mode. The CPU can perform certain operations only while running in the kernel mode. This design prevents user programs from accidentally doing tasks that could adversely affect the system operation.

- **System call (syscall) interface**: The kernel also provides a system call *application programming interface* that acts as the entry point for processes to request the kernel to perform various tasks.

- **Syscall wrapper APIs**: A user program cannot directly make a system call in the way normal functions are called because they cannot be resolved by the linker. So, architecture-specific assembly language code is needed to make system calls into the kernel. Such code is made available through wrapper libraries, which are platform-specific. For Unix/Linux/POSIX systems, this library is `libc` (or `glibc`). For the Windows operating system, there are equivalent APIs.

- **Rust Standard Library**: The Rust Standard Library is the primary interface for Rust programs into the kernel functions of an operating system. It uses `libc` (or another platform-specific equivalent library) internally to invoke system calls. The Rust Standard Library is cross-platform, which means that the details of how system calls are invoked (or which wrapper libraries are used) are abstracted away from the Rust developer. There are ways to invoke system calls from Rust code without using the standard library (for example, in embedded systems development), but that is beyond the scope of this book.

- **User space programs**: These are the programs that you will write as part of this book using the standard library. The *arithmetic expression evaluator* you wrote in the previous chapter is an example of this. In this chapter, you will learn how to write a feature of the template engine using the standard library, which is also a user space program.

> **Note**
>
> Not all modules and functions within the Rust Standard Library invoke system calls (for example, there are methods for string manipulation, and to handle errors). As we go through the standard library, it is important to remember this distinction.

Let's now begin our journey to understand and start using the Rust Standard Library.

Exploring the Rust Standard Library

We earlier discussed the role of the Rust Standard Library in enabling user programs to invoke kernel operations. The following are some of the notable features of the standard library, which we will refer to as `std` for brevity:

- `std` is cross-platform. It provides functionality that hides the differences among underlying platform architectures.

- `std` is available to all Rust crates by default. The `use` statement gives access to the respective modules and their constituents (traits, methods, structs, and so on). For example, the statement `use std::fs` gives access to the module providing file manipulation operations.

- `std` includes operations on standard Rust primitives (such as integers and floating-point numbers). For example, `std::i8::MAX` is a constant implemented in the standard library that specifies the maximum value that can be stored in a variable of type i8.

- It implements core data types such as *vector, strings*, and *smart pointers* such as `Box`, `Rc`, and `Arc`.

- It provides functionality for operations such as data manipulation, memory allocation, error handling, networking, I/O, concurrency, async I/O primitives, and foreign function interfaces.

The following figure shows a high-level view of the Rust standard library:

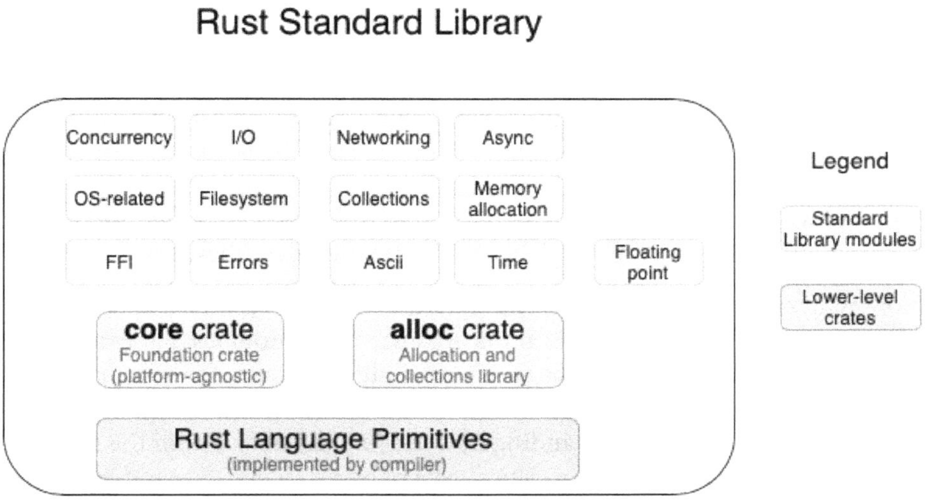

Figure 3.2 – Rust Standard Library – high-level view

The Rust Standard Library (`std`) is broadly organized as follows:

- **Rust language primitives**, which contain basic types such as signed and unsigned, integers, bool, floating point, char, array, tuple, slice, and string. Primitives are implemented by the compiler. The Rust Standard Library includes the primitives and builds on top of them.

- The **core crate** is the foundation of the Rust Standard Library. It acts as the link between the Rust language and the standard library. It provides types, traits, constants, and functions implemented on top of Rust primitives, and provides the foundational building blocks for all Rust code. The core crate can be used independently, is not platform-specific, and does not have any links to operating system libraries (such as `libc`) or other external dependencies. You can instruct the compiler to compile without the Rust Standard Library and use the core crate instead (such an environment is called `no_std` in Rust parlance, which is annotated with the `#![no_std]` attribute), and this is used commonly in embedded programming.

- The **alloc crate** contains types, functions, and traits related to memory allocation for heap-allocated values. It includes smart pointer types such as Box (`Box<T>`), reference-counted pointers (`Rc<T>`), and atomically reference-counted pointers (`Arc<T>`). It also includes and collections such as `Vec` and `String` (note that `String` is implemented in Rust as a UTF-8 sequence). This crate does not need to be used directly when the standard library is used, as the contents of the `alloc` crate are re-exported and made available as part of the `std` library. The only exception to this rule is when developing in a `no_std` environment, when this crate can be directly used to access its functionality.

- **Modules** (libraries) that are directly part of the standard library (and not re-exported from `core` or `alloc` crates) include rich functionality for operations around concurrency, I/O, file system access, networking, async I/O, errors, and OS-specific functions.

In this book, we will not directly work with the `core` or `alloc` crates, but use the Rust Standard Library modules that are a higher-level abstraction over these crates.

We will now analyze the key modules within the Rust Standard Library with a focus on systems programming. The standard library is organized into modules. For example, the functionality that enables user programs to run on multiple threads for concurrency is in the `std::thread` module, and the Rust constructs for dealing with synchronous I/O are in the `std::io` module. Understanding how the functionality within the standard library is organized across modules is a critical part of being an effective and productive Rust programmer.

Figure 3.3 shows the layout of the standard library modules organized into groups:

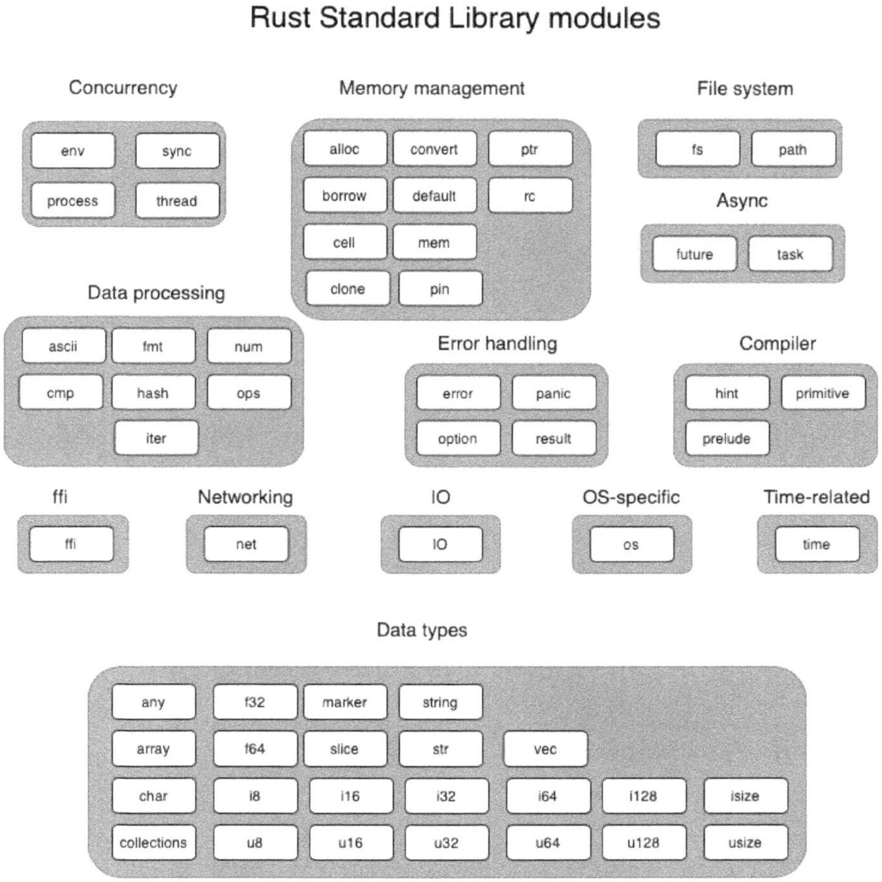

Rust Standard Library modules

Concurrency

| env | sync |
| process | thread |

Memory management

alloc	convert	ptr
borrow	default	rc
cell	mem	
clone	pin	

File system

| fs | path |

Async

| future | task |

Data processing

ascii	fmt	num
cmp	hash	ops
	iter	

Error handling

| error | panic |
| option | result |

Compiler

| hint | primitive |
| prelude | |

ffi

| ffi |

Networking

| net |

IO

| IO |

OS-specific

| os |

Time-related

| time |

Data types

any	f32	marker	string			
array	f64	slice	str	vec		
char	i8	i16	i32	i64	i128	isize
collections	u8	u16	u32	u64	u128	usize

Figure 3.3 – Rust Standard Library modules

The modules in this figure have been grouped by their primary area of focus.

How do we know, though, which of these modules is related to managing system resources? As this might be of interest for the purposes of this book, let's attempt to classify the modules further into one of these two buckets:

- **Syscalls-oriented**: These are modules that either manage system hardware resources directly or require the kernel for other privileged operations.

- **Computation-oriented**: These are the modules that are oriented towards data representation, computation, and instructions to the compiler.

Figure 3.4 shows the same module grouping as in *Figure 3.3* but segregated as **Syscalls-oriented** or **Computation-oriented**. Note that this may not be a perfect classification as not all methods in all modules marked in the **Syscalls-oriented** category involve actual system calls. But this classification can serve as a guide to find our way around the standard library:

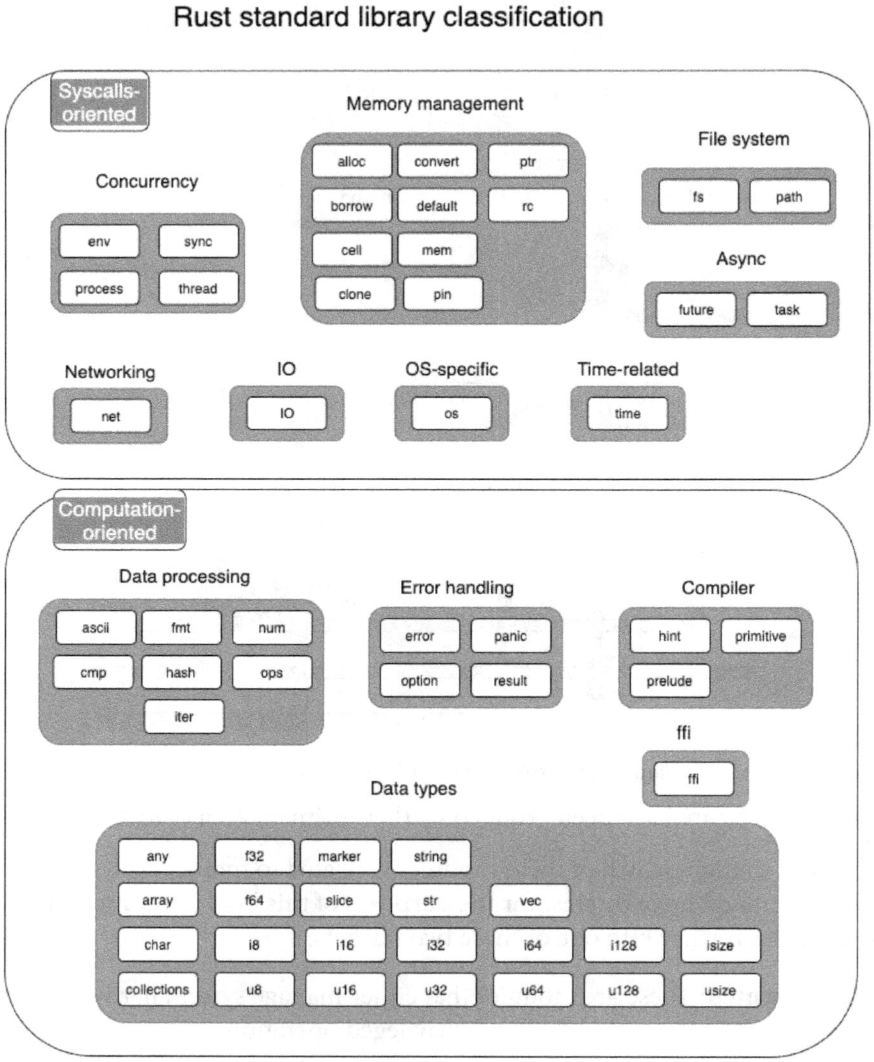

Rust standard library classification

Figure 3.4 – Rust modules with classification

Let's get to know the functionality of each module.

Computation-oriented modules

The standard library modules in this section deal *mostly* with programming constructs that deal with data processing, data modeling, error handling, and instructions to the compiler. Some of the modules may have functionality that overlaps with the syscalls-oriented category, but this grouping is based on the primary focus of each module.

Data types

The modules related to data types and structures in the Rust Standard Library are mentioned in this section. There are broadly two categories of data types in Rust. The first group comprises primitive types such as integers (signed, unsigned), floating points, and char, which are a core part of the language and compiler and the standard library adds additional functionality to those types. The second group consists of higher-level data structures and traits such as vectors and strings, which are implemented within the standard library. Modules from both these groups are listed here:

- `any`: This can be used when the type of the value passed to a function is not known at compile time. Runtime reflection is used to check the type and perform suitable processing. An example of using this would be in the logging function, where we want to customize what is logged depending on the data type.

- `array`: It contains utility functions such as comparing arrays, implemented over the primitive array type. Note that Rust arrays are value types, that is, they are allocated on the stack, and have a fixed length (not growable).

- `char`: This contains utility functions implemented over the char primitive type, such as checking for digits, converting to uppercase, encoding to UTF-8, and so on.

- `collections`: This is Rust's standard collection library, which contains efficient implementations of common collection data structures used in programming. Collections in this library include `Vectors`, `LinkedLists`, `HashMaps`, `HashSet`, `BTtreeMap`, `BTreeSet`, and `BinaryHeap`.

- `f32`, `f64`: This library provides constants specific to floating point implementations of the `f32` and `f64` primitive types. Examples of constants are `MAX` and `MIN`, which provide the maximum and minimum value of floating point numbers that can be stored by `f32` and `f64` types.

- `i8`, `i16`, `i32`, `i64`, `i128`: Signed integer types of various sizes. For example, `i8` represents a signed integer of length 8 bits (1 byte) and `i128` represents a signed integer of length 128 bits (16 bytes).

- u8, u16, u32, u64, u128: Unsigned integer types of various sizes. For example, u8 represents an unsigned integer of length 8 bits (1 byte) and u128 represents an unsigned integer of length 128 bits (16 bytes).

- isize, usize: Rust has two data types, isize and usize, that correspond to signed and unsigned integer types. The uniqueness of these types is that their size is dependent on whether the CPU uses a 32-bit or 64-bit architecture. For example, on a 32-bit system, the size of the isize and usize data types is 32 bits (4 bytes), and likewise, for 64-bit systems, their size is 64 bits (8 bytes).

- marker: Basic properties that can be attached to types (in the form of traits) are described in this module. Examples include Copy (types whose values can be duplicated by a simple copy of its bits) and Send (thread-safe types).

- slice: Contains structs and methods useful to perform operations such as iterate and split on slice data types.

- string: This module contains the String type and methods such as to_string, which allows converting a value to a String. Note that String is not a primitive data type in Rust. The primitive types in Rust are listed here: https://doc.rust-lang.org/std/.

- str: This module contains structs and methods associated with string slices such as iterate and split on str slices.

- vec: This module contains the Vector type, which is a growable array with heap-allocated contents, and associated methods for operating on vectors such as splicing and iterating. A vec module is an owned reference and a smart pointer (such as Box<T>). Note that vec was originally defined in the alloc crate, but was made available as part of both the std::vec and std::collections modules.

Data processing

This is an assorted collection of modules that provides helper methods for different types of processing such as dealing with ASCII characters, comparing, ordering, and printing formatted values, arithmetic operations, and iterators:

- ascii: Most string operations in Rust act on UTF-8 strings and characters. But in some cases, there may be a need to operate on ASCII characters only. This module provides operations on ASCII strings and characters.

- cmp: This module contains functions for ordering and comparing values, and associated macros. For example, implementing the Eq trait contained in this module allows a comparison of custom struct instances using the == and != operators.

- `fmt`: This module contains utilities to format and print strings. Implementing this trait enables printing any custom data type using the `format!` macro.

- `hash`: This module provides functionality to compute a hash of data objects.

- `iter`: This module contains the `Iterator` trait, which is part and parcel of idiomatic Rust code, and a popular feature of Rust. This trait can be implemented by custom data types for iterating over their values.

- `num`: This module provides additional data types for numeric operations.

- `ops`: This module has a set of traits that allow you to overload operators for custom data types. For example, the `Add` trait can be implemented for a custom struct and the + operator can be used to add two structs of that type.

Error handling

This group consists of modules that have functionality for error handling in Rust programs. The `Error` trait is the foundational construct to represent errors. `Result` deals with the presence or absence of errors in the return value of functions, and `Option` deals with the presence or absence of values in a variable. The latter prevents the dreaded *null value* error that plagues several programming languages. `Panic` is provided as a way to exit the program if errors cannot be handled:

- `error`: This module contains the `Error` trait, which represents the basic expectations of error values. All errors implement the trait `Error`, and this module is used to implement custom or application-specific error types.

- `option`: This module contains the `Option` type, which provides the ability for a value to be initialized to either `Some` value or `None` value. The `Option` type can be considered as a very basic way to handle errors involving the absence of values. Null values cause havoc in other programming languages in the form of null pointer exceptions or the equivalent.

- `panic`: This module provides support to deal with panic including capturing the cause of panic and setting hooks to trigger custom logic on panic.

- `result`: This module contains the `Result` type, which along with the `Error` trait and `Option` type form the foundation of error handling in Rust. `Result` is represented as `Result<T, E>`, which is used to return either values or errors from functions. Functions return the `Result` type whenever errors are expected and if the error is recoverable.

Foreign function interface (FFI)

FFI is provided by the `ffi` module. This module provides utilities to exchange data across non-Rust interface boundaries, such as working with other programming languages or to deal directly with the underlying operating system/kernel.

Compiler

This group contains modules that are related to the Rust compiler.

- `hint`: This module contains functions to hint to the compiler about how code should be emitted or optimized.

- `prelude`: The prelude is the list of items that Rust automatically imports into each Rust program. It is a convenience feature.

- `primitive`: This module re-exports Rust primitive types, normally for use in macro code.

We've so far seen the **computation-oriented** modules of the Rust standard library. Let's take a look at the **syscalls-oriented** modules now.

Syscalls-oriented modules

While the previous group of modules was related to in-memory computations, this section deals with operations that involve managing hardware resources or other privileged operations that *normally* require kernel intervention. Note that not all methods in these modules involve system calls to the kernel, but it helps to construct a mental model at the module level.

Memory management

This grouping contains a set of modules from the standard library that deal with memory management and smart pointers. Memory management includes static memory allocation (on the stack), dynamic memory allocation (on the heap), memory deallocation (when a variable goes out of scope, its destructor is run), cloning or copying values, managing raw pointers and smart pointers (which are pointers to data on the heap), and fixing memory locations for objects so that they cannot be moved around (which is needed for special situations). The modules are as follows:

- `alloc`: This module contains APIs for the allocation and deallocation of memory, and to register a custom or third-party memory allocator as the standard library's default.

- borrow: In Rust, it is common to use different representations of a given type for different use cases. For example, a value can be stored and managed as Box<T>, Rc<T>, or Arc<T>. Similarly, a string value can be stored as the String or str type. Rust provides methods that allow one type to be borrowed as some other type, by implementing the borrow method from the Borrow trait. So basically, a type is free to be borrowed as many different types. This module contains the trait Borrow, which allows the conversion of an owned value to borrowed or to convert borrowed data of any type to an owned value. For example, a value of type String (which is an owned type) can be borrowed as str.

- cell: In Rust, memory safety is based on the rule that a value can have either several immutable references to it or a single mutable reference. But there may be scenarios where a shared, mutable reference is required. This module provides shareable mutable containers that include Cell and RefCell. These types provide controlled mutability of shared types.

- clone: In Rust, primitive types such as integers are *copyable*, that is, they implement the Copy trait. This means that when assigning the value of a variable to another variable or while passing a parameter to a function, the value of the object is duplicated. But not all types can be copied, because they may require memory allocations (for example, String or Vec types where memory is allocated in the heap, rather than the stack). In such cases, a clone() method is used to duplicate a value. This module provides the Clone trait, which allows values of custom data types to be duplicated.

- convert: This module contains functionality to facilitate the conversion between data types. For example, by implementing the AsRef trait contained in this module, you can write a function that takes a parameter of type AsRef<str>, which means that this function can accept any reference that can be converted into a string reference (&str). Since both the str and String types implement the AsRef trait, you can pass either a String reference (String) or string slice reference (&str) to this function.

- default: This module has the trait Default, which is used to assign meaningful default values for data types.

- mem: This module contains memory-related functions including querying memory size, initialization, swapping, and other memory manipulation operations.

- pin: Types in Rust are movable, by default. For example, on a `Vec` type, a `pop()` operation moves a value out and a push operation may result in the reallocation of memory. However, there are situations where it is useful to have objects that have fixed memory locations and do not move. For example, self-referencing data structures such as linked lists. For such cases, Rust provides a data type that pins data to a location in memory. This is achieved by wrapping a type in the pinned pointer, `Pin<P>`, which pins the value `P` in its place in memory.

- ptr: Working with raw pointers in Rust is not common, and is used only in selective use cases. Rust allows working with raw pointers in unsafe code blocks, where the compiler does not take responsibility for memory safety and the programmer is responsible for memory-safe operations. This module provides functions to work with raw pointers. Rust supports two types of raw pointers—immutable (for example, `*const i32`) and mutable (for example, `*mut i32`). Raw pointers have no restrictions on how they are used. They are the only pointer type in Rust that can be null, and there is no automatic dereferencing of raw pointers.

- rc: This module provides single-threaded reference-counting pointers, where `rc` stands for reference-counted. A reference-counted pointer to an object of type `T` can be represented as `Rc<T>`. `Rc<T>` provides shared ownership of value `T`, which is allocated in the heap. If a value of this type is cloned, it returns a new pointer to the same memory location in the heap (does not duplicate the value in memory). This value is retained until the last `Rc` pointer that references this value is in existence, after which the value is dropped.

Concurrency

This category groups modules related to synchronous concurrent processing. Concurrent programs can be designed in Rust by spawning processes, spawning threads within a process, and having ways to synchronize and share data across threads and processes. Asynchronous concurrency is covered under the `Async` group.

- env: This module allows inspecting and manipulating a process's environment, including environment variables, the arguments of a process, and paths. This module could belong to its own category as it is widely used beyond just concurrency, but it is grouped here along with the `process` module because this module is designed to work with a *process* (for example, getting and setting the environment variables of a process or getting the command-line parameters used to start a process).

- `process`: This module provides functions for dealing with processes including spawning a new process, handling I/O, and terminating processes.

- `sync`: The sequence of instructions executed in a Rust program may vary in cases where concurrency is involved. In such cases, there may be multiple threads of execution in parallel (for example, multiple threads in a multi-core CPU), in which case synchronization primitives are needed to coordinate operations across threads. This module includes synchronization primitives such as `Arc`, `Mutex`, `RwLock`, and `Condvar`.

- `thread`: Rust's threading model consists of native OS threads. This module provides functionality to work with threads such as spawning new threads, and configuring, naming, and synchronizing them.

File system

This contains two modules that deal with filesystem operations. The `fs` module deals with methods for working with and manipulating the contents of the local file system. The `path` module provides methods to navigate and manipulate directory and file system paths programmatically:

- `fs`: This module contains operations to work with and manipulate file systems. Note that operations in this module can be used cross-platform. Structs and methods in this module deal with files, naming, file types, directories, file metadata, permissions, and iterating over entries in a directory.

- `path`: This module provides the types `PathBuf` and `Path` for working with and manipulating paths.

Input-Output

This contains the `io` module, which provides core I/O functionality. The `io` module contains common functions that are used while dealing with inputs and outputs. This includes reading and writing to I/O types, such as files or TCP streams, buffered reads and writes for better performance, and working with standard input and output.

Networking

The core networking functionality is provided by the `net` module. This module contains the primitives for TCP and UDP communications and for working with ports and sockets.

OS-specific

The OS-specific functions are provided in the `os` module. This module contains platform-specific definitions and extensions for the Linux, Unix, and Windows operating systems.

Time

The `time` module provides functions to work with system time. This module contains structs to deal with system time and to compute durations, typically used for system timeouts.

Async

Asynchronous I/O functionality is provided by the `future` and `task` modules:

- `future`: This contains the `Future` trait that serves as the foundation for building asynchronous services in Rust.

- `task`: This module provides functions needed to work with asynchronous tasks including `Context`, `Waker`, and `Poll`.

A note on the prelude module

As we've seen, Rust comes with a lot of functionality in the standard library. To use it, you have to import the respective modules into the programs. However, there is a set of commonly needed *traits*, *types*, and *functions* that Rust automatically imports into every Rust program, so the Rust programmer does not have to manually import them. This is called the **prelude**. V1 is the first (and the current) version of the *prelude* of the Rust Standard Library. The compiler automatically adds the statement `use std::prelude::v1::*` into Rust programs. This module re-exports frequently used Rust constructs.

The list of items exported by the `prelude` module includes traits, types, and functions including `Box`, `Copy`, `Send`, `Sync`, `drop`, `Clone`, `Into`, `From`, `Iterator`, `Option`, `Result`, `String`, and `Vec`. The list of modules re-exported can be found at `https://doc.rust-lang.org/std/prelude/v1/index.html`.

This concludes the overview of the Rust Standard Library modules. The Rust Standard Library is vast and is rapidly evolving. It is highly recommended that you review the official documentation at `https://doc.rust-lang.org/std/index.html` with the understanding gained in this chapter, for specific methods, traits, data structures, and example snippets.

Let's now move on to the next section where we will put this knowledge to use by writing some code.

Building a template engine

In this section, we will look at the design of an **HTML template engine** and implement one of the features using the Rust Standard Library. Let's first understand what a template engine is.

Applications such as web and mobile apps use structured data stored in datastores such as relational databases, NoSQL databases, and key-value stores. However, there is a lot of data on the web that is unstructured. One particular example is text data that all web pages contain. Web pages are generated as HTML files that have a text-based format.

On observing closely, we can see that an HTML page has two parts: *static text literals* and *dynamic parts*. The HTML page is authored as a template with the static and dynamic parts, and the context for HTML generation comes from a data source. While generating a web page, the generator should take the static text and output it without change, while it should combine some processing and the supplied context to generate the dynamic string result. Generating HTML pages involves syscalls (to create, open, read, and write files) and computationally intensive in-memory string manipulations.

A **template engine** is the system software component that can be used to generate dynamic HTML pages in a performant manner. It contains a combination of software components including parsers, tokenizers, generators, and template files.

Figure 3.5 shows the process involved in generating HTML with a template engine:

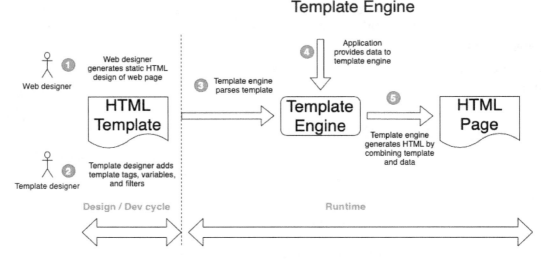

Figure 3.5 – Generating HTML with templates

To understand this better, let's take an example of an internet banking page showing a statement of transactions for a customer. This can be built using an HTML template, where:

- The static HTML includes the bank name, logo, other branding, and content that is *common to all users.*

- The dynamic portion of the web page contains the actual list of past transactions *for the logged-in user.* The transaction list varies from user to user.

The advantage of this approach is the segregation of responsibilities in the web development life cycle:

- A *frontend (web) designer* can author the static HTML with sample data using web design tools.

- A *template designer* would convert the static HTML into an HTML template embedding the metadata for the dynamic portions of the page in specific syntax.

- At runtime (when the page request comes into the server), *the template engine* takes the template file from the specified location, applies the transaction list for the logged-in user from the database, and generates the final HTML page.

Examples of popular template engines include *Jinja, Mustache, Handlebars, HAML, Apache Velocity, Twig*, and *Django*. There are differences in the architectures and syntax adopted by the various template engines.

In this book, we will write the structure for a basic template engine that uses a syntax similar to **Django templates**. *Django* is a popular web framework in Python. Commercial templating engines such as that in *Django* are full-featured and complex. It will not be possible for us to recreate them completely in this chapter, but we will build the code structure and implement a representative feature.

Types of HTML template engines

There are two types of HTML template engines, based on when the template data is parsed.

The first type of template engines parse the HTML template and convert it into code, at compilation time. Then, at runtime, dynamic data is fetched and loaded into the compiled template. These tend to have better runtime performance as part of the work is done at compilation time.

The second type of template engines do both the parsing of the template and HTML generation at runtime. We will be using this type in our project, as it is relatively simple to understand and implement.

Let's begin with the design of an HTML template file.

Template syntax and design

A template is essentially a text file. A list of common features supported by a template file is shown here:

- Literals, for example, `<h1> hello world </h1>`
- Template variables surrounded by `{{` and `}}`, for example, `<p> {{name}} </p>`
- Control logic using an `if` tag, for example, `{% if amount > 100000 %} {% endif %}`
- Loop control with a `for` tag, for example, `<ul>{% for customer in customer_list}<li>{{customer.name}}</li>{% endfor %}</ul>`
- Content import, for example, `{% include "footer.html" %}`
- Filters, for example, `{{name | upper}}`

Figure 3.6 shows a sample template and the HTML generated from the template engine:

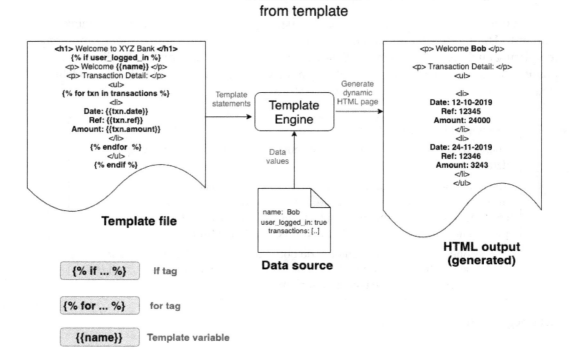

Figure 3.6 – Conceptual model of the template engine

In *Figure 3.6*, we can see the following:

- On the left-hand side, a sample template file is shown. The template file is a mix of static and dynamic content. An example of static content is `<h1> Welcome to XYZ Bank </h1>`. An example of dynamic content is `<p> Welcome {{name}} </p>`, because the value for `name` will be substituted at runtime. There are three types of dynamic content shown in the template file – an `if` tag, a `for` tag, and a template variable.

- In the middle of the figure, we can see the template engine with two sources of inputs – template file and data source. The template engine takes these inputs and generates the output HTML file.

Figure 3.7 explains the working of the template engine using an example:

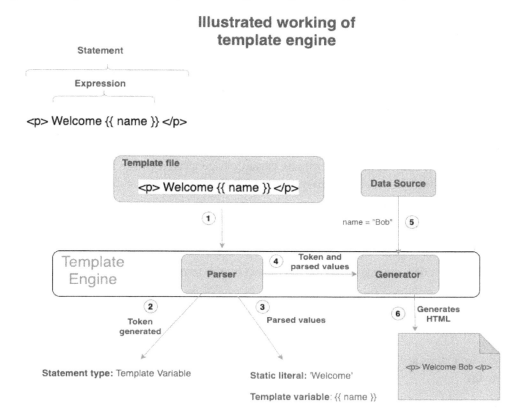

Figure 3.7 – Illustrated example for a template engine

From a design standpoint, the template engine has two parts:

- Parser
- HTML generator

Let's start by understanding the steps involved in HTML generation using the template engine.

The template file contains a set of statements. Some of these are static literals while others are placeholders for dynamic content represented using special syntax. The template engine reads each statement from the template file. Let's call each line read as a template string, henceforth. The process flow begins with the template string read from the template file:

1. The template string is fed to the parser. The template string in our example is `<p> Welcome {{name}} </p>`.

2. The parser first determines the type of template string, which is called **tokenizing**. Let's consider three types of tokens – `if` tags, `for` tags, and template variables. In this example, a token of type template variable is generated (if the template string contains a static literal, it is written to the HTML output without any changes).

3. Then the template string is parsed into a static literal, `Welcome`, and a template variable `{{name}}`.

4. The outputs of the parser (from steps 2 and 3) are passed to the HTML generator.

5. Data from a data source is passed as context by the template engine to the generator.

6. The parsed token and strings (from steps 2 and 3) are combined with the context data (from *step 5*) to produce the result string, which is written to the output HTML file.

The preceding steps are repeated for every statement (template string) read from the template file.

We cannot use the parser we created for arithmetic parsing in *Chapter 2, A Tour of the Rust Programming Language*, for this example, as we need something specific for the HTML template language syntax. We could use the general-purpose parsing libraries (for example, `nom`, `pest`, and `lalrpop` are a few popular parsing libraries in Rust), but for this book, we will custom-build a template parser. The reason for this approach is that each parsing library has its own API and grammar that we need to familiarize ourselves with. Doing that would deviate from the goal of this book, which is learning to write idiomatic code in Rust from the first principles.

First, let's create a new library project with the following:

```
cargo new --lib template-engine
```

The `src/lib.rs` file (which is automatically created by the `cargo` tool) will contain all the functionality of the template engine.

Create a new file, `src/main.rs`. The `main()` function will be placed in this file.

Let's now design the code structure for the template engine. *Figure 3.8* shows the detailed design:

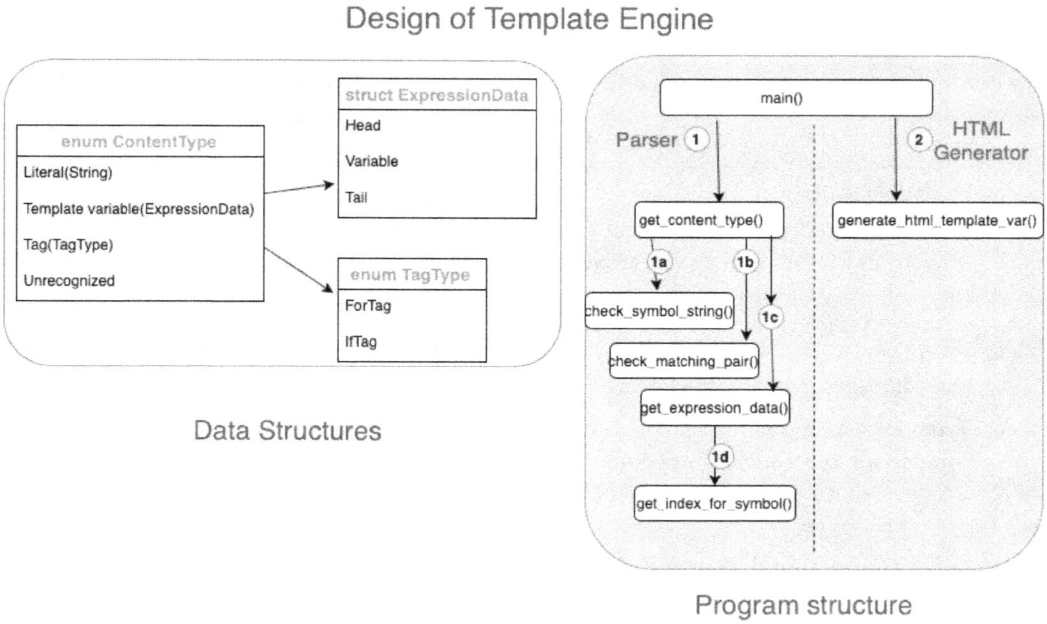

Figure 3.8: Design of the template engine

Let's cover the key data structures and functions of the template engine along with some code snippets. We will start with the data structures.

Data structures

`ContentType` is the main data structure to classify the *template string* read from the *template file*. It is represented as `enum` and contains the list of possible **token types** read from the template file. As each statement (template string) is read from the template file, it is evaluated to check if it is one of the types defined in this enum. The code for `ContentType` is as follows:

src/lib.rs

```
// Each line in input can be of one of following types
#[derive(PartialEq, Debug)]
pub enum ContentType {
    Literal(String),
    TemplateVariable(ExpressionData),
```

```
    Tag(TagType),
    Unrecognized,
}
```

Pay special attention to the annotations `PartialEq` and `Debug`. The former is used to allow content types to be compared, and the latter is used to print the values of the content to the console.

Derivable traits

The Rust compiler can automatically derive default implementations for a few traits defined in the standard library. Such traits are called *derivable traits*. To instruct the compiler to provide default trait implementations, the `#[derive]` attribute is used. Note that this can be done only for types such as custom structs and enums that you have defined, not for types defined in other libraries that you don't own.

Types for which trait implementations can be derived automatically include comparison traits such as `Eq`, `PartialEq`, and `Ord`, and others such as `Copy`, `Clone`, `Hash`, `Default`, and `Debug`.

`TagType` is a supporting data structure that is used to indicate whether a template string corresponds to a `for-tag` (repetitive loop) or `if-tag` (display control):

src/lib.rs

```
#[derive(PartialEq, Debug)]
pub enum TagType {
    ForTag,
    IfTag,
}
```

We will create a struct to store the result of the tokenization of the template string:

src/lib.rs

```
#[derive(PartialEq, Debug)]
pub struct ExpressionData {
    pub head: Option<String>,
    pub variable: String,
    pub tail: Option<String>,
}
```

Note that `head` and `tail` are of type `Option<String>` to allow for the possibility that a template variable may not contain static literal text before or after it.

To summarize, the template string is first tokenized as type `ContentType::TemplateVariable(ExpressionData)`, and `ExpressionData` is parsed into `head="Hello"`, `variable="name"`, and `tail =",welcome"`.

Key functions

Let's look at the key functions to implement the template engine:

- `Program: main()`: This is the starting point of the program. It first calls functions to tokenize and parse the template string, accepts context data to feed into the template, and then calls functions to generate the HTML using the parser outputs and context data.

- `Program: get_content_type()`: This is the entry point into the parser. It parses each line of the template file (which we refer to as the template string) and classifies it as one of the following token types: Literal, Template variable, Tag, or Unrecognized. The Tag token type can be either a `for` tag or an `if` tag. If the token is of type Template variable, it parses the template string to extract the head, tail, and template variable.

  These types are defined as part of the `ContentType` enum. Let's write a few test cases to crystallize what we would like to see as inputs and outputs to this function, and then look at the actual code for `get_content_type()`. Let's take a **test-driven development** (**TDD**) approach here.

  First, create a `tests` module by adding the following block of code in `src/lib.rs`:

  ```
  #[cfg(test)]
  mod tests {
      use super::*;
  }
  ```

Place the unit tests within this `tests` module. Each test will begin with the annotation `#[test]`.

Test case 1: To check if the content type is a literal:

src/lib.rs

```
#[test]
fn check_literal_test() {
    let s = "<h1>Hello world</h1>";
    assert_eq!(ContentType::Literal(s.to_string()),
        get_content_type(s));
}
```

This test case is to check whether the literal string stored in variable s is tokenized as `ContentType::Literal(s)`.

Test case 2: To check if the content type is of the template variable type:

src/lib.rs

```
#[test]
fn check_template_var_test() {
    let content = ExpressionData {
        head: Some("Hi ".to_string()),
        variable: "name".to_string(),
        tail: Some(" ,welcome".to_string()),
    };
    assert_eq!(
        ContentType::TemplateVariable(content),
        get_content_type("Hi {{name}} ,welcome")
    );
}
```

For the `Template String` token type, this test case checks to see if the expression in the template string is parsed into the `head`, `variable`, and `tail` components, and successfully returned as type `ContentType::TemplateVariable (ExpressionData)`.

Test case 3: To check if the content is a `ForTag`:

src/lib.rs

```
#[test]
fn check_for_tag_test() {
    assert_eq!(
        ContentType::Tag(TagType::ForTag),
        get_content_type("{% for name in names %}
            ,welcome")
    );
}
```

This test case is to check if a statement containing a `for` tag is tokenized successfully as `ContentType::Tag(TagType::ForTag)`.

Test case 4 – To check if the content contains `IfTag`:

src/lib.rs

```
#[test]
fn check_if_tag_test() {
    assert_eq!(
        ContentType::Tag(TagType::IfTag),
        get_content_type("{% if name == 'Bob' %}")
    );
}
```

This test case is to check if a statement containing an `if` tag is tokenized successfully as `ContentType::Tag(TagType::IfTag)`.

Now that we have written the unit test cases, let's write the code for the template engine.

Writing the template engine

There are two key parts to writing the template engine – the parser and HTML generator. We will start with the parser. *Figure 3.9* shows the design of the parser:

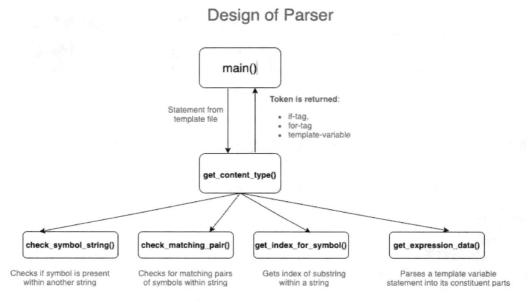

Figure 3.9: Parser design

Here is a brief description of the various methods in the parser:

- `get_content_type()`: Entry point for parser. Accepts an input statement and tokenizes it into one of an `if` tag, a `for` tag, or a template variable.

- `check_symbol_string()`: This is a supporting method that checks if a symbol is present within another string. For example, we can check if the pattern `{%` is present in a statement from the template file, and use it to determine if it is a tag statement or template variable.

- `check matching pair()`: This is a supporting method that is used to verify if a statement in a template file is syntactically correct. For example, we can check for the presence of matching pairs `{%` and `%}`. Otherwise, the statement is marked as `Unrecognized`.

- `get_index_for_symbol()`: This method returns the starting index of a substring within another string. It is used for string manipulation.

- `get_expression_data()`: This method parses a template string into its constituent parts for a token of type `TemplateString`.

Writing the parser

Let's first look at the get_content_type() method. Here is a summary of the program logic:

- for tags are enclosed by {% and %} and contain the for keyword.

- if tags are enclosed by {% and %} and contain the if keyword.

- Template variables are enclosed by {{ and }}.

Based on these rules, the statement is parsed and the appropriate token is returned – a for tag, an if tag, or a template variable.

Here is the complete code listing for the get_content_type() function:

src/lib.rs

```
pub fn get_content_type(input_line: &str) -> ContentType {
    let is_tag_expression = check_matching_pair
        (&input_line, "{%", "%}");
    let is_for_tag = (check_symbol_string(&input_line,
        "for")
        && check_symbol_string(&input_line, "in"))
        || check_symbol_string(&input_line, "endfor");
    let is_if_tag =
        check_symbol_string(&input_line, "if") ||
            check_symbol_string(&input_line, "endif");

    let is_template_variable = check_matching_pair
        (&input_line, "{{", "}}");
    let return_val;

    if is_tag_expression && is_for_tag {
        return_val = ContentType::Tag(TagType::ForTag);
    } else if is_tag_expression && is_if_tag {
        return_val = ContentType::Tag(TagType::IfTag);
    } else if is_template_variable {
        let content = get_expression_data(&input_line);
        return_val = ContentType::TemplateVariable
            (content);
    } else if !is_tag_expression && !is_template_variable {
        return_val = ContentType::Literal
            (input_line.to_string());
    } else {
```

```
            return_val = ContentType::Unrecognized;
        }
        return_val
}
```

Supporting functions

Let's now talk about supporting functions. The parser utilizes these supporting functions
to perform operations such as checking for the presence of a substring within a string,
checking for matching pairs of braces, and so on. They are needed to check whether
the template string is syntactically correct, and also to parse the template string into its
constituent parts. Before writing some more code, let's look at the test cases for these
supporting functions to understand how they will be used, and then see the code. Note
that these functions are designed to enable reuse across projects. All supporting functions
are placed in `src/lib.rs`:

- `check_symbol_string()`: Checks if a symbol string, for example, '`{%`', is
  contained within another string. Here is the test case:

```
#[test]
fn check_symbol_string_test() {
    assert_eq!(true, check_symbol_string(
        "{{Hello}}", "{{"));
}
```

Here is the code for the function:

```
pub fn check_symbol_string(input: &str, symbol: &str)
-> bool {
input.contains(symbol)
}
```

The standard library provides a straightforward way to check for a substring within
a string slice.

- `check_matching_pair()`: This function checks for matching symbol strings.
  Here is the test case:

```
#[test]
fn check_symbol_pair_test() {
    assert_eq!(true, check_matching_pair(
        "{{Hello}}", "{{", "}}"));
}
```

In this test case, we pass matching tags, '{{' and '}}', to this function, and check if both are contained within another string expression, "{{Hello}}".

Here is the code for the function:

```
pub fn check_matching_pair(input: &str, symbol1: &str,
    symbol2: &str) -> bool {
    input.contains(symbol1) && input.contains(symbol2)
}
```

In this function, we are checking if the two matching tags are contained within the input string.

- get_expression_data(): This parses an expression with a template variable, parses it into head, variable, and tail components, and returns the results. Here is the test case for this function:

```
#[test]
fn check_get_expression_data_test() {
    let expression_data = ExpressionData {
        head: Some("Hi ".to_string()),
        variable: "name".to_string(),
        tail: Some(" ,welcome".to_string()),
    };

    assert_eq!(expression_data,
        get_expression_data("Hi {{name}}
        ,welcome"));
}
```

Here is the code for the function:

```
pub fn get_expression_data(input_line: &str) ->
ExpressionData {
    let (_h, i) = get_index_for_symbol(input_line,
    '{');
    let head = input_line[0..i].to_string();
    let (_j, k) = get_index_for_symbol(input_line,
        '}');
    let variable = input_line[i + 1 + 1..k]
        .to_string();
    let tail = input_line[k + 1 + 1..].to_string();

    ExpressionData {
        head: Some(head),
        variable: variable,
```

```
            tail: Some(tail),
        }
    }
```

- `get_index_for_symbol`: This function takes two parameters and returns the index where the second value is found within the first value. This makes it easy to split the template string into three parts – head, `variable`, and `tail`. Here is the test case:

```
#[test]
fn check_get_index_for_symbol_test() {
    assert_eq!((true, 3), get_index_for_symbol("Hi
        {name}, welcome", '{'));
}
```

We see the code for the function in the following snippet. This makes use of the `char_indices()` method on the slice available as part of the standard library, and converts the input string into an iterator that is capable of tracking indices. We then iterate over the input string and return the index of the symbol when found:

```
pub fn get_index_for_symbol(input: &str, symbol: char)
    -> (bool, usize) {
    let mut characters = input.char_indices();
    let mut does_exist = false;
    let mut index = 0;
    while let Some((c, d)) = characters.next() {
        if d == symbol {
            does_exist = true;
            index = c;
            break;
        }
    }
    (does_exist, index)
}
```

This concludes the code for the `Parser` module. Let's now look at the main function that ties all the pieces together.

The main() function

The `main()` function is the entry point into the template engine. *Figure 3.10* shows the design of the `main()` function:

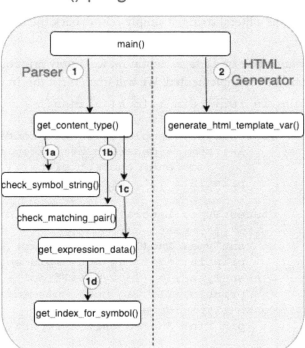

Figure 3.10: The main() function

The `main()` function performs the coordination role tying all pieces together. It invokes the parser, initializes the context data, and then invokes the generator:

- **Pass context data**: It creates a `HashMap` to pass values for the template variables mentioned in the template. We add values for `name` and `city` to this `HashMap`. The `HashMap` is passed to the generator function along with the parsed template input:

```
let mut context: HashMap<String, String> =
    HashMap::new();
context.insert("name".to_string(),
    "Bob".to_string());
context.insert("city".to_string(),
    "Boston".to_string());
```

- **Invoke parser and generator**: The parser is invoked by the call to the
  `get_context_data()` function for each line of input read from the
  command line (standard input).

  a) If the line contains template variable, it invokes the HTML generator
  `generate_html_template_var()` to create the HTML output.

  b) If the line contains a literal string, it simply echoes back the input HTML
  literal string.

  c) If the line contains `for` or `if` tags, right now, we simply print out a statement
  that the feature is not yet implemented. We will implement this in future chapters:

```rust
for line in io::stdin().lock().lines() {
    match get_content_type(&line?.clone()) {
        ContentType::TemplateVariable(content) => {
            let html = generate_html_template_var
                (content, context.clone());
            println!("{}", html);
        }
        ContentType::Literal(text) => println!
            ("{}", text),
        ContentType::Tag(TagType::ForTag) =>
            println!("For Tag not implemented"),
        ContentType::Tag(TagType::IfTag) =>
            println!("If Tag not implemented"),
        ContentType::Unrecognized =>
            println!("Unrecognized input"),
    }
}
```

- **Read template strings from the command-line**: A template engine in production
  would read inputs from a template file stored somewhere on the local file system of
  the server. However, since we have not yet covered file systems in this book, we will
  accept template strings as inputs through a command line (standard input) from
  the user. The `io::stdin()` function creates a new handle to the standard input of
  the current process. The standard input is read one line at a time using the following
  `for` loop, which is then passed on to the parser for processing:

```rust
for line in io::stdin().lock().lines() {..}
```

Here is the complete code listing for the `main()` function:

src/main.rs

```rust
use std::collections::HashMap;
use std::io;
use std::io::BufRead;
use template_engine::*;

fn main() {
    let mut context: HashMap<String, String> =
        HashMap::new();
    context.insert("name".to_string(), "Bob".to_string());
    context.insert("city".to_string(),
        "Boston".to_string());

    for line in io::stdin().lock().lines() {
        match get_content_type(&line.unwrap().clone()) {
            ContentType::TemplateVariable(content) => {
                let html = generate_html_template_var
                    (content, context.clone());
                println!("{}", html);
            }
            ContentType::Literal(text) => println!("{}",
                text),
            ContentType::Tag(TagType::ForTag) =>
                println!("For Tag not implemented"),
            ContentType::Tag(TagType::IfTag) =>
                println!("If Tag not implemented"),
            ContentType::Unrecognized =>
                println!("Unrecognized input"),
        }
    }
}
```

The implementation for the `generate_html_template_var()` function is shown here:

src/lib.rs

```rust
use std::collections::HashMap;
pub fn generate_html_template_var(
    content: ExpressionData,
    context: HashMap<String, String>,
) -> String {
    let mut html = String::new();

    if let Some(h) = content.head {
        html.push_str(&h);
    }

    if let Some(val) = context.get(&content.variable) {
        html.push_str(&val);
    }

    if let Some(t) = content.tail {
        html.push_str(&t);
    }

    html
}
```

This function constructs the output `html` statement consisting of *head*, *text content*, and *tail*. To construct the text content, the template variables are replaced with the values from the context data. The constructed `html` statement is returned from the function.

The complete code from this chapter can be found at `https://github.com/PacktPublishing/Practical-System-Programming-for-Rust-Developers/tree/master/Chapter03`.

Executing the template engine

We have, for now, the outline and foundations for a basic template engine that can deal with two kinds of input – static literals and template variables.

Let's execute the program and run some tests:

1. Build and run the project with the following:

    ```
    >cargo run
    ```

2. **Test for the literal string**: You can enter the literal string `<h2> Hello, welcome to my page </h2>`. You will see the same string printed out as there is no transformation to be done.

3. **Test for the template variable**: Enter a statement with the name or city variable (as mentioned in the main program) such as `<p> My name is {{name}} </p>` or `<p> I live in {{city}} </p>`. You will see `<p> My name is Bob </p>` or `<p> I live in Boston </p>` printed out corresponding to the input. This is because we initialized the variable `name` to `Bob` and `city` to `Boston` in the `main()` program. You are encouraged to enhance this code to add support for two template vars in a single HTML statement.

4. **Test for tag and if tag**: Enter a statement enclosed within `{%` and `%}`, and containing either the string `for` or `if`. You will see one of the following messages printed out to the terminal: `For Tag not implemented` or `If Tag not implemented`.

You are encouraged to write the code for the `for` tag and `if` tag as an exercise. Ensure to check for the right sequence of symbols. For example, an invalid format such as `{% for }%` or `%} if {%` should be rejected.

Even though we are not able to implement more features of the template engine, in this chapter, we have seen how to use the Rust Standard Library in a real-life use case. We have primarily used the `io`, `collections`, `iter`, and `str` modules from the Rust Standard Library to implement the code in this chapter. As we go through future chapters, we will cover more of the standard library.

Summary

In this chapter, we reviewed the overall structure of the Rust Standard Library and classified the modules of the standard library into different categories for better understanding. You got a brief introduction to the modules in areas of concurrency, memory management, file system operations, data processing, data types, error handling, compiler-related, FFI, networking, I/O, OS-specific, and time-related features.

We looked at what a template engine is, how it works, and defined the scope and requirements of our project. We designed the template engine in terms of Rust data structures (enum and struct) and Rust functions. We saw how to write code for parsing templates and to generate HTML for statements involving template variables. We executed the program providing input data and verified the generated HTML in the terminal (command line).

In the next chapter, we will take a closer look at the Rust Standard Library modules that deal with managing process environment, command-line arguments, and time-related functionality.

Further reading

- **Django template language**: `https://docs.djangoproject.com/en/3.0/ref/templates/language/`

- **Rust Standard Library**: `https://doc.rust-lang.org/std/index.html`

4
Managing Environment, Command Line, and Time

In the previous chapter, we looked at how the Rust Standard Library is structured. We also wrote a portion of a basic template engine that can generate dynamic HTML page components given an HTML template and data. From here onward, we will start to deep-dive into specific modules of the standard library grouped by functional areas.

In this chapter, we will look at Rust Standard Library modules that pertain to working with system environment, command-line, and time-related functions. The goal of this chapter is for you to gain more proficiency in working with *command-line parameters, path manipulation, environment variables*, and *time measurements*.

What is the benefit of learning about these?

Working with *command-line arguments* is a required skill for writing any program that accepts user inputs from the command line.

Imagine how you would write a tool (such as **find** or **grep**) that deals with searching for files and patterns within folders and subfolders. This requires knowledge of *path manipulation*, including navigating paths and reading and manipulating path entries.

Learning to use *environment variables* is an essential part of separating the code from the configuration, which is a good practice for any kind of program.

Learning to work with time is required for programs that deal with timestamps of resources and activities. Learning how to do *time measurements* to record time intervals between events is needed for benchmarking the time taken for various operations.

In this chapter, you will learn the following skills:

- Writing Rust programs that can discover and manipulate the system environment and filesystem across Linux, Unix, and Windows platforms
- Creating programs that can use command-line arguments to accept configuration parameters and user inputs
- Capturing elapsed time between events

These are relevant skills to have for systems programming in Rust. We will learn these topics in a practical way by developing a command-line application for image processing. Along the way, we will see more details about the `path`, `time`, `env`, and `fs` modules of the Rust Standard Library.

First, let's see what we will be building.

Imagine that we had a tool for bulk image resizing – tool that would look through a filesystem directory on a desktop or server, pull out all the image files (for instance, `.png` and `.jpg`), and resize all of them to predefined sizes (for example, small, medium, or large).

Think about how helpful such a tool would be for freeing up space on the hard disk, or for uploading pictures to show in a mobile or web app. We will be building such a tool. Fasten your seat belts.

We will cover the topics in the following order:

- Project scope and design overview
- Coding the image resizing library
- Developing the command-line application

Technical requirements

The GitHub repo for the code in this chapter can be found at `https://github.com/PacktPublishing/Practical-System-Programming-for-Rust-Developers/tree/master/Chapter04`.

Project scope and design overview

In this section, we will first define what we are going to build and look at the technical design. We will then code a Rust library for image processing. Finally, we will build a command-line application that accepts user inputs through the command line and uses the image resizing library we have built to perform user-specified commands.

What will we build?

In this subsection, we will describe the functional requirements, technical requirements, and project structure for the tool we are building.

Functional requirements

We will build a command-line tool that performs the following two operations:

- **Image resize**: Resizes one or more images in a source folder to a specified size
- **Image stats**: Provides some statistics on the image files present in the source folder

Let's name the tool **ImageCLI**. *Figure 4.1* shows the two main features of the tool:

ImageCLI tool - Features

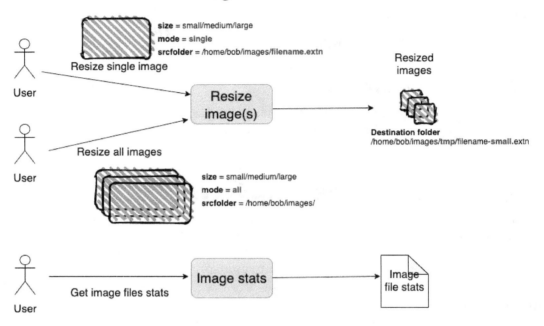

Figure 4.1 – Features of ImageCLI tool

Users will be able to resize images using this tool. The user can ask to resize either a single image or multiple images. Supported *input* image formats are JPG and PNG. The supported *output* image format is PNG. The tool will accept three command-line parameters as follows:

- **Size**: This is the desired output size of the image. If the user specifies `size = small`, the output image will have *200* pixels of width; for `size = medium`, the output file will have *400* pixels of width; and for `size = large`, the output will have *800* pixels of width. For example, if the input image is a JPG file with a total size of 8 MB, it can be resized to approximately < 500 KB in size by specifying `size = medium`.

- **Mode**: The mode indicates whether the user wants to resize one image file or multiple files. The user specifies `mode = single` for resizing a single file, or `mode = all` for resizing all image files in a specified folder.

- **Source folder**: The value specified by the user for the source folder has a different meaning depending on whether mode = single or mode = all is chosen. For mode = single, the user specifies the value of srcfolder as the full path of the image file with its filename. For mode = all, the user specifies, for the value of srcfolder, the full path of the folder (the one containing the image files) without any image filenames. For example, if mode = single and srcfolder = /user/bob/images/image1.png are used, the tool will resize the single image file of image1.png, contained in the /user/bob/images folder. If mode = all and srcfolder = /user/bob/images are used, the tool will resize *all* the image files contained in the /user/bob/images source folder.

For our image stats functionality, users will also be able to specify a srcfolder containing the image files and get back the number of image files in that folder, along with the total size of all those image files. For example, if srcfolder=/user/bob/images is used, the image stats option will give a result similar to the following: **The folder contains 200 image files with total size 2,234 MB**.

Non-functional requirements

The following are a list of non-functional (technical) requirements for the project:

- The tool will be packaged and distributed as a binary and it should work on three platforms: Linux, Unix, and Windows.

- We should be able to measure the time taken to resize the images.

- User inputs for specifying command-line flags must be *case-insensitive* for ease of use.

- The tool must be able to display meaningful error messages to the user.

- The core functionality of image resizing must be separate from the **command-line interface (CLI)**. This way, we have the flexibility of reusing the core functionality with a desktop graphical interface or as part of a web backend in a web application.

- The project will be organized as a **library** containing the image processing functionality and a **binary** that provides the CLI to read and parse user input, provide error messages, and display output messages to the user. The binary will make use of the library for core image processing.

Project structure

Let's create the project skeleton so we can visualize the project structure better. Create a new `lib` project using `cargo`. Let's name the CLI tool as `imagecli` using the following command:

```
cargo new --lib imagecli && cd imagecli
```

Here is the project structure:

Figure 4.2 – Cargo project structure

Set up the project structure as follows:

1. Under the `src` folder, create a subfolder called `imagix` (for image magic!) to host the library code. Under the `imagix` subfolder, create four files: `mod.rs`, which is the entry point into the `imagix` library, `resize.rs` to host the code related to image resizing, `stats.rs` to host the code for image file statistics, and `error.rs` to contain the custom error type and error handling code.

2. Under the `src` folder, create a new file called `imagecli.rs`, which will contain the code for the CLI.

In this subsection, we have seen the feature requirements for the tool and the desired project structure. In the next subsection, we will look at the design for the tool.

Technical design

In this subsection, we will look at the high-level design of the tool, primarily focusing on the image processing feature. We will design the specifics of the CLI in the *Developing the command-line application and testing* section.

Our project comprises our reusable imagix library containing the core functionality for image resizing and statistics, and a binary executable, imagecli, with a CLI. This is depicted in *Figure 4.3*:

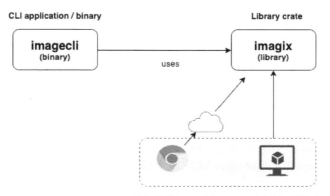

Figure 4.3 – CLI tool with a reusable library

If the library is designed right, it can be reused in the future for other types of clients; for example, the application can be provided with a graphical user interface (instead of a CLI) as a desktop application, or can even be made accessible from a browser-based HTML client app.

Before we begin the design, let's try to visualize a few of the key technical challenges we have to overcome and solve:

- **Resizing a single image:**

  How do we resize a larger image to a smaller, user-specified size, programmatically?

  How do we create a /tmp/ subfolder to store the resized images?

  How do we measure the time taken for image resizing?

- **Resizing multiple images**:

  How do we iterate through the source folder provided by the user to identify all the image files and invoke the image resizing function for each entry?

- **Getting image statistics**:

  How do we scan through the user-provided source folder, count only the number of image files, and get the aggregate file size of all image files in that folder?

- **Path manipulation**:

  How do we manipulate paths so that the output file is stored in the tmp subfolder?

The preceding points can be grouped into three broad categories of concerns for design purposes:

- Image resizing logic
- Path manipulation and directory-iteration logic
- Measuring time taken for image resizing

Image processing is a highly-specialized domain in itself, and it is beyond the scope of this book to cover the techniques and algorithms involved. Given the complexity and scope of the image processing domain, we will use a third-party library that will implement the needed algorithms and provide us with a nice API to call.

For this purpose, we will use the image-rs/image open source crate that is written in Rust. The crate docs are at the following link: https://docs.rs/image/

Let's look at how we can design the imagix library using the image crate.

The image crate is fully featured and has many image processing functions. We will however use only a small subset of features for our project. Let's recall our three key requirements for image processing: the ability to *open an image file and load it into memory*, the ability to *resize the image to a desired size*, and the ability to *write the resized image from memory into a file* on the disk. The following methods in the image-rs/image crate address our needs:

- image::open(): This function opens an image at the specified path. It automatically detects the format of the image from the image's file extension. The image data is read from the file and converted into a DynamicImage type stored in memory.

- DynamicImage::thumbnail(): This function scales an image down to a specified size (width and height) and returns a new image while preserving the aspect ratio. It uses a fast integer algorithm, which is a sinusoidal transformation technique. This is an **in-memory operation**.

- `DynamicImage::write_to()`: This function encodes an image and writes it to any object that implements the `std::io::write` trait, which in our case will be an output *file handle*. We will use this method to write the resized image to a file.

This should be adequate for our image processing requirements in this project. For the other two concerns around path manipulation and time measurements, we will use the Rust Standard Library, which is described in the next subsection.

Using the Rust Standard Library

For developing the image resizing tool, we will be using both external crates and the Rust Standard Library. In the previous section, we saw how we plan to use the `image` crate.

In this section, we will cover the features of the Rust Standard Library that we will be using to build our project. There are three key areas where we will need the standard library:

- The *path manipulation and directory iteration* functionality is needed in order to search through a directory, locate the image files, and create a new subfolder.

- We need to get tool configuration options from the user. We will evaluate two approaches – getting this information through *environment variables* and getting it through *command-line parameters*. We will choose one of the options.

- We want to *measure the time taken* for the image resizing tasks.

Let's take a look at each of these areas in detail.

Path manipulation and directory iteration

For path manipulation, we will use the `std::path` module from the Rust Standard Library. For directory iteration, we will use the `std::fs` module.

Why do we need to manipulate paths?

The source image files for resizing are stored in the *source folder*. The destination path for the resized image files is the `tmp` subfolder (within the *source folder*). Before writing each resized image file to disk, we have to construct the path where the file is to be stored. For example, if the path for the source file is `/user/bob/images/image1.jpg`, the destination path for the resized image will be `/user/bob/images/tmp/image1.jpg`. We have to construct the destination path programmatically, and then call the method on the `image` crate to store the image on the destination path.

The Rust Standard Library supports path manipulation functionality through two data types: `Path` and `PathBuf`, both part of the `std::path` module. See the sidebar for more details on how to construct and manipulate `paths` using the standard library.

The std::path module of the Rust Standard Library

This module provides cross-platform path manipulation functions.

A path points to a filesystem location by following a directory tree. An example of a path in Unix systems is /home/bob/images/. An example of a path on the Windows operating system could be c:\bob\images\image1.png.

There are two main types in the std::path module that are commonly used—Path and PathBuf.

For parsing the path and its components (read operations), Path is used. In Rust parlance, it is a **path slice** (like a string slice, which is a reference to a string).

For modifying existing paths or to construct new paths, PathBuf is used. PathBuf is an **owned**, **mutable path**.

Path is used for read operations and PathBuf for read and write operations on paths.

Here is how to construct a new path from a string:

```
let path_name = Path::new("/home/alice/foo.txt");
```

In path_name, /home/alice represents the parent, foo is the file stem, and txt is the file extension. We will be making use of the file_stem() and extension() methods on the Path type.

The pop() and push() methods on the PathBuf type are used to truncate and append components to a path.

Let's create a new PathBuf path with the following code:

```
let mut path_for_editing = PathBuf::from("/home/
bob/file1.png")
```

path_for_editing.pop() truncates this path to its parent, that is, "/home/bob".

Now, push() can be used to append a new component to PathBuf. For example, continuing from PathBuf with the value "/home/bob", push("tmp") will append tmp to "/home/bob" path and return "/home/bob/tmp".

We will be using the pop() and push() methods in our project to manipulate paths.

Let's next look at how to perform the directory operations needed for our project.

When the user specifies mode=all, our requirement is to iterate through all the files in the specified source folder and filter the list of image files for processing. For iterating over directory paths, we will use the read_dir() function in the std::fs module.

Let's see an example of how to use this function:

```rust
use std::fs;

fn main() {
    let entries = fs::read_dir("/tmp").unwrap();
    for entry in entries {
        if let Ok(entry) = entry {
            println!("{:?}", entry.path());
        }
    }
}
```

The following is the explanation for the preceding code:

1. `fs:read_dir()` takes a source folder path and returns `std::fs::ReadDir`, which is an iterator over entries in the directory.

2. We then use a `for` loop to extract each directory entry (which is wrapped in a `Result` type), and print out its value.

This is the code we will use to get entries in a directory and do further processing.

Apart from reading a directory for its contents, we also need to check for the presence of a `tmp` subfolder under the source folder and create it if it does not already exist. We will use the `create_dir()` method from the `std::fs` module to create a new subdirectory.

We will see more details of the `std::fs` module in a later chapter.

Time measurement

For measuring time, we can use the `std::time` module.

The `std::time` module in the Rust Standard Library has several time-related functions including getting the *current system time*, creating a *duration* to represent a span of time, and measuring the *time elapsed* between two specific time instants. Some examples of using the `time` module are provided in the following.

To get the current system time, we can write the following code:

```rust
use std::time::SystemTime;
fn main() {
    let _now = SystemTime::now();
}
```

Here is how to get the elapsed time from a given point in time:

```
use std::thread::sleep;
use std::time::{Duration, Instant};
fn main() {
    let now = Instant::now();
    sleep(Duration::new(3, 0));
    println!("{:?}", now.elapsed().as_secs());
}
```

`Instant::now()` is used to indicate the starting point of the time to be measured. The time duration between this point and the point at which `now.elapsed()` is called represents the time taken for the operation(s). Here, we are simulating a delay using the `sleep()` function from the `std::thread` module.

Working with environment variables

In this subsection, we will learn how to use the Rust Standard Library, along with a third-party helper crate, to store the values in environment variables and use them in the program:

1. Create a new project with the following line of code:

    ```
    cargo new read-env && cd read-env
    ```

    It is easier to work with environment variables from a `.env` file (instead of setting them in the console), so let's add a popular crate for this purpose, called `dotenv`, in `Cargo.toml`:

    ```
    [dependencies]
    dotenv = "0.15.0"
    ```

    Depending on when you are reading this book, you may have a later version of this tool available, which you may choose to use.

2. In `main.rs`, add the following code:

    ```
    use dotenv::dotenv;
    use std::env;

    fn main() {
    dotenv().ok();
    ```

```
for (key, value) in env::vars() {
    println!("{}:{}", key, value);
}
}
```

In the preceding code, we import the `std::env` module and also the `dotenv::dotenv` module.

The following statement loads the environment variables from an `.env` file:

```
dotenv().ok();
```

The `for` loop in the previous code block iterates through the environment variables in a loop and prints them to the console. `env:vars()` returns an iterator of key-value pairs for all environment variables of the current process.

3. To test this, let's create a new `.env` file in the project root and make the following entries:

```
size=small
mode=single
srcfolder=/home/bob/images/image1.jpg
```

4. Replace the `srcfolder` value with your own. Run the program with the following command:

```
cargo run
```

You will see the environment variables from the `.env` file printed out, along with the others associated with the process.

5. To access the value of any particular environment variable, the `std::env::var()` function can be used, which takes the key of the variable as a parameter. Add the following statement to the `main()` function and see the value of the `size` variable printed out:

```
println!("Value of size is {}",
    env::var("size").unwrap());
```

We have seen how to use *environment variables* to accept user inputs for image processing. Let's see how to accept user inputs with *command-line* parameters.

Working with command-line parameters

In this subsection, we will learn to read command-line parameters using the `std::env` module of the Rust Standard Library:

1. The `std::env` module supports command-line parameters through `std::env::args()`. Create a new Cargo project. Add the following line to the `main()` function in `src/main.rs`:

```rust
use std::env;
fn main() {
    for argument in env::args() {
        println!("{}", argument);
    }
}
```

2. Execute the code with `cargo run small all /tmp`.

3. The three parameters passed to the program will be printed out to the console. To access individual parameters by index, add the following code to `main.rs`:

```rust
use std::env;
fn main() {
    let args: Vec<String> = env::args().collect();
    let size = &args[1];
    let mode = &args[2];
    let source_folder = &args[3];
    println!(
        "Size:{},mode:{},source folder: {}",
        size, mode, source_folder
    );
}
```

4. Run the program with `cargo run small all /tmp`.

The individual values for `size`, `mode`, and `source_folder` will be printed out as shown here:

```
Size:small,mode:all,source folder: /tmp
```

Of the two approaches we have seen – that is, using *environment variables* and *command-line parameters* – the latter is more suitable for accepting inputs from end users, while the environment variable approach is more suitable for developers configuring the tool.

However, for a user-friendly interface, the bare-bones functionality offered by `std::env::args` is inadequate. We will use a third-party crate called **StructOpt** to improve the user interaction with the CLI.

This concludes the deep dive into the Rust Standard Library modules for path manipulation, time measurement, and reading environment and command-line parameters.

Here is a summary of the design approaches we have discussed, for the `imagix` library:

- **Resizing a single image**:

   How do we resize a larger image to a user-specified size, programmatically?

   We will use the `image-rs/image` crate.

   How do we create a `/tmp/` subfolder to store the resized images?

   We will use the `std::fs::create_dir()` method.

- **Resizing multiple images**:

   How do we iterate through the source folder provided by the user to identify all the image files and invoke the image resizing function?

   We will use `std::fs::read_dir()` method.

   How do we manipulate paths so that the output file is stored in the `tmp` subfolder?

   We will use the `std::path::Path` and `std::path::PathBuf` types.

- **Getting image statistics**:

   How do we scan through the user-provided source folder, count only the number of image files, and get the aggregate file size of all image files in that folder?

   We will use the `std::path::Path` type and the `std::fs::read_dir()` method.

- **Metrics for benchmarking**:

   How do we measure the time taken for image resizing?

   We will use the `std::time::Duration` and `std::time::Instant` modules.

- **Reading command-line parameters**:

   Use the `StructOpt` crate.

With this, we conclude this section on addressing project scope and design for the imagix library. We are now ready to start writing the code for the image processing library in the next section.

Coding the imagix library

In this section, we'll write the code for the image resizing and image statistics functionalities. Let's first look at the code structure.

The module structure of the imagix library is summarized in *Figure 4.4*:

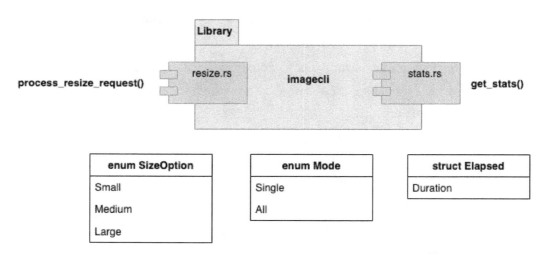

Figure 4.4 – Modules of the imagix library

The imagix library will consist of two modules, **resize** and **stats**, represented by resize.rs and stats.rs respectively. There are two enums, SizeOption and Mode, for representing the variants for *size option* and *mode* respectively. The user will specify one of the variants of the SizeOption enum to indicate the desired output image size, and one of the variants of the Mode enum to indicate whether one or multiple images need to be resized. There is also struct Elapsed for capturing elapsed time of the image resizing operation.

The resize module has the process_resize_request() public function, which is the main entry point into the imagix library for resizing images.

The stats module has a get_stats() public function.

An overview of the overall code organization of the project is shown in *Figure 4.5*:

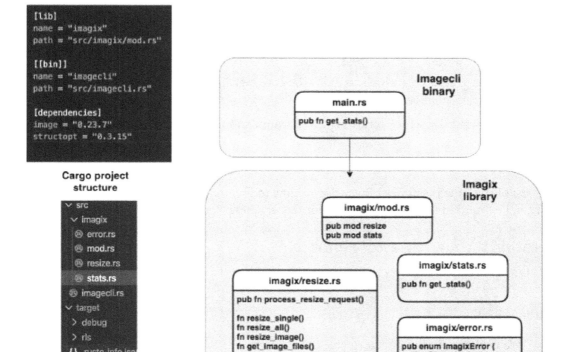

Figure 4.5 – Code organization

Figure 4.5 shows the following:

- The configuration and dependency entries needed in the `Cargo.toml` file
- The Cargo project's code tree structure
- The list of source files of the `imagix` library along with a list of the key functions
- The `imagecli.rs` file, which represents the command-line wrapper over the `imagix` library, and the code execution entry point in our tool

Let's first add the two external crates to `Cargo.toml` in the `imagecli` project folder root:

```
[dependencies]
image = "0.23.12"
structopt = "0.3.20"
```

In this section, we will walk through the code snippets for the following methods:

- `get_image_files()`, which demonstrates path navigation
- `resize_image()`, which contains the core logic for image resizing using the image crate, and for time measurements
- `get_stats()`, which returns the total count and the total size of image files in a folder
- Custom error handling methods

The rest of the code is standard Rust (not specific to the topics this chapter is focused on) and can be found in the code repository for this chapter.

Iterating through directory entries

In this subsection, let's review the code for `get_image_files()`. This is the method that retrieves the list of image files contained in a source folder.

The logic for this method is described here:

1. We first retrieve the directory entries in the source folder and collect them in a *vector*.
2. We then iterate over entries in the vector and filter for only the image files. Note that we are only focusing on PNG and JPG files in this project, but it can be extended to other types of image files too.
3. A list of image files is returned from this method.

The code listing is shown here:

src/imagix/resize.rs

```
pub fn get_image_files(src_folder: PathBuf) ->
    Result<Vec<PathBuf>, ImagixError> {
    let entries = fs::read_dir(src_folder)
```

```
    .map_err(|e| ImagixError::UserInputError("Invalid
        source folder".to_string()))?
    .map(|res| res.map(|e| e.path()))
    .collect::<Result<Vec<_>, io::Error>>()?
    .into_iter()
    .filter(|r| {
        r.extension() == Some("JPG".as_ref())
            || r.extension() == Some("jpg".as_ref())
            || r.extension() == Some("PNG".as_ref())
            || r.extension() == Some("png".as_ref())
    })
    .collect();
Ok(entries)
}
```

The code uses the read_dir() method to iterate through directory entries and collects the results in a Vector. The Vector is then converted into an iterator, and the entries are filtered to return only image files. This gives us the set of image files to work with, for resizing. In the next subsection, we will review the code to perform the actual resizing of the images.

Resizing images

In this subsection, we will review the code for resize_image(). This method performs the resizing of images.

The logic for this method is as follows:

1. The method accepts a source image filename with the full source folder path, resizes it as a .png file, and stores the resized file in a /tmp subfolder under the source folder.

2. First, the source filename is extracted from the full path. The file extension is changed to .png. This is because our tool will only support output files in .png format. As an exercise, you can add support for other image format types.

3. Then the destination file path is constructed with the /tmp prefix, as the resized image will need to be stored in the tmp subfolder under the source folder. To achieve this, we first need to check whether the tmp folder already exists. If not, it has to be created. The logic for constructing the path with the tmp subfolder and for creating the tmp subfolder is shown in the previous code listing.

4. Finally, we need to resize the image. For this, the source file is opened, the resize function is called with requisite parameters, and the resized image is written to the output file.

5. The time taken for image resizing is calculated using the `Instant::now()` and `Elapsed::from()` functions.

The code listing is shown here. For purposes of explanation, the code listing has been split into multiple snippets.

The code listed here accepts three input parameters – the size, source folder, and an entry of type `PathBuf` (which can refer to the full path of an image file). The file extension is changed to `.png` as this is the output format supported by the tool:

```
fn resize_image(size: u32, src_folder: &mut PathBuf) ->
    Result<(), ImagixError> {
    // Construct destination filename with .png extension
    let new_file_name = src_folder
        .file_stem()
        .unwrap()
        .to_str()
        .ok_or(std::io::ErrorKind::InvalidInput)
        .map(|f| format!("{}.png", f));
```

The code snippet here appends the suffix `/tmp` to the file path entry in order to create the destination folder path. Note that due to a limitation in the standard library, the filename is first constructed as `tmp.png`, which is subsequently changed to reflect the final resized image filename:

```
// Construct path to destination folder i.e. create /tmp
// under source folder if not exists
let mut dest_folder = src_folder.clone();
dest_folder.pop();
dest_folder.push("tmp/");
if !dest_folder.exists() {
    fs::create_dir(&dest_folder)?;
}
dest_folder.pop();
dest_folder.push("tmp/tmp.png");
dest_folder.set_file_name(new_file_name?.as_str());
```

The code here opens the image file and loads the image data into memory. The /tmp subfolder is created under the source folder. Then, the image is resized and written to the output file in the destination folder. The time taken for the resizing operation is recorded and printed out:

```
let timer = Instant::now();
let img = image::open(&src_folder)?;
let scaled = img.thumbnail(size, size);
let mut output = fs::File::create(&dest_folder)?;
scaled.write_to(&mut output, ImageFormat::Png)?;
println!(
    "Thumbnailed file: {:?} to size {}x{} in {}. Output
    file
    in {:?}",
    src_folder,
    size,
    size,
    Elapsed::from(&timer),
    dest_folder
    );
    Ok(())
}
```

We have now seen the code for resizing images. Next, we will look at the code for generating image stats.

Image statistics

In the previous subsection, we looked at the code for image resizing. In this subsection, we will see the logic for generating image statistics. This method will count the number of image files in a specified source folder, and measure their total file size.

The logic of the get_stats() method that we will use is described as follows:

1. The get_stats() method takes a source folder as its input parameter and returns two values: the number of image files in the folder, and the total aggregate size of all image files in the folder.

2. Get a list of image files in the source folder by calling the get_image_files() method.

3. The `metadata()` function in the `std::path` module allows us to query a file or directory for its metadata information. In our code, as we iterate through the directory entries, we aggregate the sizes of all files in one variable, `sum`. The `sum` variable is returned from the function along with the count of image file entries.

The code listing is provided here:

src/imagix/stats.rs

```
pub fn get_stats(src_folder: PathBuf) -> Result<(usize,
    f64), ImagixError> {
    let image_files = get_image_files
        (src_folder.to_path_buf())?;
    let size = image_files
        .iter()
        .map(move |f| f.metadata().unwrap().len())
        .sum::<u64>();
    Ok((image_files.len(), (size / 1000000) as f64))
}
```

We have covered the code for the image processing functionality. We will now cover some details of our custom error handling for the project.

Error handling

Let's now take a look at our error handling design.

As a part of our project, there may be many failure conditions that we have to handle. Some of them are given here:

- The source folder given by the user may be invalid.
- The specified file may not be present in the source folder.
- Our program may not have permission to read and write files.
- User inputs for size or mode may be incorrect.
- There may be errors during image resizing (for example, a corrupt file).
- There may be other types of internal processing errors.

Let's define a custom error type to handle all these different types of errors in a unified manner, and provide the error as output to the users of our library:

src/imagix/error.rs

```
pub enum ImagixError {
    FileIOError(String),
    UserInputError(String),
    ImageResizingError(String),
    FormatError(String),
}
```

The names of the errors are mostly self-explanatory. FormatError is any error encountered while converting or printing values of parameters. The goal of defining this custom error type is that the various types of errors that may be encountered during processing, such as errors in user input, the inability to read through a directory or write to a file, an error in image processing, and so on, are converted into our custom error type.

It is not enough to just define a custom error type. We also have to ensure that when errors happen in due course of the program's operation, these errors are translated into the custom error type. For example, an error in reading an image file raises an error defined in the std::fs module. This error should be caught and transformed into our custom error type. This way, regardless of whether there is an error in file operations or error processing, the program uniformly propagates the same custom error type for handling by the frontend interface to the user (in the case of this project, it is the command line).

For the conversion of various types of errors into ImagixError, we will implement the From trait. We will also implement the Display trait for our error type so that the errors can be printed out to the console.

Within each of the methods in the project modules, at the failure points, you will notice that ImagixError is raised and propagated back to the calling function. The source code can be found in the source folder for this chapter in the Packt code repository.

This concludes the error handling subsection of the code.

This also concludes this section on coding the imagix library. We have only walked through key code snippets as it isn't practical to print out the entire code listing inline in the chapter. I would urge the reader to go through the entire source code to understand how the various features are translated into idiomatic Rust code.

In the next section, we will build the command-line application that wraps this library and provides the user interface.

Developing the command-line application and testing

In the previous section, we built the library for image resizing. In this section, we will review the design and key parts of the code for the main command-line application.

Let's begin with some automated unit tests to test the image resizing functionality in `resize.rs`: This way we can confirm that the image resizing library works independently of any calling function.

Two test cases are shown here in the following code—one to resize a single image, and the other to resize multiple images. You can replace the source folder and filenames in the code with your own:

src/imagix/resize.rs

```
#[cfg(test)]
mod tests {
    use super::*;
    #[test]
    fn test_single_image_resize() {
        let mut path = PathBuf::from("/tmp/images/
            image1.jpg");
        let destination_path = PathBuf::from(
            "/tmp/images/tmp/image1.png");
        match process_resize_request(SizeOption::Small,
            Mode::Single, &mut path) {

            Ok(_) => println!("Successful resize of single
                image"),

            Err(e) => println!("Error in single image:
                {:?}", e),
        }
```

```
        assert_eq!(true, destination_path.exists());
    }
    #[test]
    fn test_multiple_image_resize() {
        let mut path = PathBuf::from("/tmp/images/");
        let _res = process_resize_request(
            SizeOption::Small, Mode::All, &mut path);
        let destination_path1 = PathBuf::from(
            "/tmp/images/tmp/image1.png");
        let destination_path2 = PathBuf::from(
            "/tmp/images/tmp/image2.png");
        assert_eq!(true, destination_path1.exists());
        assert_eq!(true, destination_path2.exists());
    }
}
```

Place the image1.jpg and image2.jpg files in /tmp/images and execute the tests with the following command:

```
cargo test
```

You can see the tests pass successfully. You can also inspect the resized images.

As an exercise, you can add the test cases for the image stats function as well.

We can now conclude that the imagix library works as intended. Let's now move on to designing the command-line application.

We shall first look at the CLI requirements.

Designing the command-line interface

In this subsection, we will look at the design of the CLI. By design, we mean finalizing the structure of the CLI that the user will use. The CLI should be intuitive to use for the end user. The CLI must also accommodate some flexibility in its performing of different types of operations.

The imagecli CLI will use a command-subcommand model like git.

The CLI command structure is shown in *Figure 4.6*:

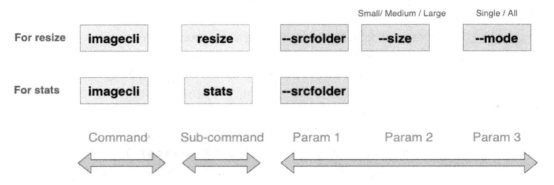

Figure 4.6 – Design of CLI commands

Here are some examples of commands with parameters that the user can specify:

- For resizing images, the command is `cargo run --release resize` with three parameters.

- For image statistics, the command is `cargo run --release stats` with one parameter.

- For resizing a single image the command is `cargo run --release resize --size small --mode single --srcfolder <path-to-image-file/file-name.extn>`.

- For resizing multiple images, we use the `cargo run --release resize --size medium --mode all --srcfolder <path-to-folder-containing-images>` command.

- For image statistics, the `cargo run --release  stats --srcfolder <path-to-folder-containing-images>` command is used.

The `imagecli main()` function parses the command-line parameters, handles user and processing errors with suitable messages to the user, and invokes the respective functions from the `imagix` library.

Let's do a quick recap. To resize images, we need to know the following from the user:

- The mode (single or multiple files)
- The output size of the image file (small/medium/large)
- The source folder where the image file (or files) is located

In this section, we designed the CLI for the tool. In the previous sections, we built the imagix library to resize images. We will now move on to the last part of the project, which is to develop the main command-line binary application that ties all the pieces together and accepts user inputs from the command-line.

Coding the command-line binary using structopt

In the previous section, we designed the interface for the command-line tool. In this section, we will see the code for the main() function that accepts user inputs from the command line and invokes the imagix library. This main() function will be compiled and built into the command-line binary tool. The user will invoke this executable for resizing images and provide the necessary command-line parameters.

The main() function will be located in src/imagecli.rs, as we want the command-line tool binary name to be imagecli.

Let's now review the code snippets for the command-line application. The main() function is located in the src/imagecli.rs file:

1. We will start with the imports section. Note the imports of the imagix library that we have written, and structOpt for command-line argument parsing:

```
mod imagix;
use ::imagix::error::ImagixError;
use ::imagix::resize::{process_resize_request, Mode,
    SizeOption};
use ::imagix::stats::get_stats;
use std::path::PathBuf;
use std::str::FromStr;
use structopt::StructOpt;
// Define commandline arguments in a struct
```

2. We will now see the definition of the command-line parameters for the tool. For this we will use the `structopt` syntax. Refer to documentation at `https://docs.rs/structopt`. Basically, we have defined an `enum` called `Commandline` and defined two subcommands, `Resize` and `Stats`. `Resize` takes three arguments: `size`, `mode` and `srcfolder` (the source folder). `Stats` takes one argument: `srcfolder`:

```rust
#[derive(StructOpt, Debug)]
#[structopt(
    name = "resize",
    about = "This is a tool for image resizing and
        stats",
    help = "Specify subcommand resize or stats. For
        help, type imagecli resize --help or
        imagecli stats --help"
)]
enum Commandline {
    #[structopt(help = "
            Specify size(small/medium/large),
            mode(single/all) and srcfolder")]

    Resize {
        #[structopt(long)]
        size: SizeOption,
        #[structopt(long)]
        mode: Mode,
        #[structopt(long, parse(from_os_str))]
        srcfolder: PathBuf,
    },
    #[structopt(help = "Specify srcfolder")]
    Stats {
        #[structopt(long, parse(from_os_str))]
        srcfolder: PathBuf,
    },
}
```

3. We can now review the code for the `main()` function. Here, we basically accept the command-line inputs (validated by `StructOpt`) and invoke the suitable methods from our `imagix` library. If the user specifies the `Resize` command, the `process_resize_request()` method of the `imagix` library is invoked. If the user specifies the `Stats` command, the `get_stats()` method of the `imagix` library is invoked. Any errors are handled with suitable messages:

```
fn main() {
    let args: Commandline = Commandline::from_args();
    match args {
        Commandline::Resize {
            size,
            mode,
            mut srcfolder,
        } => {
            match process_resize_request(size, mode,
                &mut src_folder) {
                Ok(_) => println!("Image resized
                    successfully"),
                Err(e) => match e {
                    ImagixError::FileIOError(e) =>
                        println!("{}", e),
                    ImagixError::UserInputError(e) =>
                        println!("{}", e),
                    ImagixError::ImageResizingError(e)
                        => println!("{}", e),

                    _ => println!("Error in
                        processing"),
                },
            };
        }
        Commandline::Stats { srcfolder } => match
            get_stats(srcfolder) {
            Ok((count, size)) => println!(
                "Found {:?} image files with aggregate
```

```
                        size of {:?} MB",
                        count, size
                    ),
                Err(e) => match e {
                    ImagixError::FileIOError(e) =>
                        println!("{}", e),
                    ImagixError::UserInputError(e) =>
                        println!("{}", e),
                    _ => println!("Error in processing"),
                },
            },
        }
    }
```

4. Build the app with the following command:

```
cargo build --release
```

The reason to use the release builds is that there is a considerable time difference in resizing images between the debug and release builds (the latter being much faster).

You can then execute and test the following scenarios at the Terminal. Ensure to place one or more .png or .jpg files in the folder that you specify in --srcfolder flag:

- **Resize a single image**:

```
cargo run --release resize --size medium --mode single
--srcfolder <path-to-image-file>
```

- **Resize multiple files**:

```
cargo run --release resize --size small --mode all
--srcfolder <path-to-image-file>
```

- **Generate image stats**:

```
cargo run --release  stats --srcfolder <path-to-image-
folder>
```

In this section, we have built a tool for image resizing that works from a CLI. As an exercise, you can experiment by adding additional features, including adding support for more image formats, changing the size of the output file, or even providing the option to encrypt the generated image file for additional security.

Summary

In this chapter, we learned to write Rust programs that can discover and manipulate the system environment, directory structures, and filesystem metadata in a cross-platform manner, using the `std::env`, `std::path`, and `std::fs` modules. We looked at how to create programs that can use command-line arguments or environment variables to accept configuration parameters and user inputs. We saw the use of two third-party crates: the `StructOpt` crate to improve the user interface of the tool, and `image-rs/image` to do the image resizing.

We also learned how to use the `std:time` module to measure the time taken for specific processing tasks. We defined a custom error type to unify error handling in the library. In this chapter, we were also introduced to file handling operations.

In the next chapter, we will take a detailed look at doing advanced memory management with the standard library.

Section 2: Managing and Controlling System Resources in Rust

This section covers how to interact with the kernel in Rust for managing memory, files, directories, permissions, terminal I/O, the process environment, process control and relationships, handling signals, inter-process communications, and multithreading. Example projects include a tool to compute Rust source file metrics, a text viewer, a custom shell, and a multithreaded version of the Rust source file metrics tool.

This section comprises the following chapters:

- *Chapter 5, Memory Management in Rust*
- *Chapter 6, Working with Files and Directories*
- *Chapter 7, Implementing Terminal I/O in Rust*
- *Chapter 8, Working with Processes and Signals*
- *Chapter 9, Managing Concurrency*

5
Memory Management in Rust

In *Section 1*, *Getting Started with Systems Programming in Rust*, we covered Cargo (the Rust development toolkit), a tour of the Rust language, an introduction to the Rust Standard Library, and standard library modules for managing process environment, command-line, and time-related functions. While the focus of *Section 1*, *Getting Started with Systems Programming in Rust*, was to provide an overview of the landscape and the foundation for system programming in Rust, *Section 2*, *Manage and Control System Resources in Rust*, gets into the details of how to manage and control system resources in Rust, including memory, files, terminals, processes, and threads.

We are now entering *Section 2*, *Manage and Control System Resources in Rust*, of the book. *Figure 5.1* provides the context for this section:

Managing system resources

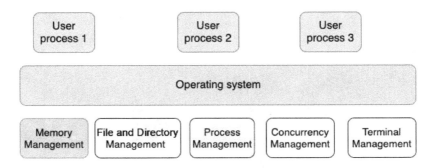

Figure 5.1 – Managing system resources

In this chapter, we will focus on memory management. The following are the key learning outcomes for this chapter:

- The basics of **operating system (OS)** memory management
- Understanding the memory layout of Rust programs
- The Rust memory management lifecycle
- Adding a dynamic data structure to a template engine

We will begin the chapter with an overview (or a refresher for those already familiar with the topic) of the general principles of memory management in OSes, including the memory management lifecycle and the layout of a process in memory. We will then cover the memory layout of a running Rust program. This will cover how a Rust program is laid out in memory and the characteristics of the heap, stack, and static data segments. In the third section, we learn about the Rust memory management lifecycle, how it differs from other programming languages, and how memory is allocated, manipulated, and released in Rust programs. Lastly, we will enhance the template engine that we started to build in *Chapter 3*, *Introduction to the Rust Standard Library and Key Crates for Systems Programming*, with a dynamic data structure.

Technical requirements

Rustup and Cargo must be installed in a local development environment.

The complete code for this chapter can be found at `https://github.com/ PacktPublishing/Practical-System-Programming-for-Rust- Developers/tree/master/Chapter05`.

The basics of OS memory management

In this section, we will go into the fundamentals of memory management in modern OSes. Those already familiar with this topic can skim through this section quickly as a refresher.

Memory is among the most fundamental and critical resources available to a running program (process). Memory management deals with the allocation, use, manipulation, ownership transfer, and eventual release of memory used by a process. Without memory management, executing a program is not possible. Memory management is performed by a combination of components, such as the kernel, program instructions, memory allocators, and garbage collectors, but the exact mechanism varies across programming languages and OSes.

In this section, we will look at the memory management lifecycle and then learn the details of how memory is laid out for a process by the operating system.

The memory management lifecycle

In this section, we will cover the different activities associated with memory management:

1. The memory management lifecycle *begins* when a binary executable is run. The operating system allocates a virtual memory address space for the program and initializes various segments of memory based on the instructions in the binary executable.

2. Memory management activities *continue* as the program processes various inputs coming in from I/O devices such as files, networks, and standard input (from the command line).

3. The memory management lifecycle *ends* when the program is terminated (or if the program ends abnormally due to error).

Figure 5.2 shows a typical memory management cycle:

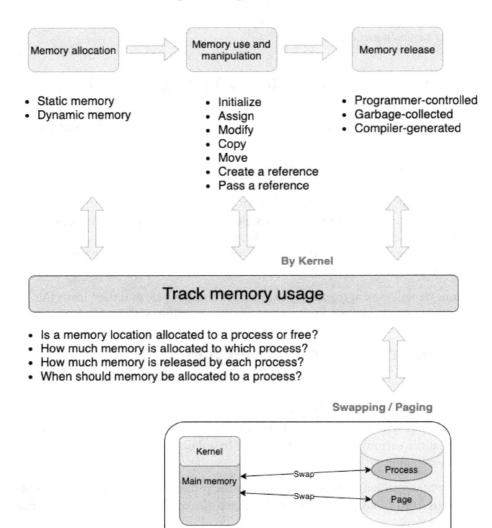

Figure 5.2 – Memory lifecycle

Memory management essentially involves four components—**allocation**, **use and manipulation**, **deallocation/release**, and **tracking usage**:

- **Memory allocation**: This is explicitly done in low-level programming languages by programmers, but is performed transparently in high-level languages. Memory allocated can either be of a *fixed-size* (where the size of a data type is determined at compilation time, such as integers, Booleans, or fixed-size arrays) or *dynamically-sized* (where the memory is increased or decreased or relocated dynamically at runtime, for example, resizable arrays).

- **Memory use and manipulation**: The following steps are typical activities performed in a program:

  1. Defining a named memory area of a particular type (for example, declaring a new variable x of type integer)

  2. Initializing a variable

  3. Modifying the value of the variable

  4. Copying or moving values to another variable

  5. Creating and manipulating references to values

- **Memory release**: This is explicitly performed by the programmer in low-level languages, but is handled automatically in high-level languages such as Java, Python, JavaScript, and Ruby using a component called the **garbage collector**.

- **Memory tracking**: This is done at the kernel level. A program invokes *system calls* to allocate and deallocate memory. System calls are executed by the *kernel*, which keeps track of memory allocations and releases per process.

- **Swapping/paging**: This is also done by the *kernel*. Modern OSes virtualize physical memory resources. Processes do not directly interact with actual physical memory addresses. The kernel assigns virtual address space to each process. The total sum of virtual address space allocated to all processes in a system can be more than the amount of physical memory available in the system, but the processes don't know (or care) about this. The OS manages this using virtual memory management, which ensures that the processes are insulated from each other, and programs have access to the committed memory over their lifetime. Swapping and paging are techniques in **virtual memory management**.

Paging and swapping

How does the operating system map the virtual memory address space to physical memory? To achieve this, the virtual address space allocated to programs is split into fixed-size pages (for example 4 KB or 8 KB chunks). A **page** is a fixed-length contiguous block of virtual memory. Thus the virtual memory allocated to a program is divided into multiple fixed-length pages. The corresponding unit on the physical RAM is a **page frame**, which is a fixed-length block of RAM. Multiple page-frames add up to the total physical memory on a system.

At any point in time, only some of the *virtual pages* of a program need to be present in the *physical page frames*. The rest are stored on disk in the *swap area*, which is a reserved area of the disk. The kernel maintains a page table to track the location of each page in the virtual memory space allocated to a program. When a program tries to access a memory location on a page, and if the page is not on the page frame, the page is located on disk and is then swapped into the main memory. Likewise, unused pages in RAM are swapped back into the disk (secondary storage) to make space for active processes. This process is called **paging**.

If the same technique is applied at the process level (rather than the page level), it is called **swapping**, where the pages of one process are swapped from memory to disk to make way for another process to be loaded into memory.

This aspect of memory management that deals with mapping physical RAM to virtual address space is called **virtual memory management**. This ensures that processes have access to adequate memory as needed, and are also isolated from each other and from the kernel. This way, a program cannot accidentally (or deliberately) write to the memory space of the kernel or another process, protecting against memory corruption, undefined behavior, and security issues.

We have learned about the memory management lifecycle of a process. Let's now understand how a program is laid out in memory by the operating system.

The process memory layout

We will now look at the structure of the virtual address space allocated by the kernel to a single process. *Figure 5.3* shows the memory layout for a process on **Linux**, but similar mechanisms exist for **Unix** and **Windows** OS variants:

Process memory layout

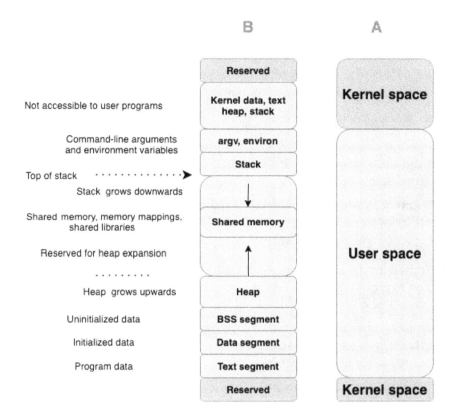

Figure 5.3 – Process memory layout

A **process** is a running program. When a program is started up, the operating system loads it into memory, gives it access to the command-line parameters and environment variables, and starts executing the program instructions.

The operating system allocates the process some amount of memory. Such allocated memory has a structure associated with it, which is called the **memory layout** of the process. The memory layout of a process contains several **memory regions** (also called **segments**), which are nothing but blocks of *memory pages* (which was described in the previous subsection). These segments are shown in *Figure 5.3*, and described next.

The portion of *Figure 5.3* marked **A** shows that the overall virtual memory space allocated to a process is split into **Kernel space** and **User space**. Kernel space is the area of memory where the portion of the kernel is loaded that assists the program in managing and communicating with hardware resources. This includes kernel code, the kernel's own memory area, and space marked **Reserved**. In this chapter, we will focus only on the **User space**, as that is the area that is actually used by the program. The kernel space of virtual memory is not accessible to the program.

The user space is segregated into several memory segments, which are described here:

- **Text segment** contains the program's code and other read-only data such as *string literals* and *const parameters*. This portion is directly loaded from the program binary (executable or library).

- **Data segment** stores global and static variables that are initialized with non-zero values.

- **BSS segment** contains uninitialized variables.

- **Heap** is used for dynamic memory allocation. The address space of the process continues to grow as memory gets allocated on the heap. The heap grows upward, which means new items are added at addresses greater than previous items.

- **Stack** is used for *local variables*, and also *function parameters* (in some platform architectures). Stacks grow downwards, which means that items put earlier in the stack occupy lower address spaces.

> Tip
> Note that the stack and the heap are allocated at opposite ends of the process address space. As the *stack size* increases, it grows downwards, and as the *heap size* increases, it grows upwards. In the event that they meet, a stack overflow error occurs or a memory allocation call on the heap will fail.

- In between the stack and the heap, there is also the area where any **shared memory** (memory shared across processes), **shared libraries** used by the program, or **memory-mapped** areas (areas of memory that reflect a file on a disk) are located.

- Above the stack, there is a segment where **command-line arguments** passed to the program and the **environment variables** set for the process are stored.

Memory management is a complex topic and a lot of details have been left out in the interest of keeping the discussion focused on memory management in Rust. However, the basics of virtual memory management and virtual memory addresses described earlier are critical for understanding the next section on how Rust performs memory management.

Understanding the memory layout of Rust programs

In the previous section, we discussed the fundamentals of memory management in modern OSes. In this section, we will discuss how a running Rust program is laid out in memory by the operating system, and the characteristics of the different parts of the virtual memory are used by Rust programs.

Rust program memory layout

In order to understand how Rust achieves the combination of low-memory footprint, memory safety, and performance, it is necessary to understand how Rust programs are laid out in memory and how they can be controlled programmatically.

A low-memory footprint depends on the efficient management of memory allocations, the copying of values, and deallocations. Memory safety deals with ensuring that there is no unsafe access to values stored in memory. Performance depends on understanding the implications of storing a value in the stack versus the heap versus the static data segment. Where Rust shines is that all these tasks are not fully left to the programmer like in C/C++. The Rust compiler and its ownership system does a lot of the heavy-lifting, preventing entire classes of memory bugs. Let's now look at the topic in detail.

The memory layout of a Rust program is shown in *Figure 5.4*:

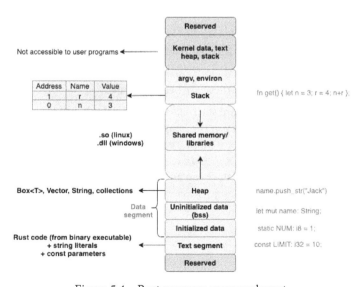

Figure 5.4 – Rust program memory layout

Let's walk through this figure to understand the memory layout of a Rust program:

- **Rust process**: When a Rust executable binary (for example, created using `cargo build`) is read into system memory by the kernel and executed, it becomes a process. The operating system assigns each process its own private user space so that different Rust processes don't interfere with each other accidentally.

- **Text segment**: Executable instructions of the Rust program are placed here. This is placed below the stack and heap to prevent any overflows from overwriting it. This segment is *read-only* so that its contents are not accidentally overwritten. However, multiple processes can *share* the text segment. Let's take the example of a text editor written in Rust running in *process 1*. If a second copy of the editor is to be executed, then the system will create a new process with its own private memory space (let's call it *process 2*), but will not reload the program instruction of the editor. Instead, it will create a reference to the text instructions of *process 1*. But the rest of the memory (the data, stack, and so on) is not shared across processes.

- **Data segment**: The data segment can be divided into *initialized variables* (such as variables declared as static), *uninitialized variables* (also known as **bss** or **block started by symbol**), and the *heap*. During execution, if the program asks for more memory, it is allocated in the *heap* area. The heap is thus associated with *dynamic memory allocation*.

Dynamic lifetime versus dynamic size

In Rust, *dynamic memory* is required for variables that have a **dynamic lifetime** or **dynamic size**.

Examples of Rust types with a *dynamic lifetime* are `Rc` (single-threaded reference-counting pointer) and `Arc` (thread-safe reference counting pointer).

Examples of types in Rust with a *dynamic size* are `Vectors`, `Strings`, and other `collection` types, and these are heap-allocated.

Primitive types such as integers are stack-allocated by default, but the programmer can allocate memory in the heap by using a `Box<T>` type (for example, `let y =3` allocates memory for integer y on the stack and initializes it to 3, whereas `let x: Box<i32> = Box::new(3)` allocates a value for integer x on the heap and initializes it to 3).

- **Stack segment**: The stack is the region of the process memory that stores *temporary (local) variables, function parameters*, and the *return address* of the instruction (which is to be executed after the function call is over). By default, all memory allocations in Rust are on the stack. Whenever a function is called, its variables get memory-allocated on the stack. Memory allocation happens in contiguous memory locations one above the other, in a *stack data structure*.

To summarize, here is how the virtual memory allocated to a running Rust program looks:

- The *code instructions* of a Rust program go into the *text segment* area.

- The *primitive data types* are allocated on the *stack*.

- The static variables are located in the *data segment*.

- The *heap-allocated values* (values whose size is not known at compilation time, such as vectors and strings) are stored in the *heap area of the data segment*.

- The *uninitialized variables* are in the *BSS segment*.

Of these, the Rust programmer does not have much control over the *text* segment and *BSS* segments, and only primarily works with the *stack*, *heap*, and *static* areas of memory. In the next section, we will delve into the characteristics of these three memory areas.

The characteristics of stack, heap, and static memory

We have seen how the different types of variables declared in a Rust program are allocated in different regions of the process space. Of the three memory segments, we have discussed – **text**, **data**, and **stack** – the text area is not under the control of the Rust programmer, but the programmer has the flexibility to decide whether to place a value (that is, allocate memory) on the stack, heap, or as a static variable. However, there are strong implications of this decision because the stack, static variables, and the heap are managed quite differently, and their lifetimes are also different. Understanding these trade-offs is an important part of writing any Rust program. Let's look at them more closely.

Table 5.1 summarizes the characteristics of stack-allocated versus heap-allocated versus static-segment memory. Recall from *Figure 5.4* that stack-allocated memory belongs to the *stack segment*, and heap and static variables belong to the *data segment* of virtual memory address space:

Attribute	Stack	Heap	Static
Memory allocation	Automatic, by default	Manual – by the programmer	Automatic – when the program is loaded into memory
Memory deallocation	Automatic	The Rust compiler generates code to call the destructor when a variable goes out of scope	Automatic – when the program terminates
Size	There is a system limit on stack size (OS-dependent) per process	The heap can grow to the maximum size of the virtual memory allocated by the operating system	Fixed
Speed	Very fast access	Relatively slow access	Fast, as it is at a fixed memory location
Memory fragmentation	Space is managed efficiently by the OS, without fragmentation	Memory may become fragmented as blocks are allocated and released	Not applicable as memory is not released or reallocated for a lifetime of programs
Scope of variables	Only local variables can be stored	Values can be accessed globally in the program	Values can be accessed globally
Size of variables	Variable size is fixed; cannot store collections that can dynamically grow in size	Resizing of variables possible (for example, a new element can be appended to a vector)	Fixed
Lifetime	Variables live only until the end of the surrounding function or block	The lifetime of the allocation in the heap depends on the lifetime of the box values pointing to it	Lasts for the lifetime of the program

Attribute	Stack	Heap	Static
Read/write	Read-only by default; mut to be specified for write	Read-only by default; mut to be specified for write	Read-only by default. Should be encapsulated in a mutex for write
Memory reuse	Memory reused by CPU	Memory can be reused by the programmer	Memory allocated at a fixed location; cannot be allocated or released by the programmer

Table 5.1 – Characteristics of the stack, heap, and static memory areas

Is it important to understand the memory locations of values?

For people who have worked with other high-level programming languages, understanding whether a variable was stored in the stack, heap, or static data segments won't have really been necessary, as the language compiler, runtime, and garbage collector will have abstracted away these details and made it easy for the programmer.

But in Rust, especially for writing system-oriented programs, awareness of the memory layout and the memory model is necessary to select appropriate and efficient data structures for various parts of the system design. And in many cases, this knowledge is necessary even to get the Rust program to compile!

In this section, we have covered the memory layout of Rust programs and understood the characteristics of the stack and data segment memory areas. In the next section, we will provide an overview of the Rust memory management lifecycle and a comparison with other programming languages. We will also look at the three steps of the Rust memory management lifecycle in detail.

The Rust memory management lifecycle

Computer programs can be modeled as finite state machines. A running program accepts different forms of inputs (for example, file inputs, command-line arguments, network calls, interrupts, and so on) and transitions from one state to another. Take the case of a device driver. It can be in either of the following states: *uninitialized*, *active*, or *inactive*. When a device driver is just booted up (loaded into memory), it is in the *uninitialized* state. When the device registers are initialized and ready to accept events, it goes into the *active* state. It can be put in suspended mode and not ready to accept inputs, in which case it goes into the *inactive* state. You can extend this concept further. For a communications device like a serial port, the device driver can be in the *sending* or *receiving* state. Interrupts can trigger the transitions from one state to another. Likewise, every kind of program, whether it is a kernel component, command-line tool, network server, or an e-commerce application, can be modeled in terms of states and transitions.

Why is the discussion around state important for memory management? Because, state is represented in a program by the programmer as a set of variables with values, and these values are stored in the virtual memory of a running program (process). Since a program goes through numerous state transitions (top social media site programs handle several hundred million state transitions per day), all this state and these transitions are represented in memory and then persisted to disk. Every component of the modern layered application stack (including frontend apps, backend servers, the network stack, other system programs, and operating system kernel utilities) needs to be able to efficiently allocate, use, and release memory. Hence, it is important to understand how the memory layout of a program changes over its lifetime, and what the programmer can do to make it efficient.

With this background, let's move on to an overview of the Rust memory management lifecycle.

Overview of the Rust memory management lifecycle

Let's now compare the memory management lifecycle for other programming languages with Rust. Let's also take a look at *Figure 5.5*, which shows how memory management in Rust works, in comparison with other programming languages:

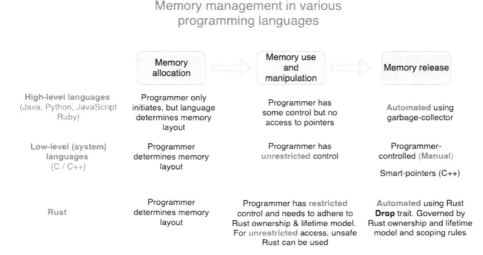

Figure 5.5 – Memory management in other programming languages

In order to appreciate the Rust memory model, it is important to understand how memory management is done in other programming languages. *Figure 5.5* shows how two sets of programming languages—high-level and low-level—manage memory and compare it with Rust.

There are three main steps in the memory management lifecycle:

1. Memory allocation
2. Memory use and manipulation
3. Memory release (deallocation)

The way these three steps are performed varies across programming languages.

High-level languages (such as Java, JavaScript, and Python) hide a lot of the details of memory management from the programmer (who has limited control), automate memory deallocation using a garbage collector component, and do not provide direct access to memory pointers to the programmer.

Low-level (also known as system) programming languages such as C/C++ provide a complete degree of control to the programmer but do not provide any safety nets. Managing memory efficiently is left solely to the skills and meticulousness of the developer.

Rust combines the best of both worlds. A Rust programmer has full control over memory allocation, being able to manipulate and move around values and references in memory, but is subjected to strict Rust ownership rules. Memory deallocation is automated by the compiler-generated code.

> **High-level versus low-level programming languages**
>
> Note that the terms **high-level** and **low-level** are used to classify programming languages based on the level of abstraction provided to the programmer. Languages that provide higher-level programming abstractions are easier to program in and take away many of the hard responsibilities around memory management, at the cost of lack of control for the programmer.
>
> On the other hand, system languages such as C and C++ provide full control and responsibility to the programmer to manage memory and other system resources.

We have seen an overview of the memory management approaches of Rust versus other programming languages. Let's now see them in more detail in the following subsections.

Memory allocation

Memory allocation is the process of storing a value (it can be an integer, string, vector, or higher-level data structures such as network ports, parsers, or e-commerce orders) to a location in memory. As part of memory allocation, a programmer instantiates a data type (primitive or user-defined) and assigns an initial value to it. The Rust program invokes system calls to allocate memory.

In higher-level languages, the programmer declares variables using the specified syntax. The language compiler (in conjunction with the language runtime) handles the allocation and exact location of the various data types in virtual memory.

In C/C++, the programmer controls memory allocation (and reallocation) through the system call interfaces provided. The language (compiler, runtime) does not intervene in the programmer's decision.

In Rust, by default, when the programmer initializes a data type and assigns it a value, the operating system allocates memory on the stack. This applies to all primitive types (integers, floating points, char, Boolean, fixed-length arrays), function local variables, function parameters, and other fixed-length data types (such as smart pointers). But the programmer has the option to explicitly place a primitive data type on the heap by using `Box<T>` smart pointers. Secondly, all dynamic values (for example, strings and vectors whose size changes at runtime) are stored on the heap, and the smart pointer to this heap data is placed on the stack. To summarize, for fixed-length variables, values are stored on the stack, variables with a dynamic length are allocated memory on the heap segment, and a pointer to the starting location of heap-allocated memory is stored on the stack.

Let's now look at some additional information about memory allocation.

All data types declared in a Rust program have their size calculated at compile time; they are not dynamically allocated or freed. So what, then, is dynamic?

When there are values that change over time (for example, a `String` whose value is not known at compile time or a collection where the number of elements is not known upfront), these are allocated at runtime on the heap, but a reference to such data is stored as a pointer (which has a fixed size) on the stack.

For example, run the following code:

```
use std::mem;
fn main() {
    println!("Size of string is {:?}",
        mem::size_of::<String>());
}
```

When you run this program on a 64-bit system, the size of `String` will be printed as **24**, meaning it takes 24 bytes. Have you noticed that we are printing the size of `String` without even creating a string variable or assigning a value to it? This is because Rust does not care how long a string is, in order to compute its size. Sound strange? This is how it works.

In Rust, `String` is a smart pointer. This is illustrated in *Figure 5.6*. It has three components: a **pointer to bytes** (stored in heap), a **length**, and **capacity**. Each of these three components has a size of one **machine-word** each, so in the case of 64-bit architectures, each of these 3 components of the `String` smart pointer occupies 64 bits (or 8 bytes), hence the total size occupied by a variable of the `String` type is 24 bytes. This is regardless of the actual value contained in the string, which is stored in the heap, while the smart pointer (24 bytes) is stored on the stack. Note that even though the size of the `String` smart pointer is fixed, the actual size of the memory allocated on the heap may vary as the value of string changes during program runtime.

String smart pointer in Rust

(example for 64-bit arch)

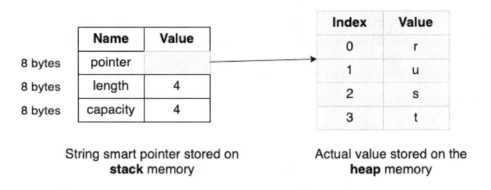

String smart pointer stored on **stack** memory

Actual value stored on the **heap** memory

In 64-bit computer architectures, machine word size = 64 bits (8 bytes)

Figure 5.6 – Structure of a String smart pointer in Rust

In this subsection, we have discussed various aspects of memory allocation in a Rust program. In the next subsection, we will look at the second step of the memory management lifecycle, which is about memory manipulation and use within the Rust program.

Memory use and manipulation

Memory use and manipulation refer to program instructions such as modifying the value assigned to a variable, copying a value to another variable, moving the ownership of a value from one variable to another, and creating new references to an existing value. In Rust, copy, move, and clone are three fundamental memory manipulation operations. The move operation transfers ownership of data from one variable to another. The copy operation allows a value associated with a variable to be duplicated with a bit-wise copy. Implementing the clone trait on a data type allows the duplication of values instead of move semantics.

All primitive data types (such as integers, bools, and chars) implement the copy trait by default. This means assigning a variable of the primitive data type to another variable of same type copies the value (duplicates). User-defined data types such as structs can implement copy if all their data members also implement the copy trait.

Anything that does not implement copy is moved by default. For example, for the Vec data type, all operations (for example, passing a Vec value as a function argument, returning a Vec from a function, assignment, pattern matching) are *move* operations. Rust does not have a Move trait explicitly because it is the default.

For non-copy data types, move is the default behavior. To implement arbitrary copy operations on non-copy types, the clone trait can be implemented on the type.

More details can be found in the Rust book at https://doc.rust-lang.org/book/. In high-level languages, the programmer can initialize a variable, assign values to variables, and copy values to other variables. Generally, high-level languages do not have explicit pointer semantics or arithmetic but use references. The difference is that a pointer refers to the exact memory address of a value, but references are aliases for another variable. While the programmer uses reference semantics, the language internally implements pointer operations.

In C/C++, the programmer can also initialize variables, and assign and copy values. In addition, pointer operations are possible. Pointers allow you to write directly to any memory allocated by the process. The problem with this model is that this gives rise to several types of memory safety issues, such as free-after-use, double-free, and buffer overflows.

In Rust, memory use and manipulation are governed by certain rules:

- First, all variables in Rust are immutable by default. If a value contained in a variable needs to be altered, the variable has to be declared explicitly as mutable (with the mut keyword).

- Secondly, there are ownership rules that apply to data access, which are listed in a later subsection.

- Third, there are rules of references (borrowing) that apply when it comes to sharing a value with one or more variables, which is also covered later.

- Fourth, there are lifetimes, which give information to the compiler about how two or more references relate to each other. This helps the compiler prevent memory safety issues by checking if the references are valid.

These concepts and rules make programming in Rust very different (and more difficult at times) from other programming languages. But it is also these very concepts that impart super-powers to Rust in areas of memory and thread-safety. Importantly, Rust provides these benefits without runtime costs.

Let's now recap the Rust rules for ownership and for borrowing and references in the subsections that follow.

Rust ownership rules

Ownership is arguably Rust's most unique feature. It gives memory safety to Rust programs without an external garbage collector or relying entirely on the programmer's skillset. There are three ownership rules in Rust, which are listed here. More details can be found at the following link: https://doc.rust-lang.org/book/ch04-01-what-is-ownership.html.

The rules governing Rust ownership

In Rust, every value has an owner. At any point in time, for a given value, there can be only one owner. A value is dropped (the memory associated with it is deallocated) when its owner goes out of scope. Some examples of the scope of a variable are a function, a for loop, a statement, or an arm of a match expression. More details on scope can be found here: https://doc.rust-lang.org/reference/destructors.html#drop-scopes.

The really interesting aspect of Rust is that these ownership rules are not meant for the programmer to memorize, but the Rust compiler enforces these rules. Another significant implication of these ownership rules is that the same rules also ensure thready safety, in addition to memory safety.

Rust borrowing and references

In Rust, references simply borrow a value and are indicated by the & symbol. They basically allow you to refer to a value without taking ownership of the value. This is unlike smart pointers such as `String`, `Vector`, `Box`, and `Rc`, which own the value they point to.

Taking a reference to a value is called **borrowing**, which is a temporary reference to an object, but it has to be returned and cannot be destroyed by the borrower (only the owner can deallocate memory). If there are multiple borrows of a value, the compiler ensures that all borrows end before the object is destroyed. This eliminates memory errors such as **use-after-free** and **double-free** errors.

More details on Rust borrowing and references can be found at `https://doc.rust-lang.org/book/ch04-02-references-and-borrowing.html`.

The rules governing Rust references

A value stored in memory can either have one mutable reference to it or any number of immutable references (but not both).

References must always be valid. The borrow checker portion of the Rust compiler stops compilation if invalid references are found in code. When it's ambiguous, the Rust compiler also asks the programmer to explicitly specify the lifetime of references.

In this subsection, we have covered several rules governing the manipulation of variables and values in memory and the rules governing them. In the next subsection, we will look at the last aspect of the memory management lifecycle, which is about deallocating memory after use.

Memory deallocation

Memory deallocation deals with the question of how to release memory back to the operating system from the Rust program. Stack-allocated values are automatically released, as this is a managed-memory area. Static variables have a lifetime until the end of the program, so they get released automatically when the program terminates. The real question around memory release applies to heap-allocated memory.

Some of these values may not be required to be held in memory until the end of the program, in which case they can be released. But the mechanism of such memory release varies widely across different programming language groups:

- Higher-level languages do not require the programmers to explicitly release memory when they are no longer needed. Instead, they use a mechanism called **garbage collection**. In this model, a runtime component called **garbage collector** analyzes the *heap-allocated* memory of the process, determines the unused objects using specialized algorithms, and deallocates them. This helps improve memory safety, prevents memory leaks, and makes programming easier for developers.

- In C/C++, the deallocation of memory is the responsibility of the programmer. Forgetting to release memory causes **memory leaks**. Accessing values after memory has been released causes memory safety issues. In large, complex code bases, or in code maintained by multiple people, this causes serious issues.

- Rust takes a very different approach to memory deallocation. Rust neither has a **garbage collector** (**GC**) nor does it require the programmer to explicitly remember to release heap-allocated memory. Instead, Rust uses a technique called **Resource Acquisition Is Initialization** (**RAII**), which is a rather strange name for a technique that calls the destructor and releases memory when a variable goes out of scope. The programmer can implement the destructor (the `Drop` trait) for a type, and that will be called by the compiler-generated code. The benefit of this approach is that it gives fine-grained memory control (like C/C++) while freeing the Rust programmer from having to manually deallocate memory (like high-level languages), without the drawbacks of the garbage collector (latency and unpredictable GC pauses).

- Note that in Rust, only the owner of a value can release the memory associated with it. References do not own the data they point to, so cannot deallocate memory. But smart pointers own the data they point to. The compiler generates code that calls the `drop` method from the `Drop` trait associated with the smart pointer when the smart pointer goes out of scope.

- Also, these memory deallocation rules apply only to heap-allocated memory as the other two types of memory segments (stack and statics) are managed directly by the operating system.

We have so far seen the rules governing memory allocation, manipulation, and release in Rust programs. All these collectively aim to achieve the primary goal of memory safety without an external garbage collector, which is truly one of the highlights of the Rust programming language. The following callout section describes the various types of memory vulnerabilities and how Rust prevents them.

What is memory safety?

Memory safety simply means that in any possible execution path of a program, there is no access to invalid memory. The following are some of the prominent categories of memory safety bugs:

- **Double-free**: Attempting to release the same memory location(s) more than once. This can result in undefined behavior or memory corruption. Rust ownership rules allow the release of memory only by the owner of a value, and at any point, there can be only one owner of a value allocated in the heap. Rust thus prevents this class of memory safety bugs.

- **Use-after-free**: A memory location is accessed after it has been released by the program. The memory being accessed may have been allocated to another pointer, so the original pointer to this memory may inadvertently corrupt the value at the memory location causing undefined behavior or security issues through arbitrary code execution. Rust reference and lifetime rules enforced by the borrow checker in the compiler always ensure that a reference is valid before use. Rust borrow checker prevents a situation where a reference outlives the value it points to.

- **Buffer overflow**: The program attempts to store a value in memory beyond the allocated range. This can corrupt data, cause a program to crash, or result in the execution of malicious code. Rust associates capacity with a buffer and performs bounds check on access. So, in safe Rust code, it is not possible to overflow a buffer. Rust will panic if you attempt to write out of bounds.

- **Uninitialized memory use**: The program reads data from a buffer that was allocated but not initialized with values. This causes undefined behavior because the memory location can hold indeterminate values. Rust prevents reading from uninitialized memory.

- **Null pointer dereference**: The program writes to memory with a null pointer, causing segmentation faults. A null pointer is not possible in safe Rust because Rust ensures that a reference does not outlive the value it refers to, and Rust's lifetime rules require functions manipulating references to declare how the references from input and output are linked, using lifetime annotations.

We have thus seen how Rust achieves memory safety through its unique system of immutable-by-default variables, ownership rules, lifetimes, reference rules, and borrow-checker.

With this, we conclude this section on the Rust memory management lifecycle. In the next section, we will implement a dynamic data structure in Rust.

Implementing a dynamic data structure

In this section, we will enhance the template engine from *Chapter 3, Introduction to the Rust Standard Library and Key Crates for Systems Programming*, to add support for multiple template variables in one statement. We will achieve this by converting a static data structure into a dynamic data structure.

We will refresh our memory with the model of the template engine shown in *Figure 5.7*:

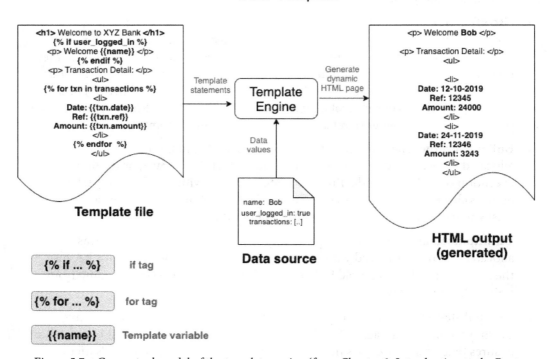

Figure 5.7 – Conceptual model of the template engine (from Chapter 3, Introduction to the Rust Standard Library and Key Crates for Systems Programming)

You will recall that we implemented a template engine in *Chapter 3, Introduction to the Rust Standard Library and Key Crates for Systems Programming*, to parse an input statement with a template variable and convert it into a dynamic HTML statement using context data provided. We will enhance the template variable feature in this section. We will first discuss the design changes and then implement the code changes.

Changes to the design of the template engine

In *Chapter 3*, *Introduction to the Rust Standard Library and Key Crates for Systems Programming*, we implemented the **template variable** content type, wherein the following was input at the command line:

```
<p> Hello {{name}} </p>
```

This will generate the following HTML statement:

```
<p> Hello Bob </p>
```

We provided the value of name=Bob as context data in the main() program.

Let's enhance the feature for the template variable content type in this chapter. So far, our implementation works if there is *one* template variable. But if there is more than one template variable (as provided in the following example), it does not yet work.

Our expectation is that the following code should work, assuming we provide the values of city=Boston and name=Bob as context data in the main() program:

```
<p> Hello {{name}}. Are you from {{city}}? </p>
```

This will generate the following HTML statement:

```
<p> Hello Bob. Are you from Boston? </p>
```

You will notice that there are two template variables in the input statement here—name and city. We will have to enhance our design to support this, starting with the ExpressionData struct, which stores the result of the parsing of the template-variable statement.

Let's look at the data structure ExpressionData. We can start with the code from Chapter03 located at https://github.com/PacktPublishing/Practical-System-Programming-for-Rust-Developers/tree/master/Chapter03:

```rust
#[derive(PartialEq, Debug)]
pub struct ExpressionData {
    pub head: Option<String>,
    pub variable: String,
    pub tail: Option<String>,
}
```

In our implementation, the input value of `<p> Hello {{name}}. How are you? </p>` will be tokenized into the `ExpressionData` struct as follows:

```
Head = Hello
Variable = name
Tail = How are you?
```

In the preceding design, we allowed the following format:

```
<String literal> <template variable> <String literal>
```

The string literal before the `template variable` was mapped to the `Head` field in `ExpressionData`, and the string literal after the `template variable` was mapped to the `Tail` field of `ExpressionData`.

As you can see, we have made provision for only one `template variable` in the data structure (the `variable` field is of type `String`). In order to accommodate multiple `template variable` in a statement, we must alter the struct, to allow the `variable` field to store more than one `template variable` entry.

In addition to allowing multiple template variables, we also need to accommodate a more flexible structure of input statements. In our current implementation, we accommodate one string literal before `template variable`, and one literal after it. But in the real world, an input statement can have any number of string literals, as shown in the following example:

```
<p> Hello , Hello {{name}}. Can you tell me if you are living
    in {{city}}? For how long? </p>
```

So, we have the following changes to make to our template engine:

- Allow for the parsing of more than one template variable per statement
- Allow for the parsing of more than two string literals in the input statement

To allow for these changes, we have to redesign the `ExpressionData` struct. We also need to modify the methods that deal with `ExpressionData` to implement the parsing functionality for these two changes.

Let's review the summary of changes to be made to the design, which is shown in *Figure 5.8*. This figure is from *Chapter 3, Introduction to the Rust Standard Library and Key Crates for Systems Programming*, but the components to be changed are highlighted in the figure:

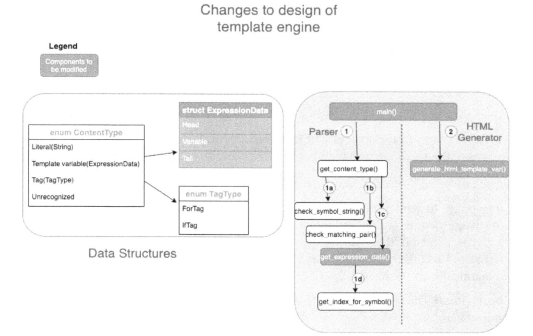

Figure 5.8 – Changes to the design of the template engine

In this subsection, we designed a dynamic data structure for the template engine we are building throughout several chapters of the book. In the next subsection, we will write the code to implement this.

Coding the dynamic data structure

As indicated in *Figure 5.7*, we will be modifying the following components of the template engine in this chapter:

- The `ExpressionData` struct
- The `get_expression_data()` function
- The `generate_html_template_var()` function
- The `main()` function

We will start with the changes to the `ExpressionData` struct:

src/lib.rs

```rust
#[derive(PartialEq, Debug, Clone)]
pub struct ExpressionData {
    pub expression: String,
    pub var_map: Vec<String>,
    pub gen_html: String,
}
```

We have fully revamped the structure of `ExpressionData`. It now has three fields. The descriptions of the fields are provided here:

- `expression`: The expression input by the user is stored here.

- `var_map`: Instead of a single `String` field as earlier, we now have a vector of strings to store *multiple template variables* in a statement. We have used a vector instead of the array because we do not know at compile time how many template variables there will be in the user input. For vectors, memory is allocated dynamically on the heap.

- `gen_html`: The generated HTML statement corresponding to the input is stored here.

> **What are dynamic data structures?**
>
> **Dynamic data structures** are data structures that can grow and shrink as needed. Memory blocks are allocated on the heap, which is tied together by the definition of the data structure. When the data is no longer needed, the memory is deallocated and reused. In our revised template engine, `ExpressionData` is an example of a dynamic data structure. It is dynamic because the memory allocation for the field `var_map` changes dynamically at runtime depending on how many *template variables* are present in the input, and the total length of the *expression* field (which is based on the count and length of the string literals in the input statement). Expression data is an example of a user-defined data structure that is associated with smart pointers as its field members contain dynamic values.

Due to this change to the structure of `ExpressionData`, we have to alter the following two functions: `get_expression_data()` and `generate_html_template_var()`:

src/lib.rs

```
pub fn get_expression_data(input_line: &str) -> ExpressionData
{
    let expression_iter = input_line.split_whitespace();
    let mut template_var_map: Vec<String> = vec![];
    for word in expression_iter {
        if check_symbol_string(word, "{{") &&
            check_symbol_string(word, "}}") {
            template_var_map.push(word.to_string());
        }
    }
    ExpressionData {
        expression: input_line.into(),
        var_map: template_var_map,
        gen_html: "".into(),
    }
}
```

In the preceding code, we are doing the following:

- Splitting the input statement into words separated by whitespace (`expression_iter`)

- Iterating through the words to parse only the template variables

- Adding the template variables to a vector of strings `template_var_map.push(word.to_string());`

- Constructing the `ExpressionData` struct and returning from the function

> **Dynamic memory allocation**
>
> In the preceding function, the following statement shows dynamic memory allocation:
>
> ```
> template_var_map.push(word.to_string());
> ```
>
> This statement adds each template variable found in the input statement to a collection of vectors, which is then stored in the `ExpressionData` struct. Each `push()` statement on the vector is translated by the Rust Standard Library into a memory allocation—**syscall**—to the operating system, which allocates memory on the heap segment. Because memory is thus dynamically allocated, `ExpressionData` is a dynamic data structure. Likewise, when the variable of type `ExpressionData` goes out of scope, memory is deallocated for all the elements of the struct (including the vector of strings).

We will now modify the function that generates HTML output:

src/lib.rs

```rust
pub fn generate_html_template_var(
    content: &mut ExpressionData,
    context: HashMap<String, String>,
) -> &mut ExpressionData {
    content.gen_html = content.expression.clone();
    for var in &content.var_map {
        let (_h, i) = get_index_for_symbol(&var, '{');
        let (_j, k) = get_index_for_symbol(&var, '}');
        let var_without_braces = &var[i + 2..k];
        let val = context.get(var_without_braces).unwrap();
        content.gen_html = content.gen_html.replace(var, val);
    }
    content
}
```

This function accepts two inputs—the `ExpressionData` type and the `context` HashMap. Let's understand the logic through an example. Let's also assume the following input values are passed to the function:

- The expression field of `content` has `<p> {{name}} {{city}} </p>`.
- The following values are contained in the `var_map` field of `content`: `[{{name}},{{city}}]`
- The following context data is passed to the function in the `content` HashMap: `name=Bob` and `city=Boston`.

Here is the processing that we perform in the function:

1. We iterate through the list of template variables contained in the `var_map` field of `content`.

2. For each iteration, we first strip out the leading and trailing curly braces from the template variable values stored in the `var_map` field of `content`. So `{{name}}` becomes `name` and `{{city}}` becomes `city`. We then look them up in the `context` HashMap and retrieve the value (yielding `Bob` and `Boston`).

3. The last step is to replace all instances of `{{name}}` in the input string with `Bob` and all instances of `{{city}}` with `Boston`. The resultant string is stored in the `gen_html` field of the `content` struct, which is of type `ExpressionData`.

And finally, we will modify the `main()` function as follows. The main change in the `main()` function, compared to *Chapter 3, Introduction to the Rust Standard Library and Key Crates for Systems Programming*, is the change in the parameters to be passed to the `generate_hml_template_var()` function:

src/main.rs

```
use std::collections::HashMap;
use std::io;
use std::io::BufRead;
use template_engine::*;
fn main() {
    let mut context: HashMap<String, String> = HashMap::new();
    context.insert("name".to_string(), "Bob".to_string());
    context.insert("city".to_string(), "Boston".to_string());
```

```
    for line in io::stdin().lock().lines() {
        match get_content_type(&line.unwrap().clone()) {
            ContentType::TemplateVariable(mut content) => {
                let html = generate_html_template_var(&mut
                    content, context.clone());
                println!("{}", html.gen_html);
            }
            ContentType::Literal(text) => println!("{}",
                text),
            ContentType::Tag(TagType::ForTag) => println!("For
                Tag not implemented"),
            ContentType::Tag(TagType::IfTag) => println!("If
                Tag not implemented"),
            ContentType::Unrecognized => println!(
                "Unrecognized input"),
        }
    }
}
```

With these changes, we can run the program with `cargo run`, and enter the following in the command line:

```
<p> Hello {{name}}. Are you from {{city}}? </p>
```

You will see the following generated HTML statement displayed on your terminal:

```
<p> Hello Bob. Are you from Boston? </p>
```

In this section, we converted the `ExpressionData` struct from a static to a dynamic data structure, and modified the associated functions to add the following features to the template engine:

- Allow for the parsing of more than one template variable per statement
- Allow for the parsing of more than two string literals in the input statement

Now, let's end the chapter with a summary.

Summary

In this chapter, we looked in depth at the memory layout of a standard process in the Linux environment, and then the memory layout of a Rust program. We compared the memory management lifecycle in different programming languages and how Rust takes a different approach to memory management. We learned how memory is allocated, manipulated, and released in a Rust program, and looked at the rules governing memory management in Rust, including ownership and reference rules. We looked at the different types of memory safety issues and how Rust prevents them from using its ownership model, lifetimes, reference rules, and borrow checker.

We then returned to our template engine implementation example from `Chapter 03` and added a couple of features to the template engine. We achieved this by converting a static data structure into a dynamic data structure and learned how memory is allocated dynamically. Dynamic data structures are very useful in programs that deal with external inputs, for example, in programs that accept incoming data from network sockets or file descriptors, where it is not known in advance what the size of incoming data will be, which is likely to be the case for most real-world complex programs that you will be writing using Rust over the course of your professional career.

This concludes the memory management topic. In the next chapter, we will take a closer look at the Rust Standard Library modules that deal with file and directory operations.

Further reading

Understanding Ownership in Rust: `https://doc.rust-lang.org/book/ch04-00-understanding-ownership.html`

6
Working with Files and Directories in Rust

In the previous chapter, we looked at the details of how Rust uses memory, a key system resource.

In this chapter, we will look at how Rust interacts with another important class of system resources – **files** and **directories**. The Rust Standard Library offers a rich set of abstractions that enable platform-independent file and directory operations.

For this chapter, we will review the basics of how files are managed by Unix/Linux, and master the key APIs that the Rust Standard Library provides to deal with *files*, *paths*, *links*, and *directories*.

Using the Rust Standard Library, we will implement a shell command, `rstat`, that counts the total number of lines of Rust code in a directory (and its subfolders), and provides a few additional source code metrics.

We will cover the topics in the following order:

- Understanding Linux system calls for file operations
- Doing file I/O in Rust

- Learning directory and path operations
- Setting hard links, symbolic links, and performing queries
- Writing a shell command in Rust (project)

Technical requirements

Verify that `rustc`, and `cargo` have been installed correctly with the following command:

```
rustc --version
cargo --version
```

The Git repo for the code in this chapter can be found at `https://github.com/PacktPublishing/Practical-System-Programming-for-Rust-Developers/tree/master/Chapter06`.

Understanding Linux system calls for file operations

In this section, we will look at the terminology and basic mechanisms associated with managing file system resources at the operating system level. We will use Linux/Unix as an example, but similar concepts apply to other operating systems.

So, what do you think a file is?

A **file** is just a set of bytes. A **byte** represents a unit of information—it can be a number, text, video, audio, image, or any other such digital content. The bytes are organized in a *linear array* called a **byte stream**. There is no other expectation in terms of the structure or contents of a file, as far as the operating system is concerned. It is the *user application* that does the interpretation of the file and its contents.

A **user application** is a program that is not a part of the operating system kernel. An example of a user application is an image viewer that interprets the bytes of data as an image. Since files are resources that are managed by the operating system, any user programs that we write must know how to interact with the operating system through system calls. A file can be read from, written to, or executed. An example of a file that can be executed is the binary executable (object) file, generated by software build systems such as **Make** or **Cargo**.

Another aspect that is unique to Linux/Unix is the philosophy that *everything is a file.* Here, *everything* refers to system resources. There can be many types of files on Linux/Unix:

- **Regular files**, which we use to store text or binary data
- **Directories**, which contain listings of names and references to other files
- **Block device files**, for example, a hard disk, a tape drive, USB cameras
- **Character device files**, for example, a terminal, a keyboard, a printer, a sound card
- **Named pipes**, an in-memory inter-process communication mechanism
- **Unix domain sockets**, also a form of inter-process communication
- **Links**, such as hard links and symbolic links

In this chapter, we will focus on files, directories, and links. However, the universality of the Unix I/O model means that the same set of system calls used to open, read, write, and close regular files can also be used on any other types of files such as **device files**. This is achieved in Linux/Unix by standardizing the system calls, which are then implemented by various filesystems and device drivers.

Linux/Unix also provides a unified **namespace** for all its files and directories. Files and directories organized into a hierarchy are called a **filesystem**. Many different filesystems can be added to or removed from the namespace through **mounting** and **unmounting**. For example, a CD-ROM drive can be mounted at /mnt/cdrom, which becomes the location to access the root of the filesystem. The root directory of a "filesystem" can be accessed at the mount point.

The **mount namespace** of a process is the set of all mounted filesystems it sees. A process that makes system calls for file operations operates on the set of files and directories that it sees as a part of its mount namespace.

The Unix/Linux system calls (**Application Programming Interface - API**) model for file operations hinges on four operations: **open**, **read**, **write**, and **close**, all of which work with the concept of **file descriptors**. What is a file descriptor?

A file descriptor is a handle to a file. Opening a file returns a file descriptor, and other operations such as reading, writing, and closing use the file descriptor.

> **More about file descriptors**
>
> File operations such as read and write are performed by processes. A process performs these operations by invoking system calls on the kernel. As soon as a file is opened by a process, the kernel records it in a *file table*, where each entry contains details of the open file including the **file descriptor (fd)** and **file position**. Each Linux process has a limit on the number of files it can open.
>
> To the kernel, all open files are referred to by file descriptors. When a process opens an existing file or creates a new file, the kernel returns a file descriptor to the process. By default, when a process is started from a shell, three file descriptors are automatically created: `open: 0 - standard input (stdin)`, `1- standard output (stdout)`, and `2-standard error (stderr)`.
>
> The kernel maintains a table of all open file descriptors. If the process opens or creates a file, the kernel allocates the next free file descriptor from the pool of free file descriptors. When a file is closed, the file descriptor is released back to the pool and is available for re-allotment.

Let's now look at the common *system calls* associated with file operations, which the operating system exposes:

- `open()`: This system call opens an existing file. It can also create a new file if the file does not exist. It accepts a pathname, the mode in which the file is to be opened, and flags. It returns a file descriptor that can be used in subsequent system calls to access the file:

```
int open(const char *pathname, int flags, ... /* mode_t
    mode */);
```

There are three basic modes in which to open a file – *read only*, *write only*, and *read-write*. In addition, flags are specified as arguments to the `open()` system call. An example of a flag is `O_CREAT`, which tells the system call to create a file if the file does not exist, and returns the file descriptor.

If there is an error in opening a file, `-1` is returned in place of the file descriptor, and the error number (`errno`) returned specifies the reason for the error. File open calls can fail for a variety of reasons including a *permissions error* and the *incorrect path* being specified in an argument to a system call.

- `read()`: This system call accepts three arguments: a *file descriptor*, the *number of bytes* to be read, and the *memory address of the buffer* into which the data read is to be placed. It returns the number of bytes read. `-1` is returned in the event of an error when reading the file.

- write(): This system call is similar to read(), in that it also takes three parameters – a *file descriptor*, a *buffer pointer* from which to read the data, and the *number of bytes* to read from the buffer. Note that successful completion of the write() system call does not guarantee that the bytes have been written to disk immediately, as the kernel performs buffering of I/O to disk for performance and efficiency reasons.

- close(): This system call accepts a *file descriptor* and releases it. If a close() call is not explicitly invoked for a file, all open files are closed when the process terminates. But it is good practice to release file descriptors (when no longer needed) for reuse by the kernel.

- lseek(): For each open file, the kernel keeps track of a file offset, which represents the location in the file at which the next read or write operation will happen. The system call lseek() allows you to reposition the file offset to any location in the file. The lseek() system call accepts three arguments – the file descriptor, an offset, and a reference position. The reference position can take three values – *start of file*, *current cursor position*, or *end of file*. The offset specifies the number of bytes relative to the reference position that the file offset should be pointed to, for the next read() or write().

This concludes the overview of terminologies and key concepts of how operating systems manage files as system resources. We have seen the main system calls (syscalls) in Linux for working with files. We will not be directly using these syscalls in this book. But we will work with these syscalls indirectly, through the Rust Standard Library modules. The Rust Standard Library provides higher-level *wrappers* to make it easier to work with these syscalls. These *wrappers* also allow Rust programs to work without necessarily understanding all the differences in syscalls across different operating systems. However, gaining basic knowledge of how operating systems manage files gives us a glimpse into what goes on under the hood when we use the Rust Standard Library for file and directory operations.

In the next section, we will cover how to do file I/O in Rust.

Doing file I/O in Rust

In this section, we will look at the Rust method calls that let us work with files in Rust programs. The Rust Standard Library spares the programmer from having to work with system calls directly and provides a set of wrapper methods exposing APIs for common file operations.

The primary module in the Rust Standard Library for working with files is `std::fs`. The official documentation for `std::fs` can be found here: `https://doc.rust-lang.org/std/fs/index.html`. This documentation provides the set of methods, structs, enums, and traits that collectively provide features for working with files. It helps to study the structure of the `std::fs` module to gain a deeper understanding. However, for those starting out with exploring system programming in Rust, it is more useful to begin with a mental model of what kinds of things a programmer would like to do with files, and map it back to the Rust Standard Library. This is what we will do in this section. The common lifecycle operations for a file are shown in *Figure 6.1*.

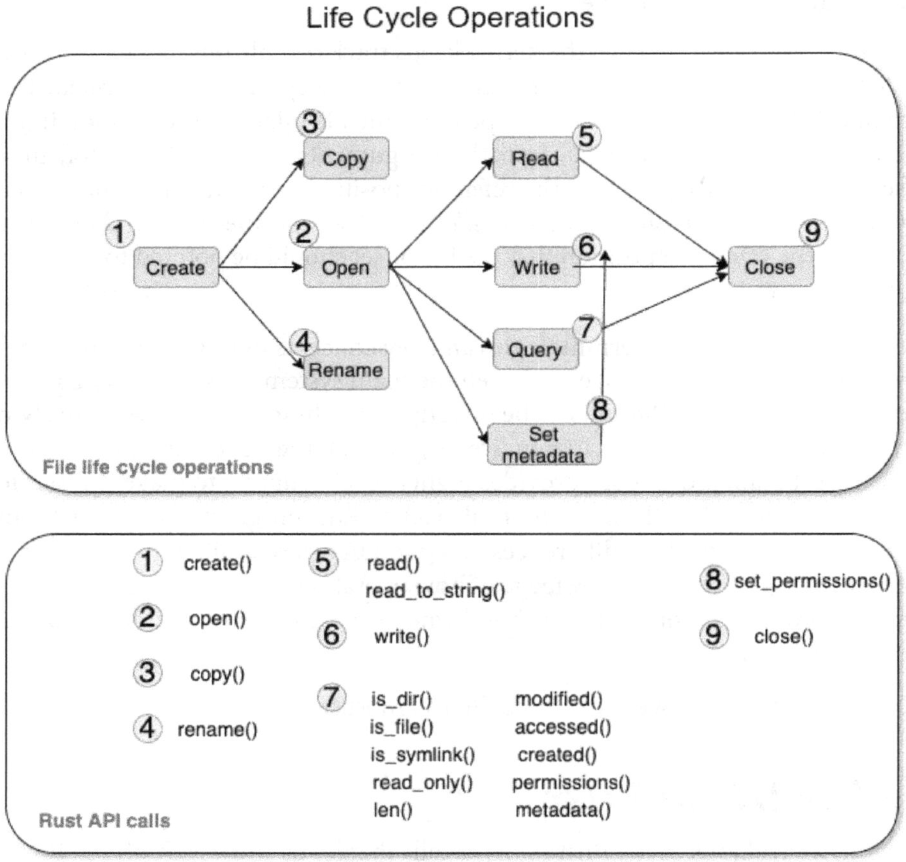

Life Cycle Operations

Figure 6.1 – Common file life cycle operations

The common things programmers like to do with files include creating a file, opening and closing files, reading and writing files, accessing metadata about files, and setting file permissions. These are shown in *Figure 6.1*. Descriptions of how to perform each of these file operations using the Rust Standard Library are provided here:

- **Create**: The *create* operation simply creates a new file with the *specified name*, at the *specific location* in the filesystem. The corresponding function call in the `std::fs` module is `File::create()`, which allows you to create a new file and write to it. Custom permissions for the file to be created can be specified using the `std::fs::OpenOptions` struct. An example of a *create* operation using the `std::fs` module is shown in the code snippet here:

```rust
use std::fs::File;
fn main() {
    let file = File::create("./stats.txt");
}
```

- **Open**: The *open* operation opens an existing file, given the *full path* to the file in the filesystem. The function call to be used is `std::fs::File::open()`. This opens a file in *read-only* mode by default. The `std::fs::OpenOptions` struct can be used to set *custom permissions* to create the file. Two methods to open a file are shown below. The first function returns a `Result` type, which we are just handling using `.expect()`, which panics with a message if the file is not found. The second function uses `OpenOptions` to set additional permissions on the file to be opened. In the example shown, we are opening a file for the *write* operation, and also are asking for the file to be created if not present already:

```rust
use std::fs::File;
use std::fs::OpenOptions;
fn main() {
    // Method 1
    let _file1 = File::open("stats1.txt").expect("File
        not found");
    // Method 2
    let _file2 = OpenOptions::new()
        .write(true)
        .create(true)
        .open("stats2.txt");
}
```

- **Copy**: This is simply a byte-by-byte copy of the contents of one file to another. The `std::fs::copy()` function can be used to copy the contents of one file to another, overwriting the latter. An example is shown here:

```
use std::fs;
fn main() {
    fs::copy("stats1.txt", "stats2.txt").expect("Unable
        to copy");
}
```

- **Rename**: This is an operation that renames a specified file to a new name. Errors can occur if the *from file* does not exist, or if permissions are insufficient. In Rust, the `std::fs::rename()` function can be used for this purpose. If the *to* file exists, it is replaced. One thing to note is that there can be more than one filesystem mounted (at various points) within the *mount namespace* of a process, as seen in the previous section. The `rename` method in Rust will work only if both the *from* and *to* file paths are in the same filesystem. An example of usage of the `rename()` function is shown here:

```
use std::fs;
fn main() {
    fs::rename("stats1.txt", "stats3.txt").expect("Unable
        to rename");
}
```

- **Read**: The *read* operation takes a *filename with its path* and reads the contents. In the `std::fs` module, there are two functions available: `fs::read()` and `fs::read_to_string()`. The former reads the contents of a file into a `bytes` `vector`. It pre-allocates a buffer based on file size (when available). The latter reads the contents of a file directly into a string. Examples are shown here:

```
use std::fs;
fn main() {
    let byte_arr = fs::read("stats3.txt").expect("Unable
        to read file into bytes");
    println!(
        "Value read from file into bytes is {}",
        String::from_utf8(byte_arr).unwrap()
    );
    let string1 = fs::read_to_string("stats3.txt").
```

```
        expect("Unable to read file into string");
    println!("Value read from file into string is {}",
        string1);
}
```

In the code snippet shown for `fs::read()`, we convert the `byte_arr` into a string for printing purposes, as printing out a byte array is not human-readable.

- **Write**: The *write* operation writes the contents of a buffer into a file. In `std::fs`, the `fs::write()` function accepts a *filename* and a *byte slice*, and writes the *byte slice* as the contents of the file. An example is shown here:

```
use std::fs;
fn main() {
    fs::write("stats3.txt", "Rust is exciting,isn't
        it?").expect("Unable to write to file");
}
```

- **Query**: These operations deal with obtaining metadata about files. There are several query methods available on files in the `std::fs` module. The functions `is_dir()`, `is_file()`, and `is_symlink()` respectively check whether a file is a *regular file*, *directory*, or a *symlink*. The `modified()`, `created()`, `accessed()`, `len()`, and `metadata()` functions are used to retrieve file metadata information. The `permissions()` function is used to retrieve a list of permissions on the file.

A few examples of the usage of query operations are shown here:

```
use std::fs;
fn main() {
    let file_metadata = fs::metadata("stats.txt").
        expect("Unable to get file metadata");
    println!(
        "Len: {}, last accessed: {:?}, modified : {:?},
        created: {:?}",
        file_metadata.len(),
        file_metadata.accessed(),
        file_metadata.modified(),
        file_metadata.created()
    );
    println!(
```

```
            "Is file: {}, Is dir: {}, is Symlink: {}",
            file_metadata.is_file(),
            file_metadata.is_dir(),
            file_metadata.file_type().is_symlink()
    );
    println!("File metadata: {:?}",fs::metadata
        ("stats.txt"));
        println!("Permissions of file are: {:?}",
            file_metadata.permissions());
}
```

- **Metadata**: Metadata for a file includes details about a file such as *file type, file permissions, last accessed time, created time*, and so on. Permissions for a file can be set for a file using set_permissions(). An example is shown here, where, after setting the file permission to read-only, the write operation to the file fails:

```
use std::fs;
fn main() {
    let mut permissions = fs::metadata("stats.txt").
        unwrap().permissions();
    permissions.set_readonly(true);
    let _ = fs::set_permissions("stats.txt",
        permissions).expect("Unable to set permission");

    fs::write("stats.txt", "Hello- Can you see me?").
        expect("Unable to write to file");
}
```

- **Close**: In Rust, files are automatically closed when they go out of scope. There is no specific close() method in the Rust Standard Library to close files.

In this section, we saw the key function calls from the Rust Standard Library that can be used to perform *file manipulation* and *query* operations. In the next section, we will take a look at how the Rust Standard Library can be used for *directory* and *path* operations.

Learning directory and path operations

The kernel in Linux (and other Unix variants) maintains a single directory tree structure visible to a process, which is hierarchical and contains all files in that namespace. This hierarchical organization contains both individual files, directories, and links (for example, a symbolic link).

In the previous section, we looked at *files* and file operations in Rust. In this section, we will take a closer look at *directory* and *path* operations. In the next section, we will cover *links*.

A *directory* is a special file that contains a list of filenames with references (**inodes**) to the corresponding files. Directories can point to regular files or other directories. It is this connection between directories that establishes the overall directory hierarchy in a namespace. For example, / represents the root directory, and /home and /etc will link to / as the *parent* directory. (Note that in some operating systems, such as Microsoft Windows variants, each disk device has its own hierarchy of files, and there is not a single unified namespace.) Each directory contains at least two entries – a *dot entry* pointing to itself and a *dot-dot* directory, which is a link to its parent directory:

Common directory and path operations

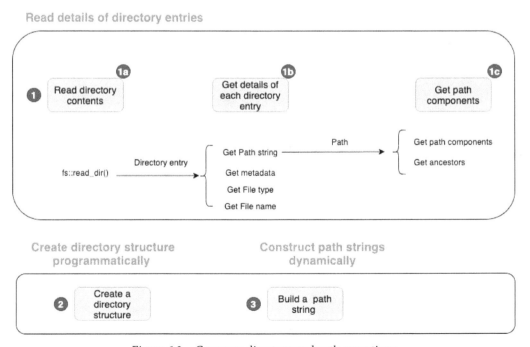

Figure 6.2 – Common directory and path operations

In the Rust Standard Library, the `std::fs` module contains methods to work with directories, and the `std::path` module contains methods to work with *paths*.

Just as in the previous section, we will look at the common programming tasks involving *directory* and *path* manipulations. These are shown in *Figure 6.2* and detailed here:

1. **Read details of directory entries**: In order to write system programs that deal with files and directories, it is necessary to understand how to read through the structure of a directory, retrieve the directory entries, and get their metadata. This is achieved by using functions in the `std::fs` module. The `std::fs::read_dir()` function can be used to iterate through and retrieve the entries in a directory. From the directory entry thus retrieved, the metadata details of the directory entry can be obtained with the functions `path()`, `metadata()`, `file_name()`, and `file_type()`. Examples of how to do this are shown here:

```rust
use std::fs;
use std::path::Path;
fn main() {
    let dir_entries = fs::read_dir(".").expect("Unable to
        read directory contents");
    // Read directory contents
    for entry in dir_entries {
        //Get details of each directory entry
        let entry = entry.unwrap();
        let entry_path = entry.path();
        let entry_metadata = entry.metadata().unwrap();
        let entry_file_type = entry.file_type().unwrap();
        let entry_file_name = entry.file_name();
        println!(
            "Path is {:?}.\n Metadata is {:?}\n File_type
            is {:?}.\n Entry name is{:?}.\n",
            entry_path, entry_metadata, entry_file_type,
            entry_file_name
        );
    }
}
```

```
// Get path components
let new_path = Path::new("/usr/d1/d2/d3/bar.txt");
println!("Path parent is: {:?}", new_path.parent());
for component in new_path.components() {
    println!("Path component is: {:?}", component);
}
}
```

Next, we'll look at how to construct directory trees programmatically.

2. **Create directory structure programmatically**: If there is a need to create a directory structure programmatically in the filesystem, it is possible using the std::fs module. The Rust std::fs:DirBuilder struct provides methods to recursively construct a directory structure. An example of creating a directory structure recursively is shown here:

```
use std::fs::DirBuilder;
fn main() {
    let dir_structure = "/tmp/dir1/dir2/dir3";
    DirBuilder::new()
        .recursive(true)
        .create(dir_structure)
        .unwrap();
}
```

Note that there are two other functions also available to create directories. create_dir() and create_dir_all() in std::fs can be used for this purpose.

Likewise, the functions remove_dir() and remove_dir_all() in the std::fs module can be used to delete directories.

Next, we'll look at how to construct path strings dynamically.

3. **Construct path strings dynamically**: A pathname is a string consisting of a series of components separated by slashes. Each component represents a directory name, except the component following the final slash, which represents the file. For example, in the pathname /usr/bob/a.txt, usr and bob represent directories, while a.txt represents a file. The Rust Standard Library provides facilities to construct a path string (representing the full path to a file or a directory) programmatically. This is available in std::path::PathBuf. An example of how to construct a path dynamically is shown here:

```
use std::path::PathBuf;
fn main() {
    let mut f_path = PathBuf::new();
    f_path.push(r"/tmp");
    f_path.push("packt");
    f_path.push("rust");
    f_path.push("book");
    f_path.set_extension("rs");
    println!("Path constructed is {:?}", f_path);
}
```

In the code shown, a new variable of type PathBuf is constructed, and the various path components are dynamically added to create a fully qualified path.

This concludes this subsection on directory and path operations with the Rust Standard Library.

In this section, we looked at how to use the Rust Standard Library to read through directory entries, get their metadata, construct a directory structure programmatically, get path components, and build a path string dynamically.

In the next section, we will look at how to work with *links* and *queries*.

Setting hard links, symbolic links, and performing queries

We saw earlier that a directory is treated in a file system similarly to a regular file. But it has a different file type, and it contains a list of filenames with their inodes. **Inodes** are data structures that contain metadata about a file such as an inode number (to uniquely identify the file), permission, ownership, and so on. In Unix/Linux, the first column in the output of an `ls -li` command shows the inode number corresponding to a file, as shown here:

```
256029 drwxrwxr-x. 3 ap ap 4096 Aug 20 12:53 rust
```

Figure 6.3 – Inode numbers visible in the file listing

Since a directory contains a listing that maps *filenames* with *inode numbers*, there can be multiple filenames that map to the same inode number. Such multiple names are called **hard links**, or simply **links**. Hard links in Unix/Linux are created using the `ln` shell command. Not all non-UNIX filesystems support such hard links.

Within a file system, there can be many *links* to the same file. All of them are essentially the same, as they point to the same file. Most files have a *link count* of 1 (meaning there is a single directory entry for that file), but a file can have a *link count* > 1 (for example, if there are two links pointing to the same *inode* entry, there will be two directory entries for that file, and the *link count* will be 2). The kernel maintains this *link count*.

A *hard link* has a limitation in that they can refer only to files within the same file system because inode numbers are unique only within a file system. There is another type of link called a **symbolic link** (also called a **soft link**), which is a special type of file that contains the name of another file. In Linux/Unix, symbolic links are created using the `ln -s` command. Since a symbolic link refers to a filename instead of an inode number, it can refer to a file in another filesystem. Also, unlike hard links, symbolic links can be created in directories.

In the following points, we will see the methods in the Rust Standard Library that can be used to create and query hard links and symbolic links (symlinks):

- **Create a hard link**: The Rust `std::fs` module has a function, `fs::hard_link`, that can be used to create a new hard link on the file system. An example is shown here:

```
use std::fs;
fn main() -> std::io::Result<()> {
    fs::hard_link("stats.txt", "./statsa.txt")?; // Hard
```

```
                                    // link stats.txt to statsa.txt
    Ok(())
}
```

- **Create and query a symlink**: The APIs to create a `symlink` using the Rust Standard Library vary by platform. On Unix/Linux, the `std::os::unix::fs::symlink` method can be used. On windows, there are two APIs – `os::windows::fs::symlink_file` to create a *symbolic link* to a file, or `os::windows::fs::symlink_dir` to create a `symlink` to a directory. An example of creating a `symlink` on Unix-like platforms is shown here:

```
use std::fs;
use std::os::unix::fs as fsunix;
fn main() {
    fsunix::symlink("stats.txt", "sym_stats.txt").
        expect("Cannot create symbolic link");
    let sym_path = fs::read_link("sym_stats.txt").

        expect("Cannot read link");
    println!("Link is {:?}", sym_path);
}
```

The `fs::read_link` function can be used to read a symbolic link as shown in the code.

With this, we conclude the subsection on working with links in the Rust Standard Library. We have so far seen how to work with files, directories, paths, and links in Rust. In the next section, we will build a small shell command that demonstrates the practical use of the Rust Standard Library for file and directory operations.

Writing a shell command in Rust (project)

In this section, we will use our knowledge of the Rust Standard Library on file and directory operations that we learned in previous sections to implement a shell command.

What will the shell command do?

The shell command will be called **rstat**, short for **Rust source statistics**. Given a directory as an argument, it will generate a *file count* of Rust source files, and source code metrics such as the *number of blanks*, *comments*, and *actual lines of code* within the directory structure.

Here is what you will type:

```
cargo run --release -- -m src .
```

Here is an example of the result you will see from this shell command:

```
Summary stats: SrcStats { number_of_files: 7, loc: 187,
comments: 8, blanks: 20 }
```

This section is structured as four sub-sections. In the first sub-section, we will see an overview of the code structure and a summary of steps to build this shell command. Then, in three different subsections, we will review the code for the three source files corresponding to error handling, source metric computation, and the main program.

Code overview

In this subsection, we will look at how the code is structured for the shell command. We will also review a summary of the steps to build the shell command. Let's get started.

The code structure is shown in *Figure 6.4*:

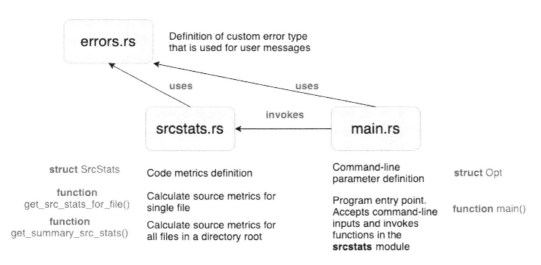

Figure 6.4 – Shell command code structure

Here is a summary of the steps to build the shell command. The source code snippets are shown later in this section:

1. Create project: Create a new project with the following command and change directory into the `rstat` directory:

```
cargo new rstat && cd rstat
```

2. Create source files: Create three files under the `src` folder – `main.rs`, `srcstats.rs`, and `errors.rs`.

3. Define custom error handling: In `errors.rs`, create a struct, `StatsError`, to represent our custom error type. This will be used to unify error handling in our project and to send messages back to the user. Implement the following four traits on `struct StatsError`: `fmt::Display`, `From<&str>`, `From<io::Error>`, and `From<std::num::TryFromIntError>`.

4. Define logic for computing source stats: In `srcstats.rs`, create a struct, `SrcStats`, to define the source metrics to be computed. Define two functions: `get_src_stats_for_file()` (which accepts a filename as an argument and computes the source metrics for that file) and `get_summary_src_stats()` (which takes a directory name as an argument and computes source metrics for all files in that directory root).

5. Write the main() function to accept command-line parameters:

   In `main.rs`, define a `Opt` struct to define command-line parameters and flags for the shell command. Write the `main()` function, which accepts a source directory name from the command line and invokes the `get_summary_src_stats()` method in the `srcstats` module. Ensure to include **structopt** in `Cargo.toml` under dependencies.

6. Build the tool with the following command:

```
cargo build --release
```

7. Run the shell command with the following command:

```
cargo run --release -- -m src <src-folder>
```

   Alternatively, add the `rstat` binary to the path, and set `LD_LIBRARY PATH` to run the shell command like this:

```
target/debug/rstat -m src <src-folder>
```

In Unix environments, `LD_LIBRARY_PATH` can be set as shown here (equivalent commands can be used for Windows):

```
export LD_LIBRARY_PATH=$(rustc --print sysroot)/lib:$LD_
LIBRARY_PATH
```

8. View the consolidated source stats printed to the terminal and confirm the metrics generated.

Let's now look at the code snippets for the steps listed previously. We will start by defining custom error handling.

Error handling

While executing our shell command, several things can go wrong. The source folder specified may be invalid. The permissions may be insufficient to view the directory entries. There can be other types of I/O errors such as those listed here: `https://doc.rust-lang.org/std/io/enum.ErrorKind.html`. In order for us to give a meaningful message back to the user, we will create a custom error type. We will also write conversion methods that will automatically convert different types of I/O errors into our custom error type by implementing various `From` traits. All this code is stored in the `errors.rs` file. Let's review the code snippets from this file in two parts:

*   Part 1 covers the definition of the custom error type and `Display` trait implementation.

*   Part 2 covers the various `From` trait implementations for our custom error type.

Part 1 of the `errors.rs` code is shown here:

src/errors.rs (part-1)

```
use std::fmt;
use std::io;


#[derive(Debug)]
pub struct StatsError {
    pub message: String,
}

impl fmt::Display for StatsError {
    fn fmt(&self, f: &mut fmt::Formatter) -> Result<(),
```

```
        fmt::Error> {
        write!(f, "{}", self)
    }
}
```

Here the `StatsError` struct is defined with a field `message` that will be used to store the error message, which will get propagated to the user in case of errors. We have also implemented the `Display` trait to enable the error message to get printed to the console.

Let's now see part 2 of the `errors.rs` file. Here, we implement the various `From` trait implementations, as shown here. Code annotations are numbered, and are described after the code listing:

src/errors.rs (part-2)

```
impl From<&str> for StatsError {              <1>
    fn from(s: &str) -> Self {
        StatsError {
            message: s.to_string(),
        }
    }
}
impl From<io::Error> for StatsError {         <2>
    fn from(e: io::Error) -> Self {
        StatsError {
            message: e.to_string(),
        }
    }
}
impl From<std::num::TryFromIntError> for StatsError {   <3>
    fn from(_e: std::num::TryFromIntError) -> Self {
        StatsError {
            message: "Number conversion error".to_string(),
        }
    }
}
```

The source code annotations (shown with numbers) are detailed here:

1. Helps to construct a `StatsError` from a string

2. Converts `IO:Error` to `StatsError`

3. Used to check for errors while converting `usize` into `u32`

In this section, we reviewed the code for the `errors.js` file. In the next section, we will see the code for the computation of source code metrics.

Source metric computation

In this section, we will look at the code for the `srcstats.rs` file. The code snippets for this file are shown in the following order in separate parts:

- *Part 1*: Module imports

- *Part 2:* Definition of the `SrcStats` struct

- *Part 3*: Definition of the `get_summary_src_stats()` function

- *Part 4:* Definition of the `get_src_stats_for_file()` function

Let's look at *part 1*. The module imports are shown here. The descriptions corresponding to code annotation numbers are shown after the code listing:

src/srcstats.rs (part-1)

```
use std::convert::TryFrom;        <1>
use std::ffi::OsStr;              <2>
use std::fs;                      <3>
use std::fs::DirEntry;            <4>
use std::path::{Path, PathBuf};<5>
use super::errors::StatsError;  <6>
```

The descriptions for the numbered code annotations are listed here:

- `TryFrom` is used to capture any errors in converting `usize` to `u32`.

- `OsStr` is used to check for files with the `.rs` extension.

- `std::fs` is the main module in the Rust Standard Library for file and directory operations.

- `DirEntry` is a struct used by Rust Standard Library to denote individual directory entries.

- `Path` and `PathBuf` are used to store path names. `&Path` is similar to `&str` and `PathBuf` is similar to `String`. One is a reference and another is an owned object.

- Any errors in reading files or computations are converted to the custom error type `StatsError`. This is imported in this line.

We will now look at *part 2*. The definition of the struct to store computed metrics is covered here.

The struct `SrcStats` contains the following source metrics, which will be generated by our shell command:

- The number of Rust source files

- A count of lines of code (excluding comments and blanks)

- The number of blank lines

- The number of comment lines (single-line comments that begin with `//`; note that we are not considering multi-line comments in the scope of this tool)

The Rust data structure to hold the computed source file metrics is shown next:

src/srcstats.rs (part-2)

```rust
// Struct to hold the stats
#[derive(Debug)]
pub struct SrcStats {
    pub number_of_files: u32,
    pub loc: u32,
    pub comments: u32,
    pub blanks: u32,
}
```

Let's look at *part 3*, which is the main function that computes summary statistics. As this code is a bit long, we will look at this in three parts:

- Part 3a of the code snippet shows variable initialization.

- Part 3b of the code snippet shows the main code that recursively retrieves the Rust source files within a directory.

- In part 3c, we iterate through the list of Rust files and invoke the `get_src_stats_for_file()` method to compute source metrics for each file. The results are consolidated.

Part 3a of the `get_summary_src_stats()` method is shown here:

src/srcstats.rs (part 3a)

```
pub fn get_summary_src_stats(in_dir: &Path) ->
    Result<SrcStats, StatsError> {
    let mut total_loc = 0;
    let mut total_comments = 0;
    let mut total_blanks = 0;
    let mut dir_entries: Vec<PathBuf> =
        vec![in_dir.to_path_buf()];
    let mut file_entries: Vec<DirEntry> = vec![];

    // Recursively iterate over directory entries to get flat
    // list of .rs files
```

Part 3a shows the initialization of variables representing the various metrics that will be computed by the shell command – `total_loc`, `total_comments`, and `total_blanks`. Two more variables, `dir_entries` and `file_entries`, are initialized as `vector` data types, which will be used for intermediate computations.

Part 3b of the `get_summary_src_stats()` method is shown here:

src/srcstats.rs (part-3b)

```
    while let Some(entry) = dir_entries.pop() {
        for inner_entry in fs::read_dir(&entry)? {
            if let Ok(entry) = inner_entry {
                if entry.path().is_dir() {
                    dir_entries.push(entry.path());
                } else {
                    if entry.path().extension() ==
                    Some(OsStr::new("rs")) {
                        file_entries.push(entry);
```

```
                }
            }
        }
    }
}
```

In part 3b of the code, we are iterating through the entries within the specified folder and segregating the entries of the type *directory* from the entries of the type *file*, and storing them in separate vector variables.

Part 3c of the get_summary_src_stats() method is shown here:

src/srcstats.rs (part 3c)

```
    let file_count = file_entries.len();
    // Compute the stats
    for entry in file_entries {
        let stat = get_src_stats_for_file(&entry.path())?;
        total_loc += stat.loc;
        total_blanks += stat.blanks;
        total_comments += stat.comments;
    }


    Ok(SrcStats {
        number_of_files: u32::try_from(file_count)?,
        loc: total_loc,
        comments: total_comments,
        blanks: total_blanks,
    })
}
```

We will now look at *part 4*, which is the code to compute source metrics for an individual Rust source file:

src/srcstats.rs (part-4)

```
pub fn get_src_stats_for_file(file_name: &Path) ->
    Result<SrcStats, StatsError> {
    let file_contents = fs::read_to_string(file_name)?;
    let mut loc = 0;
    let mut blanks = 0;
    let mut comments = 0;
    for line in file_contents.lines() {
        if line.len() == 0 {
            blanks += 1;
        } else if line.trim_start().starts_with("//") {
            comments += 1;
        } else {
            loc += 1;
        }
    }
    let source_stats = SrcStats {
        number_of_files: u32::try_from(file_contents.lines()
            .count())?,
        loc: loc,
        comments: comments,
        blanks: blanks,
    };
    Ok(source_stats)
}
```

In part 4, the code for the `get_src_stats_for_file()` function is shown. This function reads the source file line by line and determines whether the line corresponds to a regular line of code, or blanks, or comments. Based on this classification, the respective counters are incremented. The final result is returned as the `SrcStats` struct from the function.

This concludes the code listing for the srcstats module. In this subsection, we reviewed the code for computing source code metrics. In the next section, we will review the code for the last part of the code listing, which is the main() function.

The main() function

In this subsection, we will now look at the final part of the code, which is the main() function that represents the entry point into the binary. It performs four tasks:

1. Accepts user inputs from the command line.

2. Invokes the appropriate method to compute the source code metrics.

3. Displays the result to the user.

4. In the event of errors, a suitable error message is displayed to the user.

The code listing for the main() function is shown in two parts:

*   Part 1 shows the structure of the command-line interface for the shell command.

*   Part 2 shows the code to invoke calls for the computation of source metrics and to display the results to the user.

Part 1 of main.rs is shown here. We will use the structopt crate to define the structure of the command line inputs to be accepted from the user.

Add the following to the Cargo.toml file:

```
[dependencies]
structopt = "0.3.16"
```

The code listing for *part 1* is shown here:

src/main.rs (part-1)

```
use std::path::PathBuf;
use structopt::StructOpt;
mod srcstats;
use srcstats::get_summary_src_stats;
mod errors;
use errors::StatsError;
```

```
#[derive(Debug, StructOpt)]
#[structopt(
    name = "rstat",
    about = "This is a tool to generate statistics on Rust
        projects"
)]
struct Opt {
    #[structopt(name = "source directory",
        parse(from_os_str))]
    in_dir: PathBuf,
    #[structopt(name = "mode", short)]
    mode: String,
}
```

In part 1 of the code shown, a data structure, Opt, is defined, which contains two fields – in_dir, representing the path to the input folder (for which source metrics are to be computed), and a field, mode. The value for mode in our example is src, which indicates that we want to compute source code metrics. In the future, additional modes can be added (such as the object mode to compute object file metrics such as the size of the executable and library object files).

In *part 2* of this code, we read the source folder from user's command-line argument, and invoke the get_summary_src_stats() method from the srcstats module, which we reviewed in the previous subsection. The metrics returned by this method are then shown to user in the terminal. *Part 2* of the code listing is shown here:

src/main.rs

The main function code is as follows:

```
fn main() -> Result<(), StatsError> {
    let opt = Opt::from_args();
    let mode = &opt.mode[..];
    match mode {
        "src" => {
            let stats = get_summary_src_stats(&opt.in_dir)?;
            println!("Summary stats: {:?}", stats);
        }
```

```
        _ => println!("Sorry, no stats"),
    }
    Ok(())
}
```

Part 2 shows the `main()` function, which is the entry point into our shell command. The function accepts and parses command-line parameters, and invokes the `get_summary_src_stats()` function, passing the *source folder* specified by the user as a function parameter. The results, containing consolidated source code metrics, are printed to the console.

Build and run the tool with the following commands:

```
cargo run --release -- -m src <src-folder>
```

`<source-folder>` is the location of the Rust project or source files and `-m` is the command-line flag to be specified. It will be `src`, to indicate that we want source code metrics.

If you want to run the stats for the current project, you can do so with the following:

```
cargo run --release -- -m src .
```

Note the dot (`.`) in the command, which indicates we want to run the command for the current project folder.

You will see the source code metrics displayed on the terminal.

As an exercise, you can extend this shell command to generate metrics on the binary files generated for a Rust project. To invoke this option, allow the user to specify the –m flag as `bin`.

This concludes the section on developing a shell command, which demonstrated file and directory operations in Rust.

Summary

In this chapter, we reviewed the basics of file management at the operating system level, and the main system calls to work with files. We then learned how to use the Rust Standard Library to open and close a file, read and write to a file, query file metadata, and work with links. After file operations, we learned how to do directory and path operations in Rust. In the third section, we saw how to create hard links and soft (symbolic) links using Rust, and how to query `symlinks`.

We then developed a shell command that computed source code metrics for Rust source files within a directory tree. This project illustrated how to perform various file and directory operations in Rust using a practical example, and reinforced the concepts of the Rust Standard Library for file I/O operations.

Continuing with the topic of I/O, in the next chapter, we will learn the basics of terminal I/O and the features Rust provides to work with pseudo terminals.

7
Implementing Terminal I/O in Rust

In the previous chapter, we looked at how to work with files and directories. We also built a shell command in Rust that generates consolidated source code metrics for Rust source files in a project directory.

In this chapter, we will look at building **terminal-based applications** in Rust. Terminal applications are an integral part of many software programs, including **games**, **text editors**, and **terminal emulators**. For developing these types of programs, it helps to understand how to build customized terminal interface-based applications. This is the focus of this chapter.

For this chapter, we will review the basics of how terminals work, and then look at how to perform various types of actions on a terminal, such as setting colors and styles, performing cursor operations (such as clearing and positioning), and working with keyboard and mouse inputs.

We will cover the topics in the following order:

- Introducing terminal I/O fundamentals
- Working with the terminal UI (size, color, styles) and cursors
- Processing keyboard inputs and scrolling
- Processing mouse inputs

A bulk of this chapter will be dedicated to explaining these concepts through a practical example. We will build a mini text viewer that will demonstrate key concepts of working with terminals. The text viewer will be able to load a file from disk and display its contents on the terminal interface. It will also allow a user to scroll through the contents using the various arrow keys on the keyboard, and display information on the header and footer bar.

Technical requirements

The Git repo for the code in this chapter can be found at `https://github.com/PacktPublishing/Practical-System-Programming-for-Rust-Developers/tree/master/Chapter07/tui`.

For those working on the Windows platform, a virtual machine needs to be installed for this chapter, as the third-party crate used for terminal management does not support the Windows platform (at the time of writing this book). It is recommended to install a virtual machine such as VirtualBox or equivalent running Linux for working with the code in this chapter. Instructions to install VirtualBox can be found at `https://www.virtualbox.org`.

For working with terminals, Rust provides several features to read keypresses and to control *standard input* and *standard output* for a process. When a user types characters in the command line, the bytes generated are available to the program when the user presses the *Enter* key. This is useful for several types of programs. But for some types of programs, such as games or text editors, which require more fine-grained control, the program must process each character as it is typed by the user, which is also known as **raw mode**. There are several third-party crates available that make raw mode processing easy. We will be using one such crate, **Termion**, in this chapter.

Introducing terminal I/O fundamentals

In this section, we'll cover the key characteristics of terminals, see an overview of the Termion crate, and define the scope of what we will be building in this project.

Let's first look at some fundamentals of terminals.

Characteristics of terminals

Terminals are devices with which users can interact with a computer. Using a terminal, a user can get command-line access to interact with the computer's operating system. A shell typically acts as the controlling program to drive the terminal on one hand and the interface with the operating system on the other hand.

Originally, UNIX systems were accessed using a terminal (also called a console) connected to a serial line. These terminals typically had a *24 x 80* row x column character-based interface, or in some cases, had rudimentary graphics capabilities. In order to perform operations on the terminal, such as clearing the screen or moving the cursor, specific escape sequences were used.

There are two modes in which terminals can operate:

- **Canonical mode**: In canonical mode, the inputs from the user are processed line by line, and the user has to press the *Enter* key for the characters to be sent to the program for processing.

- **Noncanonical or raw mode**: In raw mode, terminal input is not collected into lines, but the program can read each character as it is typed by the user.

Terminals can be either physical devices or virtual devices. Most terminals today are **pseudo-terminals**, which are virtual devices that are connected to a terminal device on one side, and to a program that drives the terminal device on the other end. Pseudo-terminals help us write programs where a user on one host machine can execute a *terminal-oriented program* on another host machine using network communications. An example of a pseudo-terminal application is **SSH**, which allows a user to log in to a remote host over a network.

Terminal management includes the ability to perform the following things on a terminal screen:

- **Color management**: Setting various foreground and background colors on the terminal and resetting the colors to default values.

- **Style management**: Setting the style of text to *bold*, *italics*, *underline*, and so on.

- **Cursor management**: Setting the cursor at a particular position, saving the current cursor position, showing and hiding a cursor, and other special features, such as blinking cursors.

- **Event handling**: Listening and responding to keyboard and mouse events.

- **Screen handling**: Switching from main to alternate screens and clearing the screen.

- **Raw mode**: Switching a terminal to raw mode.

In this chapter, we will use a combination of the Rust standard library and the Termion crate to develop a terminal-oriented application. Let's see an overview of the Termion crate in the next section.

The Termion crate

The Termion crate provides the features listed in the previous section, while also providing the user with easy-to-use command-line interfaces. We will be using many of these features in this chapter.

> **Why use an external crate for terminal management?**
>
> While it is technically possible to work at the byte level using the Rust standard library, it is cumbersome. External crates such as Termion help us group individual bytes to keypresses, and also implement many of the commonly used terminal management functions, which allows us to focus on the higher-level, user-directed functionality.

Let's discuss a few terminal management features of the Termion crate. The official documentation of the crate can be found at `https://docs.rs/termion/`.

The Termion crate has the following key modules:

- `cursor`: For moving cursors
- `event`: For handling key and mouse events
- `raw`: To switch the terminal to raw mode
- `style`: To set various styles on text
- `clear`: To clear the entire screen or individual lines
- `color`: To set various colors to text
- `input`: To handle advanced user input
- `scroll`: To scroll across the screen

To include the Termion crate, start a new project and add the following entry to `cargo.toml`:

```
[dependencies]
termion = "1.5.5"
```

A few examples of Termion usage are shown through code snippets here:

- To get the terminal size, use the following:

```
termion::terminal_size()
```

- To set the foreground color, use the following:

```
println!("{}", color::Fg(color::Blue));
```

- To set the background color and then reset the background color to the original state, use the following:

```
println!(
    "{}Background{} ",
    color::Bg(color::Cyan),
    color::Bg(color::Reset)
);
```

- To set bold style, use the following:

```
println!(
    "{}You can see me in bold?",
    style::Bold
);
```

- To set the cursor to a particular position, use the following:

```
termion::cursor::Goto(5, 10)
```

- To clear the screen, use the following:

```
print!("{}", termion::clear::All);
```

We will use these terminal management features in a practical example in the upcoming sections. Let's now define what we are going to build in this chapter.

What will we build?

We will develop a mini text viewer application. This application provides a terminal text interface to load a document from a directory location and view the document. The user can scroll through the document using keyboard keys. We'll build this project progressively over multiple iterations of code.

Figure 7.1 shows the screen layout of what we will build in this chapter:

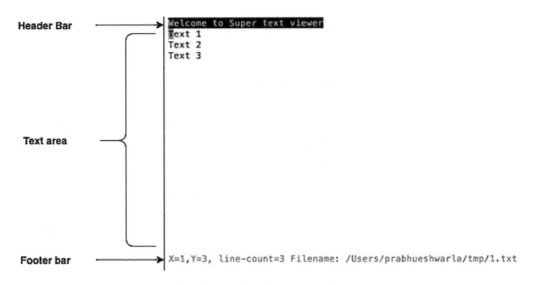

Figure 7.1 – Text viewer screen layout

There are three components in the terminal interface of the text viewer:

- **Header bar**: This contains the title of the text editor.

- **Text area**: This contains the lines of text to be displayed.

- **Footer bar**: This displays the position of the cursor, the number of lines of text in the file, and the name of the file being displayed.

The text viewer will allow the user to perform the following actions:

- Users can provide a filename as a command-line argument to display. This should be a valid filename that already exists. If the file does not exist, the program will display an error message and exit.

- The text viewer will load the file contents and display them on the terminal. If the number of lines in a file is more than the terminal height, the program will allow the user to scroll through the document, and repaint the next set of lines.

- Users can use the up, down, left, and right keys to scroll through the terminal.

- Users can press *Ctrl + Q* to exit the text viewer.

A popular text viewer would have a lot more features, but this core scope provides an adequate opportunity for us to learn about developing a terminal-oriented application in Rust.

In this section, we've learned what terminals are and what kinds of features they support. We also saw an overview of how to work with the Termion crate and defined what we will be building as part of the project in this chapter. In the next section, we'll develop the first iteration of the text viewer.

Working with the terminal UI (size, color, styles) and cursors

In this section, we will build the first iteration of the text viewer. At the end of this section, we will have a program that will accept a filename from the command line, display its contents, and display a header and footer bar. We will use a Termion crate to set the color and style, get the terminal size, position the cursor at specific coordinates, and clear the screen.

The code in this section is organized as follows:

- Writing data structures and the main() function
- Initializing the text viewer and getting the terminal size
- Displaying a document and styling the terminal color, styles, and cursor position
- Exiting the text viewer

Let's start with data structures and the main() function of the text viewer

Writing data structures and the main() function

In this section, we'll define the data structures needed to represent the text viewer in memory. We'll also write the main() function, which coordinates and invokes various other functions:

1. Create a new project and switch to the directory with the following command:

    ```
    cargo new tui && cd tui
    ```

    Here, tui stands for **terminal user interface**. Create a new file called text-viewer1.rs under src/bin.

2. Add the following to `cargo.toml`:

```
[dependencies]
termion = "1.5.5"
```

3. Let's first import the required modules from the standard library and the Termion crate:

```
use std::env::args;
use std::fs;
use std::io::{stdin, stdout, Write};
use termion::event::Key;
use termion::input::TermRead;
use termion::raw::IntoRawMode;
use termion::{color, style};
```

4. Let's next define the data structures to represent a text viewer:

```
struct Doc {
    lines: Vec<String>,
}
#[derive(Debug)]
struct Coordinates {
    pub x: usize,
    pub y: usize,
}
struct TextViewer {
    doc: Doc,
    doc_length: usize,
    cur_pos: Coordinates,
    terminal_size: Coordinates,
    file_name: String,
}
```

This code shows three data structures defined for the text viewer:

The document that will be displayed in the viewer is defined as a `Doc` struct, which is a vector of strings.

To store cursor position *x* and *y* coordinates and to record the current size of the terminal (the total number of rows and columns of characters), we have defined a `Coordinates` struct.

The `TextViewer` struct is the main data structure representing the text viewer. The number of lines contained in the file being viewed is captured in the `doc_length` field. The name of the file to be shown in the viewer is recorded in the `file_name` field.

5. Let's now define the `main()` function, which is the entry point for the text viewer application:

```
fn main() {
    //Get arguments from command line
    let args: Vec<String> = args().collect();
    if args.len() < 2 {
        println!("Please provide file name
            as argument");
        std::process::exit(0);
    }
    //Check if file exists. If not, print error
    // message and exit process
    if !std::path::Path::new(&args[1]).exists() {
        println!("File does not exist");
        std::process::exit(0);
    }
    // Open file & load into struct
    println!("{}", termion::cursor::Show);
    // Initialize viewer
    let mut viewer = TextViewer::init(&args[1]);
    viewer.show_document();
    viewer.run();
}
```

The `main()` function accepts a filename as a command-line parameter and exits the program if the file does not exist. Furthermore, if a filename is not provided as a command-line parameter, it displays an error message and exits the program.

6. If the file is found, the `main()` function does the following:

    It first calls the `init()` method on the `TextViewer` struct to initialize the variables.

    Then, it invokes the `show_document()` method to display the contents of the file on the terminal screen.

    Lastly, the `run()` method is called, which waits for user inputs to the process. If the user presses *Ctrl + Q*, the program exits.

7. We will now write three method signatures – `init()`, `show_document()`, and `run()`. These three methods should be added to the `impl` block of the `TextViewer` struct, as shown:

```rust
impl TextViewer {
    fn init(file_name: &str) -> Self {
        //...
    }
    fn show_document(&mut self) {
        // ...
    }
    fn run(&mut self) {
        // ...
    }
}
```

So far, we've defined the data structures and written the `main()` function with placeholders for the other functions. In the next section, let's write the function to initialize the text viewer.

Initializing the text viewer and getting the terminal size

When a user starts the text viewer with a document name, we have to initialize the text viewer with some information and perform startup tasks. This is the purpose of the `init()` method.

Here is the complete code for the `init()` method:

```rust
fn init(file_name: &str) -> Self {
    let mut doc_file = Doc { lines: vec![] };          <1>
```

```
    let file_handle = fs::read_to_string(file_name)
        .unwrap();                                          <2>

    for doc_line in file_handle.lines() {                   <3>
        doc_file.lines.push(doc_line.to_string());
    }
    let mut doc_length = file_handle.lines().count();       <4>

    let size = termion::terminal_size().unwrap();           <5>
    Self {                                                  <6>
        doc: doc_file,
        cur_pos: Coordinates {
            x: 1,
            y: doc_length,
        },
        doc_length: doc_length,
        terminal_size: Coordinates {
            x: size.0 as usize,
            y: size.1 as usize,
        },
        file_name: file_name.into(),
    }
}
```

The code annotations in the init() method are described here:

1. Initialize the buffer that is used to store the file contents.

2. Read the file contents as a string.

3. Read each line from the file and store it in the Doc buffer.

4. Initialize the doc_length variable with the number of lines in the file.

5. Use the termion crate to get the terminal size.

6. Create a new struct of the TextViewer type and return it from the
    init() method.

We've written the initialization code for the text viewer. Next, we'll write the code
to display the document contents on the terminal screen, and also display the header
and footer.

Displaying a document and styling the terminal color, styles, and cursor position

We saw earlier the layout of the text viewer that we would like to build. There are three main parts of the text viewer screen layout – the header, the document area, and the footer. In this section, we'll write the primary function and supporting function to display the contents as per the defined screen layout.

Let's look at the show_document() method:

src/bin/text-viewer1.rs

```rust
fn show_document(&mut self) {
    let pos = &self.cur_pos;
    let (old_x, old_y) = (pos.x, pos.y);
    print!("{}{}", termion::clear::All,
        termion::cursor::Goto(1, 1));
    println!(
        "{}{}Welcome to Super text viewer\r{}",
        color::Bg(color::Black),
        color::Fg(color::White),
        style::Reset
    );
    for line in 0..self.doc_length {
        println!("{}\r", self.doc.lines[line as usize]);
    }

    println!(
        "{}",
        termion::cursor::Goto(0, (self.terminal_size.y - 2) as
            u16),
    );
    println!(
        "{}{} line-count={} Filename: {}{}",
        color::Fg(color::Red),
        style::Bold,
        self.doc_length,
```

```
        self.file_name,
        style::Reset
    );
    self.set_pos(old_x, old_y);
}
```

The code annotations for the `show_document()` method are described here:

1. Store the current positions of the cursor *x* and *y* coordinates in temp variables.
    This will be used to restore the cursor position in a later step.

2. Using the Termion crate, clear the entire screen and move the cursor to row 1 and
    column 1 on the screen.

3. Print the header bar of the text viewer. A background color of black and
    a foreground color of white is used to print text.

4. Display each line from the internal document buffer to the terminal screen.

5. Move the cursor to the bottom of the screen (using the terminal size *y* coordinate)
    to print the footer.

6. Print the footer text in red and with bold style. Print the number of lines in the
    document and filename to the footer.

7. Reset the cursor to the original position (which was saved to temporary variable
    in *step 1*).

Let's look at the `set_pos()` helper method used by the `show_document()` method:

src/bin/text-viewer1.rs

```
fn set_pos(&mut self, x: usize, y: usize) {
    self.cur_pos.x = x;
    self.cur_pos.y = y;
    println!(
        "{}",
        termion::cursor::Goto(self.cur_pos.x as u16,
            (self.cur_pos.y) as u16)
    );
}
```

This helper method synchronizes the internal cursor tracking field (the `cur_pos` field of the `TextViewer` struct) and the on-screen cursor position.

We now have the code to initialize the text viewer and to display the document on the screen. With this, a user can open a document in the text viewer and view its contents. But how does the user exit the text viewer? We'll find out in the next section.

Exiting the text viewer

Let's say that a key combination of *Ctrl + Q* will let the user exit the text viewer program. How can we implement this code?

To achieve this, we need a way to listen for user key strokes, and when a particular key combination is pressed, we should exit the program. As discussed earlier, we need to get the terminal into raw mode of operation, where each character is available for the program to evaluate, rather than wait for the user to press the *Enter* key. Once we get the raw characters, the rest of it becomes fairly straightforward. Let's write the code to do this in the `run()` method, within the `impl TextViewer` block, as shown:

src/bin/text-viewer1.rs

```rust
fn run(&mut self) {
    let mut stdout = stdout().into_raw_mode().unwrap();
    let stdin = stdin();
    for c in stdin.keys() {
        match c.unwrap() {
            Key::Ctrl('q') => {
                break;
            }
            _ => {}
        }
        stdout.flush().unwrap();
    }
}
```

In the code shown, we use the `stdin.keys()` method to listen for user inputs in a loop. `stdout()` is used to display text to the terminal. When *Ctrl + Q* is pressed, the program exits.

We can now run the program with the following:

```
cargo run --bin text-viewer1 <file-name-with-full-path>
```

Since we have not implemented scrolling yet, pass a filename to the program that has 24 lines or less of content (this is typically the default height of a standard terminal in terms of the number of rows). You will see the text viewer *open up* and the *header bar*, *footer bar*, and *file contents* printed to the terminal. Type *Ctrl + Q* to exit. Note that you have to specify the filename with the full file path as a command-line argument.

In this section, we learned how to get the terminal size, set the foreground and background colors, and apply bold style using the Termion crate. We also learned how to position the cursor onscreen at specified coordinates, and how to clear the screen.

In the next section, we will look at processing keystrokes for user navigation within the document displayed in the text editor and how to implement scrolling.

Processing keyboard inputs and scrolling

In the previous section, we built the first iteration of our text viewer terminal-oriented application. We were able to display a file with fewer than 24 lines and see the header and footer bar containing some information. Finally, we were able to exit the program with *Ctrl + Q*.

In this section, we will add the following features to the text viewer:

- Provide the ability to display files of any size.
- Provide the ability for the user to scroll through the document using arrow keys.
- Add cursor position coordinates to the footer bar.

Let's begin by creating a new version of the code.

Copy the original code to a new file, as shown:

```
cp src/bin/text-viewer1.rs src/bin/text-viewer2.rs
```

This section is organized into three parts. First, we'll implement the logic to respond to the following keystrokes from a user: up, down, left, right, and backspace. Next, we'll implement the functionality to update the cursor position in internal data structures, and simultaneously update the cursor position onscreen. Lastly, we'll allow scrolling through a multi-page document.

We'll begin with handling user keystrokes.

Listening to keystrokes from the user

Let's modify the `run()` method to act on user inputs and scroll through the document. We also want to record and display the current cursor position in the footer bar. The code is shown here:

src/bin/text-viewer2.rs

```rust
fn run(&mut self) {
    let mut stdout = stdout().into_raw_mode().unwrap();
    let stdin = stdin();
    for c in stdin.keys() {
        match c.unwrap() {
            Key::Ctrl('q') => {
                break;
            }
            Key::Left => {
                self.dec_x();
                self.show_document();
            }
            Key::Right => {
                self.inc_x();
                self.show_document();
            }
            Key::Up => {
                self.dec_y();
                self.show_document();
            }
            Key::Down => {
                self.inc_y();
                self.show_document();
            }
            Key::Backspace => {
                self.dec_x();
            }
            _ => {}
        }
    }
}
```

```
        stdout.flush().unwrap();
    }
}
```

Lines in bold show the changes to the run() method from the earlier version. In this code, we are listening for up, down, left, right, and backspace keys. For any of these keypresses, we are incrementing the *x* or *y* coordinate appropriately using one of the following methods: inc_x(), inc_y(), dec_x(), or dec_y(). For example, if the right arrow is pressed, the *x* coordinate of the cursor position is incremented using the inc_x() method, and if the down arrow is pressed, only the *y* coordinate is incremented using the inc_y() method. The changes to coordinates are recorded in the internal data structure (the cur_pos field of the TextViewer struct). Also, the cursor is repositioned on the screen. All these are achieved by the inc_x(), inc_y(), dec_x(), and dec_y() methods.

After updating the cursor position, the screen is refreshed fully and repainted.

Let's look at implementing the four methods to update cursor coordinates, and reposition the cursor on the screen.

Positioning the terminal cursor

Let's write the code for the inc_x(), inc_y(), dec_x(), and dec_y() methods. These should be added as a part of the impl TextViewer block of code like the other methods:

src/bin/text-viewer2.rs

```
fn inc_x(&mut self) {
    if self.cur_pos.x < self.terminal_size.x {
        self.cur_pos.x += 1;
    }
    println!(
        "{}",
        termion::cursor::Goto(self.cur_pos.x as u16,
            self.cur_pos.y as u16)
    );
}
fn dec_x(&mut self) {
```

```rust
        if self.cur_pos.x > 1 {
            self.cur_pos.x -= 1;
        }
    println!(
            "{}",
            termion::cursor::Goto(self.cur_pos.x as u16,
                self.cur_pos.y as u16)
        );
}
fn inc_y(&mut self) {
    if self.cur_pos.y < self.doc_length {
        self.cur_pos.y += 1;
    }

    println!(
            "{}",
            termion::cursor::Goto(self.cur_pos.x as u16,
                self.cur_pos.y as u16)
        );
}
fn dec_y(&mut self) {
    if self.cur_pos.y > 1 {
        self.cur_pos.y -= 1;
    }
    println!(
            "{}",
            termion::cursor::Goto(self.cur_pos.x as u16,
                self.cur_pos.y as u16)
        );
}
```

The structure of all these four methods is similar and each performs only two steps:

1. Depending on the keypress, the corresponding coordinate (*x* or *y*) is incremented or decremented and recorded in the `cur_pos` internal variable.

2. The cursor is repositioned on the screen at the new coordinates.

We now have a mechanism to update the cursor coordinates whenever the user presses the up, down, left, right, or backspace keys. But that's not enough. The cursor should be repositioned on the screen to the latest cursor coordinates. For this, we will have to update the show_document() method, which we will do in the next section.

Enabling scrolling on the terminal

We have so far implemented the code to listen for user keystrokes and reposition the cursor onscreen. Now, let's turn our attention to another major issue in the code. If we load a document that has fewer lines than the terminal height, then the code works fine. But consider a situation where the terminal has the capacity to display 24 rows of characters, and there are 50 lines in the document to be displayed on text viewer. Our code cannot handle it. We're going to fix it in this section.

To display more lines than is possible for the screen size, it is not enough to reposition the cursor. We will have to repaint the screen to fit a portion of the document in the terminal screen depending on the cursor location. Let's see the modifications needed to the show_document() method to enable scrolling. Look for the following lines of code in the show_document() method:

```
for line in 0..self.doc_length {
        println!("{}\r", self.doc.lines[line as
            usize]);
    }
```

Replace the preceding with the following code:

src/bin/text-viewer2.rs

```
if self.doc_length < self.terminal_size.y {   <1>
    for line in 0..self.doc_length {
        println!("{}\r", self.doc.lines[line as
            usize]);
    }
} else {

    if pos.y <= self.terminal_size.y {          <2>
        for line in 0..self.terminal_size.y - 3 {
            println!("{}\r", self.doc.lines[line as
                usize]);
```

```
            }
        } else {
            for line in pos.y - (self.terminal_size.y -
            3)..pos.y {
                println!("{}\r", self.doc.lines[line as
                usize]);
            }
        }
    }
```

The code annotations in the show_document() method snippet are described here:

1. First, check whether the number of lines in the input document is less than the terminal height. If so, display all lines from the input document on the terminal screen.

2. If the number of lines in the input document is greater than the terminal height, we have to display the document in parts. Initially, the first set of lines from the document are displayed onscreen corresponding to the number of rows that will fit into the terminal height. For example, if we allocate 21 lines to the text display area, then as long as the cursor is within these lines, the original set of lines is displayed. If the user scrolls down further, then the next set of lines is displayed onscreen.

Let's run the program with the following:

```
cargo run --bin text-viewer2 <file-name-with-full-path>
```

You can try two kinds of file inputs:

- A file where the number of lines is less than the terminal height
- A file where the number of lines is more than the terminal height

You can use the up, down, left, and right arrows to scroll through the document and see the contents. You will also see the current cursor position (both *x* and *y* coordinates) displayed on the footer bar. Type *Ctrl* + *Q* to exit.

This concludes the text viewer project for this chapter. You have built a functional text viewer that can display files of any size, and can scroll through its contents using the arrow keys. You can also view the current position of the cursor along with the filename and number of lines in the footer bar.

> **Note on the text viewer**
>
> Note that what we have implemented is a mini version of a text viewer in under 200 lines of code. While it demonstrates the key functionality, additional features and edge cases can be implemented by you to enhance the application and improve its usability. Furthermore, this viewer can also be converted into a full-fledged text editor. These are left to you, the reader, as an exercise.

We've completed the implementation of the text viewer project in this section. The text viewer is a classic command-line application and does not have a GUI interface where mouse inputs are needed. But it is important to learn how to handle mouse events, for developing GUI-based terminal interfaces. We'll learn how to do that in the next section.

Processing mouse inputs

Like keyboard events, the Termion crate also supports the ability to listen for mouse events, track the mouse cursor location, and react to it in code. Let's see how to do this here.

Create a new source file called `mouse-events.rs` under `src/bin`.

Here is the code logic:

1. Import the needed modules.
2. Enable mouse support in the terminal.
3. Clear the screen.
4. Create an iterator over incoming events.
5. Listen to mouse presses, release and hold events, and display the mouse cursor location on the terminal screen.

The code is explained in snippets corresponding to each of these points.

Let's first look at module imports:

1. We're importing the `termion` crate modules for switching to raw mode, detecting the cursor position, and listening to mouse events:

    ```
    use std::io::{self, Write};
    use termion::cursor::{self, DetectCursorPos};
    use termion::event::*;
    use termion::input::{MouseTerminal, TermRead};
    use termion::raw::IntoRawMode;
    ```

In the `main()` function, let's enable mouse support as shown:

```
fn main() {
    let stdin = io::stdin();
    let mut stdout = MouseTerminal::from(io::stdout().
        into_raw_mode().unwrap());
    // ...Other code not shown
}
```

To ensure that previous text on the terminal screen does not interfere with this program, let's clear the screen, as shown here:

```
writeln!(
    stdout,
    "{}{} Type q to exit.",
    termion::clear::All,
    termion::cursor::Goto(1, 1)
)
.unwrap();
```

2. Next, let's create an iterator over incoming events and listen to mouse events. Display the location of the mouse cursor on the terminal:

```
for c in stdin.events() {
    let evt = c.unwrap();
    match evt {
        Event::Key(Key::Char('q')) => break,
        Event::Mouse(m) => match m {
            MouseEvent::Press(_, a, b) |
                MouseEvent::Release(a, b) |
                MouseEvent::Hold(a, b) => {

                    write!(stdout, "{}",
                    cursor::Goto(a, b))
                    .unwrap();
                    let (x, y) = stdout.cursor_pos
                        ().unwrap();
                    write!(
                        stdout,
```

```
                    "{}{}Cursor is at:
                    ({},{}){}",
                    cursor::Goto(5, 5),
                    termion::clear::
                        UntilNewline,
                    x,
                    y,
                    cursor::Goto(a, b)
                )
                .unwrap();
            }
        },
        _ => {}
    }
}

    stdout.flush().unwrap();
}
```

In the code shown, we are listening to both keyboard events and mouse events. In keyboard events, we are specifically looking for the Q key, which exits the program. We are also listening to mouse events – press, release, and hold. In this case, we position the cursor at the specified coordinates and also print out the coordinates to the terminal screen.

3. Run the program with the following command:

```
cargo run --bin mouse-events
```

4. Click around the screen with the mouse, and you will see the cursor position coordinates displayed on the terminal screen. Press q to exit.

With this, we conclude the section on working with mouse events on the terminal. This also concludes the chapter on terminal I/O management using Rust.

Summary

In this chapter, we learned the basics of terminal management by writing a mini text viewer. We learned how to use the Termion library to get the terminal size, set the foreground and background colors, and set styles. After this, we learned how to work with cursors on the terminal, including clearing the screen, positioning the cursor at a particular set of coordinates, and keeping track of the current cursor position.

We learned how to listen to user inputs and track the keyboard arrow keys for scrolling operations, including left, right, up, and down. We wrote code to display document contents dynamically as the user scrolls through it, keeping the constraints of the terminal size in mind. As an exercise, you can refine the text viewer, and also add functionality to convert the text viewer into a full-fledged editor.

Learning these features is important to write applications such as terminal-based games, editing and viewing applications and terminal graphical interfaces, and to provide terminal-based dashboards.

In the next chapter, we will learn the basics of process management using Rust, including starting and stopping processes and handling errors and signals.

8
Working with Processes and Signals

Do you know how commands are executed when you type them into a terminal interface on your computer? Are these commands directly executed by the operating system, or is there an intermediate program that handles them? When you run a program from the command line in the foreground, and press *Ctrl + C*, who is listening to this keypress, and how is the program terminated? How can multiple user programs be run at the same time by the operating system? What is the difference between a program and a process? If you are curious, then read on.

In the previous chapter, we learned how to control and alter the terminal interface that is used to interact with the users in command-line applications.

In this chapter, we will look at *processes*, which are the second most popular abstraction in systems programming after *files*. We'll learn what processes are, how they differ from programs, how they are started and terminated, and how the process environment can be controlled. This skill is necessary if you want to write systems programs such as shells, where you want programmatic control over the life cycle of processes.

We'll also build an elementary shell program as a mini project by using the *Rust Standard Library* This will give you a practical understanding of how popular shells such as *Bourne*, *Bash*, and *zsh* work under the hood, and teach you the basics of how you can build your own customized shell environments in Rust.

We will cover these topics in the following order:

- Understanding Linux process concepts and syscalls
- Spawning new processes with Rust
- Handling I/O and environment variables for child processes
- Handling panic, errors, and signals
- Writing a basic shell program in Rust (project)

By the end of this chapter, you will have learned how to programmatically launch new programs as separate processes, how to set and adjust environment variables, how to handle errors, respond to external signals, and exit the process gracefully. You will learn how to talk to the operating system to perform these tasks using the Rust standard library. This gives you, as a system programmer, great control over this important system resource; that is, *processes*.

Technical requirements

Verify that `rustc`, and `cargo` have been installed correctly with the following command:

```
rustc -version
cargo --version
```

The Git repo for the code in this chapter can be found at `https://github.com/PacktPublishing/Practical-System-Programming-for-Rust-Developers/tree/master/Chapter08`.

> **Note**
>
> The section on signal handling requires a Unix-like development environment (*Unix*, *Linux*, or *macOS*), as Microsoft Windows does not directly have the concept of signals. If you work with Windows, download a virtual machine such as Oracle VirtualBox (`https://www.virtualbox.org/wiki/Downloads`) or use a *Docker* container to launch a *Unix/Linux* image to follow along.

Understanding Linux process concepts and syscalls

In this section, we'll cover the fundamentals of process management and get an appreciation of why it is important for systems programming. We'll look at the process life cycle, including *creating new processes*, *setting their environment parameters*, *working with their standard input and output*, and *terminating the processes*.

This section starts with understanding the differences between a *program* and a *process*. We'll then go into a few key details about the fundamentals of processes in Linux. Lastly, we'll see an overview of how to manage the process life cycle with Rust using syscalls encapsulated by the Rust standard library.

How does a program become a process?

A **process** is a running **program**. To be precise, it is an *instance* of a running program. You can have *multiple instances* of a single program running at the same time, such as starting a text editor from multiple terminal windows. Each such instance of a running program is a *process*.

Even though a process is created as a result of running (or executing) a program, the two are different. A program exists in two forms – **source code** and **machine-executable instructions** (object code or executables). A compiler (and linker) is typically used to convert the source code of a program into *machine-executable instructions*.

Machine-executable instructions contain information for the operating system on how to *load a program into memory*, *initialize* it, and *run* it. The instructions include the following:

- An executable format (for example, **ELF** is a popular executable format in Unix systems).

- The program logic to be executed by the CPU.

- The memory address of the entry point of the program.

- Some data for initializing the program variables and constants.

- Information on the location of shared libraries, functions, and variables.

When a program is started either from a command line, script, or graphical user interface, the following steps occur:

1. The operating system (kernel) allocates virtual memory to the program (which is also called the **memory layout** of the program). We saw this in *Chapter 5, Memory Management in Rust,* on how virtual memory is laid out for a program in terms of *stack*, *heap*, *text*, and *data* segments.

2. The kernel then loads the program instructions into the *text segment* of the virtual memory.

3. The kernel initializes the program variables in the *data segment*.

4. The kernel triggers the CPU to start executing the program instructions.

5. The kernel also provides the running program with access to resources it needs, such as files or additional memory.

The memory layout of a process (running program) was discussed in *Chapter 5, Memory Management*. It is reproduced here in *Figure 8.1* for reference:

Rust program memory layout

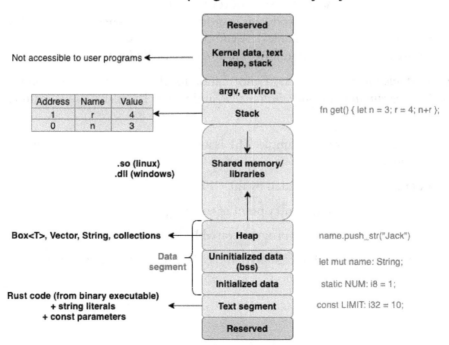

Figure 8.1 – Program memory layout

We've seen the *memory layout* of a program. What is a *process*, then?

As far as the kernel is concerned, a process is an abstraction that consists of the following:

- Virtual memory in which the program instructions and data are loaded, which is represented in the program memory layout in *Figure 8.1*.

- A set of metadata about the running program such as the *process identifier*, *system resources* associated with the program (such as a list of open files), *virtual memory tables*, and other such information about the program. What is of particular importance is the *process ID*, which uniquely identifies an instance of a running program.

> **Note**
>
> The kernel itself is the **process manager**. It allocates *process IDs* to new instances of user programs. When a system is booted up, the kernel creates a special process called `init`, which is assigned a *process ID* of *1*. The `init` process terminates only when the system is shut down and cannot be killed. All future processes are created either by the `init` process or one of its descendent processes.
>
> Thus, a program refers to instructions created by the programmer (in the source or a machine-executable format) and a process is a running instance of a program that uses system resources and is controlled by the kernel. As programmers, if we want to control a running program, we will need to use appropriate *system calls* to the kernel. The Rust standard library wraps these system calls into neat APIs for use within Rust programs, as discussed in *Chapter 3, Introduction to the Rust Standard Library*.

We've seen how programs relate to processes. Let's discuss some more details about the *characteristics of processes* in the next section.

Delving into Linux process fundamentals

In *Chapter 3, Introduction to the Rust Standard Library and Key Crates for Systems Programming*, we saw how system calls are the interface between a user program (process) and the kernel (operating system). Using system calls, a user program can manage and control various system resources such as *files*, *memory*, *devices*, and so on.

In this section, we'll look at how one running program (the parent process) can make system calls to manage the life cycle of another program (the child process). Recall that processes are also treated as system resources in Linux, just like files or memory. Understanding how one process can manage and communicate with another process is the focus of this section.

Figure 8.2 shows the key set of tasks related to process management:

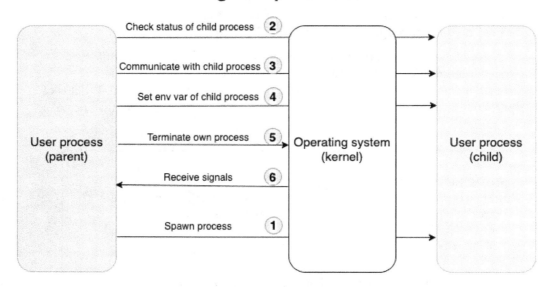

Figure 8.2 – Working with processes in Rust

Let's go over the process management tasks shown in the preceding figure. We'll see how process management is done on Linux by a non-Rust user program (for example, C/C++), and how it is different in Rust.

Creating a new process

While working with Unix/Linux, any user program that needs to create a new process has to request the kernel to do so using system calls (*syscalls*). A program (let's call it the **parent process**) can create a new process using the `fork()` syscall. The kernel duplicates the parent process and creates a *child process* with a unique ID. The child process gets an exact copy of the parent's memory space (the heap, stack, and so on). The child also gets access to the same copy of the program instructions as the parent.

After creation, a child process can choose to load a different program into its process memory space and execute it. This is accomplished using one of the `exec()` family of *syscalls*.

So, basically, the *syscall* in Unix/Linux to *create a new child process* is different from that needed to *load a new program* into the child process and execute it. However, the Rust standard library simplifies this for us and provides a uniform interface, where both these steps can be combined while creating a new child process. We'll see examples of this in the next section.

Let's go back to the question at the beginning of the chapter: *What exactly happens when you type something in the command line of a terminal?*

When you run a program by typing the program executable name in a command line, two things take place:

1. First, a new process is created using the `fork()` system call.

2. Then, the image of the new program (that is, the *program executable*) is loaded into memory and executed using the `exec()` family of calls.

What happens when you type a command in a terminal?

A terminal (as we saw in the previous chapter) provides an interface for the user to interact with the system. But there has to be something that interprets that command and executes it. This is the **shell program**. You may be familiar with one of the popular shell programs such as *Bourne shell* or *Bash shell* in Unix/Linux, or *PowerShell* in Windows. It is these programs that accept the commands from the command line and fork new processes to execute the command. For example, let's take the following command on Unix/Linux, which finds file entries in the current directory structure recursively, searches for *debug*, and returns the count of such files:

```
find *  |  grep debug  |  wc -l
```

When this command is typed into a terminal, the shell program spawns three processes to execute this command pipeline. It is this shell command that makes the system call to the kernel to create new processes, load these commands, and execute them in a sequence. The shell then returns the results of the execution and prints it to standard output.

Checking the status of a child process

Once a child process is spawned by the kernel, it returns a child *process ID*. The `wait()` and `waitpid()` syscalls can be used to check whether the child process is running by passing the *child process ID* to the call. These are helpful to synchronize the execution of the child process with the parent process. The Rust system library provides calls to wait for the child process to finish and to check its status.

Communicating using inter-process communication

Processes can communicate with each other and with the kernel (remember that the kernel is also a process) to coordinate their activities, using mechanisms such as signals, pipes, sockets, message queues, semaphores, and shared memory. In Rust also, two processes can communicate using various means including pipes, processes, and message queues. But one of the basic forms of **Inter-Process Communication** (**IPC**) between parent and child processes involves *stdin/stdout pipes*. The parent process can write to standard input and read from the child process's standard output. We'll see an example of this in a later section.

Setting environment variables

Each process also has its own set of associated environment variables. The fork() and exec() syscalls allow the passing and setting of environment variables from the parent to the child process. The values of these environment variables are stored within the virtual memory area of the process. The Rust standard library also allows the parent process to explicitly set or reset the environment variables of the child process.

Terminating a process

A process can terminate itself by using the exit() syscall, or by being killed by a signal (such as the user pressing *Ctrl* + *C*) or using the kill() syscall. Rust also has an exit() call for this purpose. Rust also provides other ways to abort a process, which we will look at in a later section.

Handling signals

Signals are used to communicate asynchronous events such as keyboard interrupts to a process. Except for two of the signals, SIGSTOP and SIGKILL, processes can either choose to ignore signals or decide how to respond to them in their own way. Handling signals directly using the Rust standard library is not developer-friendly, so for this, we can use external crates. We'll be using one such crate in a later section.

In this section, we've seen the differences between a *program* and a *process*, delved into a few of the characteristics of Linux processes, and got an overview of the kind of things we can do in Rust to interact with processes.

In the next section, we'll learn first-hand how to spawn, interact, and terminate processes using Rust by writing some code. Note that in the next few sections, only code snippets are provided. In order to execute the code, you will need to create a new cargo project and add the code shown in the `src/main.rs` file with the appropriate module imports.

Spawning processes with Rust

In the Rust standard library, `std::process` is the module for working with processes. In this section, we'll look at how to *spawn new processes*, *interact with child processes*, and *abort the current process* using the Rust standard library. The Rust standard library internally uses the corresponding Unix/Linux *syscalls* to invoke the kernel operations for managing processes.

Let's begin with launching new child processes.

Spawning new child processes

The `std::process::Command` is used to launch a program at a specified path, or to run a standard shell command. The configuration parameters for the new process can be constructed using a builder pattern. Let's see a simple example:

```
use std::process::Command;
fn main() {
    Command::new("ls")
        .spawn()
        .expect("ls command failed to start");
}
```

The code shown uses the `Command::new()` method to create a new command for execution, that takes as a parameter the name of the program to be run. The `spawn()` method creates a new child process.

If you run this program, you will see a listing of files in the current directory.

This is the simplest way to spin off a standard Unix *shell command* or a *user program* as a child process using the Rust standard library.

What if you would like to pass parameters to the shell command? Some example code is shown in the following snippet that passes arguments to the command:

```
use std::process::Command;
fn main() {
```

```
    Command::new("ls")
        .arg("-l")
        .arg("-h")
        .spawn()
        .expect("ls command failed to start");
}
```

The `arg()` method can be used to pass one argument to the program. Here we want to run the `ls -lh` command to display files in a long format with readable file sizes. We have to use the `arg()` method twice to pass the two flags.

Alternatively, the `args()` method can be used as shown here. Note that the `std::process` import and the `main()` function declaration have been removed in future code snippets to avoid repetition, but you must add them before you can run the program:

```
Command::new("ls")
        .args(&["-l", "-h"]).spawn().unwrap();
```

Let's alter the code to list the directory contents for the directory one level above (relative to the current directory).

The code shows two parameters for the `ls` command configured through the `args()` method.

Next, let's set the current directory for the child process to a non-default value:

```
    Command::new("ls")
        .current_dir("..")
        .args(&["-l", "-h"])
        .spawn()
        .expect("ls command failed to start");
```

In the preceding code, we are spawning the process to run the `ls` command in the directory one level above.

Run the program with the following command:

```
cargo run
```

You will see the listing of the parent directory displayed.

We've so far used `spawn()` to create a new child process. This method returns a handle to the child process.

There is another way to spawn a new process using `output()`. The difference is that `output()` spawns the child process and waits for it to terminate. Let's see an example:

```
let output = Command::new("cat").arg("a.txt").output().
    unwrap();
if !output.status.success() {
    println!("Command executed with failing error code");
}
println!("printing: {}", String::from_utf8(output.stdout).
    unwrap());
```

We are spawning a new process using the `output()` method to print out the contents of a file named `a.txt`. Let's create this file using the following command:

```
echo "Hello World" > a.txt
```

If you run the program, you will see the contents of the `a.txt` file printed out to the terminal. Note that we are printing out the contents of the standard output handle of the child process because that's where the output of the `cat` command is directed to by default. We'll learn more details of how to work with child processes' `stdin` and `stdout` later in this chapter.

We'll now look at how to terminate a process.

Terminating processes

We've seen how to spawn new processes. What about terminating them? For this, the Rust standard library provides two methods—`abort()` and `exit()`.

The usage of the `abort()` method is shown in the following snippet:

```
use std::process;
fn main() {
    println!("Going to abort process");
    process::abort();
    // This statement will not get executed
    println!("Process aborted");
}
```

This code aborts the current process, and the last statement will not get printed.

There is another `exit()` method similar to `abort()`, but it allows us to specify an exit code that is available to the calling process.

What is the benefit of processes returning error codes? A child process can fail due to various errors. When the program fails and the child process exits, it would be useful to the calling program or user to know the error code denoting the reason for failure. **0** indicates a successful exit. Other error codes indicate various conditions such as *data error*, *system file error*, *I/O error*, and so on. The error codes are platform-specific, but most Unix-like platforms use 8-bit error codes, allowing for error values between 0 and 255. Examples of error codes for Unix BSD can be found at `https://www.freebsd.org/cgi/man.cgi?query=sysexits&apropos=0&sektion=0&manpath=FreeBSD+11.2-stable&arch=default&format=html`.

The following is an example showing the returning of error codes from a process with the `exit()` method:

```
use std::process;
fn main() {
    println!("Going to exit process with error code 64");
    process::exit(64);
    // execution never gets here
    println!("Process exited");
}
```

Run this program on the command line in your terminal. To know the exit code of the last executed process on Unix-like systems, you can type `$?` on the command line. Note that this command may vary depending on the platform.

---

abort() versus exit()

Note that both `abort()` and `exit()` do not clean up and call any destructors, so if you want to shut down a process in a clean manner, these methods should be called only after all the destructors have been run. However, the operating system will ensure that on termination of a process, all the resources associated with it, such as memory and file descriptors, are automatically made available for re-allocation to other processes.

In this section, we've seen how to spawn and terminate processes. Let's next take a look at how to check the status of execution of a child process after it has been spawned.

Checking the status of a child process' execution

As seen earlier, when we start a new process, we also specify the program or command to be executed within the process. Frequently, we also care about whether this program or command has been executed successfully or not, in order to take suitable actions.

The Rust standard library provides a `status()` method to let us find out whether a process completed executing successfully. Some example usage is shown in the following snippet:

```
use std::process::Command;
fn main() {
    let status = Command::new("cat")
        .arg("non-existent-file.txt")
        .status()
        .expect("failed to execute cat");

    if status.success() {
        println!("Successful operation");
    } else {
        println!("Unsuccessful operation");
    }
}
```

Run this program and you will see the message **Unsuccessful operation** printed out to your terminal. Re-run the program with a valid filename and you will see the success message printed.

This concludes this section. You learned different ways to run commands in a separate child process, how to terminate them, and how to get the status of their execution.

In the next section, we'll look at how to set environment variables and work with I/O for child processes.

Handling I/O and environment variables

In this section, we'll look at how to handle I/O with child processes, and also learn to set and clear environment variables for the child process.

Why would we need this?

Take the example of a load balancer that is tasked with spawning new workers (Unix processes) in response to incoming requests. Let's assume the new worker process reads configuration parameters from environment variables to perform its tasks. The load balancer process then would need to spawn the worker process and also set its environment variables. Likewise, there may be another situation where the parent process wants to read a child process's standard output or standard error and route it to a log file. Let's understand how to perform such activities in Rust. We'll start with handling the I/O of the child process.

Handling the I/O of child processes

Standard input (`stdin`), standard output (`stdout`), and standard error (`stderr`) are abstractions that allow a process to interact with the surrounding environment.

For example, when many user processes are running at the same time, and when a user types keystrokes on a terminal, the kernel delivers the keystrokes to the standard input of the right process. Likewise, a Rust program (running as a process in a shell) can print out characters to its standard output, which is in turn read by the shell program and delivered to the terminal screen for the user. Let's learn how to work with standard input and standard output using the Rust standard library.

The `piped()` method on `std::process::Stdio` allows the child process to communicate with its parent process using a `pipe` (which is an IPC mechanism in Unix-like systems).

We'll first look at how to communicate with the standard output handle of the child process from the parent process:

```rust
use std::io::prelude::*;
use std::process::{Command, Stdio};


fn main() {
    // Spawn the `ps` command
    let process = match Command::new("ps").
    stdout(Stdio::piped()).spawn() {
        Err(err) => panic!("couldn't spawn ps: {}", err),
        Ok(process) => process,
    };
    let mut ps_output = String::new();
    match process.stdout.unwrap().read_to_string(&mut
    ps_output) {
```

```
        Err(err) => panic!("couldn't read ps stdout: {}",
            err),
        Ok(_) => print!("ps output from child process
            is:\n{}", ps_output),
    }
}
```

In the preceding code snippet, we first create a new child process to run the ps command to show a list of currently running processes. The output is, by default, sent to the child process's stdout.

In order to get access to the child process's stdout from the parent process, we create a Unix pipe using the stdio::piped() method. The process variable is the handle to the child process, and process.stdout is the handle to the child process's standard output. The parent process can read from this handle, and print out its contents to its own stdout (that is, the parent process's stdout). This is how a parent process can read the output of a child process.

Let's now write some code to send some bytes from the parent process to the standard input of the child process:

```
let process = match Command::new("rev")
    .stdin(Stdio::piped())                       <1>
    .stdout(Stdio::piped())                      <2>
    .spawn()
{
    Err(err) => panic!("couldn't spawn rev: {}", err),
    Ok(process) => process,
};
match process.stdin.unwrap().write_all

    ("palindrome".as_bytes()) {
    Err(why) => panic!("couldn't write to stdin: {}",
        why),
    Ok(_) => println!("sent text to rev command"),
}                                                <3>
let mut child_output = String::new();
match process.stdout.unwrap().read_to_string(&mut
    child_output) {
```

```
      Err(err) => panic!("couldn't read stdout: {}", err),
      Ok(_) => print!("Output from child process is:\n{}",
        child_output),
   }                                                        <4>
```

The descriptions of the numbered annotations in the preceding code are provided here:

1. Register a piped connection between the *parent process* and *standard input* of the child process.

2. Register a piped connection between the *parent process* and *standard output* of the child process.

3. Write bytes to the *standard input* of the child process.

4. Read from the *standard output* of the child process and print it to the terminal screen.

There are a few other methods available on the child process. The id() method provides the *process id* of the child process, the kill() method kills the child process, the stderr method gives a handle to the child process's *standard error*, and the wait() method makes the parent process to wait until the child process has completely exited.

We've seen how to handle I/O for child processes. Let's now learn how to work with environment variables.

Setting the environment for the child process

Let's look at how to set environment variables for the child process. The following example shows how to set the path environment variable for a child process:

```
use std::process::Command;
fn main() {
    Command::new("env")
        .env("MY_PATH", "/tmp")
        .spawn()
        .expect("Command failed to execute");
}
```

The env() method on std::process::Command allows the parent process to set the environment variable for the child process being spawned. Run the program and test it with the following command:

```
cargo run | grep MY_PATH
```

You'll see the value of the MY_PATH environment variable that was set in the program.

To set multiple environment variables, the envs() command can be used.

The environment variables for a child process can be cleared by using the env_clear() method, as shown:

```
Command::new("env")
    .env_clear()
    .spawn()
    .expect("Command failed to execute");
```

Run the program with cargo run, and you will see that *nothing* is printed out for the env command. Re-run the program by commenting out the .env_clear() statement, and you will find the env values printed to terminal.

To remove a specific environment variable, the env_remove() method can be used.

With this, we conclude this section. We've seen how to interact with standard input and standard output of a child process and to set/reset the environment variables. In the next section, we'll learn how to handle errors and signals in child processes.

Handling panic, errors, and signals

Processes can fail due to various error conditions. These have to be handled in a controlled manner. There may also be situations where we want to terminate a process in response to external inputs, such as a user pressing *Ctrl + C*. How we can handle such situations is the focus of this section.

> **Note**
> In cases when processes exit due to errors, the operating system itself performs some cleanup, such as releasing memory, closing network connections, and releasing any file handles associated with the process. But sometimes, you may want program-driven controls to handle these cases.

Failures in process execution can broadly be classified into two types – *unrecoverable errors* and *recoverable errors*. When a process encounters an unrecoverable error, there is sometimes no option but to abort the process. Let's see how to do that.

Aborting the current process

We saw how to terminate and exit from a process in the *Spawning processes with Rust* section. The abort() and exit() methods on process::Command can be used for this purpose.

In some cases, we consciously allow a program to fail under some conditions without handling it, mainly in cases of unrecoverable errors. The std::panic macro allows us to panic the current thread. What this means is that the program terminates immediately and provides feedback to the caller. But unlike the exit() or abort() methods, it unwinds the stack of the current thread and calls all destructors. Here is an example of the usage of the panic! macro:

```rust
use std::process::{Command, Stdio};
fn main() {
    let _child_process = match Command::new("invalid-command")
        .stdin(Stdio::piped())
        .stdout(Stdio::piped())
        .spawn()
    {
        Err(err) => panic!("Unable to spawn child process:
            {}", err),
        Ok(new_process_handle) => {
            println!("Successfully spawned child process");
            new_process_handle
        }
    };
}
```

Run the program with `cargo run` and you will see the error message printed out from the `panic!` macro. There is also a custom hook that can be registered that will get invoked before the standard cleanup is performed by the `panic` macro. Here is the same example, this time with a custom `panic` hook:

```
use std::panic;
use std::process::{Stdio,Command};
fn main() {
panic::set_hook(Box::new(|_| {
            println!(" This is an example of custom panic
                hook, which is invoked on thread panic, but
                before the panic run-time is invoked")
        }));
    let _child_process = match Command::new("invalid-command")
        .stdin(Stdio::piped())
        .stdout(Stdio::piped())
        .spawn()
    {
        Err(err) => panic!("Normal panic message {}", err),
        Ok(new_process_handle) => new_process_handle,
    };
}
```

On running this program, you will see the custom error hook message displayed, as we are providing an invalid command to spawn as a child process.

Note that `panic!` should be used only for non-recoverable errors. For example, if a child process tries to open a file that does not exist, this can be handled using a recoverable error mechanism such as the `Result` enum. The advantage of using `Result` is that the program can return to its original state and the failed operation can be retried. If `panic!` is used, the program terminates abruptly, and the original state of the program cannot be recovered. But there are situations where `panic!` may be appropriate such, as when a process runs out of memory in the system.

Let's next look at another aspect of process control—signal handling.

Signal handling

In Unix-like systems, the operating system can send signals to processes. Note that Windows OS does not have signals. The process can handle the signal in a way it deems fit, or even ignore the signal. There are operating-system defaults for handling various signals. For example, when you issue a kill command on a process from a shell, the SIGTERM signal is generated. The program terminates on receipt of this signal by default, and there is no special additional code that needs to be written in Rust to handle that signal. Similarly, a SIGINT signal is received when a user presses *Ctrl + C*. But a Rust program can choose to handle these signals in its own way.

However, handling Unix signals correctly is hard for various reasons. For example, a signal can occur at any time and the thread processing cannot continue until the signal handler completes execution. Also, signals can occur on any thread and synchronization is needed. For this reason, it is better to use third-party crates in Rust for signal handling. Note that even while using external crates, caution should be exercised as the crates do not solve all problems associated with signal handling.

Let's now see an example of handling signals using the signal-hook crate. Add it to dependencies in Cargo.toml as shown:

```
[dependencies]
signal-hook = "0.1.16"
```

An example code snippet is shown as follows:

```
use signal_hook::iterator::Signals;
use std::io::Error;
fn main() -> Result<(), Error> {
    let signals = Signals::new(&[signal_hook::SIGTERM,
        signal_hook::SIGINT])?;
    'signal_loop: loop {
        // Pick up signals that arrived since last time
        for signal in signals.pending() {
            match signal {
                signal_hook::SIGINT => {
                    println!("Received signal SIGINT");
                }
                signal_hook::SIGTERM => {
                    println!("Received signal SIGTERM");
```

```
                    break 'signal_loop;
                }
                _ => unreachable!(),
            }
        }
    }
    println!("Terminating program");
    Ok(())
}
```

In the preceding code, we listen for two specific signals, SIGTERM and SIGINT, within the match clause. SIGINT can be sent to the program by pressing *Ctrl + C*. The SIGTERM signal can be generated by using the kill command on a *process id* from the shell.

Now, run the program and simulate the two signals. Then, press the *Ctrl + C* key combination, which generates the SIGINT signal. You will see that instead of the default behavior (which is to terminate the program), a statement is printed out to the terminal.

To simulate SIGTERM, run a ps command on the command line of a Unix shell and retrieve the *process id*. Then run a kill command with the *process id*. You will see that the process terminates, and a statement is printed to the terminal.

> **Note**
>
> If you are using **tokio** for asynchronous code, you can use the **tokio-support** feature of signal-hook.

It is important to remember that signal handling is a complex topic, and even with external crates, care must be exercised while writing custom signal-handling code.

While handling signals or dealing with errors, it is also good practice to log the signal or error using a crate such as log for future reference and troubleshooting by system administrators. However, if you'd like a program to read these logs, you can log these messages in JSON format instead of plaintext by using an external crate such as serde_json.

This concludes this subsection on working with *panic*, *errors*, and *signals* in Rust. Let's now write a shell program that demonstrates some of the concepts discussed.

Writing a shell program in Rust (project)

We learned in the *Delving into Linux process fundamentals* section what a shell program is. In this section, let's build a shell program, adding features iteratively.

In the first iteration, we'll write the basic code to read a shell command from the command line and spawn a child process to execute the command. Next, we'll add the ability to pass command arguments to the child process. Lastly, we will personalize the shell by adding support for users to enter commands in a more natural-language-like syntax. We'll also introduce error handling in this last iteration. Let's get started:

1. Let's first create a new project:

    ```
    cargo new myshell && cd myshell
    ```

2. Create three files: `src/iter1.rs`, `src/iter2.rs`, and `src/iter3.rs`. The code for the three iterations will be placed in these files so that it will be easy to build and test each iteration separately.

3. Add the following to `Cargo.toml`:

    ```
    [[bin]]
    name = "iter1"
    path = "src/iter1.rs"

    [[bin]]
    name = "iter2"
    path = "src/iter2.rs"

    [[bin]]
    name = "iter3"
    path = "src/iter3.rs"
    ```

    In the preceding code, we specify to the Cargo tool that we want to build separate binaries for the three iterations.

We're now ready to start with the first iteration of the shell program.

Iteration 1 – Spawning a child process to execute commands

First, let's write a program to accept commands from the terminal, and then spawn a new child process to execute those user commands. Add a loop construct to continue accepting user commands in a loop until the process is terminated. The code is as follows:

src/iter1.rs

```rust
use std::io::Write;
use std::io::{stdin, stdout};
use std::process::Command;
fn main() {
    loop {
        print!("$ ");                                    <1>
        stdout().flush().unwrap();                       <2>
        let mut user_input = String::new();              <3>
        stdin()
            .read_line(&mut user_input)                  <4>
            .expect("Unable to read user input");
        let command_to_execute = user_input.trim(); <5>
        let mut child = Command::new(command_to_execute) <6>
            .spawn()
            .expect("Unable to execute command");
        child.wait().unwrap();                           <7>
    }
}
```

The numbered annotations in the preceding code are described as follows:

1. Display the $ prompt to nudge the user to enter commands.

2. Flush the stdout handle so that the $ prompt is immediately displayed on the terminal.

3. Create a buffer to hold the command entered by the user.

4. Read the user commands one line at a time.

5. Remove the newline character from the buffer (this is added when the user presses the *Enter* key to submit the command).

6. Create a new child process and pass the user commands to the child process for execution.

7. Wait until the child process completes execution before accepting additional user inputs.

8. Run the program with the following command:

```
cargo run --bin iter1
```

Type any command without arguments such as `ls` or `ps` or `du` on the $ prompt. You'll see the output of the command execution displayed on the terminal. You can continue to enter more such commands at the next $ prompt. Press *Ctrl + C* to exit the program.

We now have the first version of our shell program working, but this program will fail if parameters or flags are entered after the command. For example, typing a command such as `ls` works, but typing `ls -lah` will cause the program to panic and exit. Let's add support for command arguments in the next iteration of our code.

Iteration 2 – Adding support for command arguments

Let's add support for command arguments with the `args()` method:

src/iter2.rs

```
// Module imports not shown here
fn main() {
    loop {
        print!("$ ");
        stdout().flush().unwrap();
        let mut user_input = String::new();
        stdin()
            .read_line(&mut user_input)
            .expect("Unable to read user input");
        let command_to_execute = user_input.trim();
        let command_args: Vec<&str> =
            command_to_execute.split_whitespace().
            collect(); <1>


        let mut child = Command::new(command_args[0])
                                                    <2>
```

```
                .args(&command_args[1..])    <3>
                .spawn()
                .expect("Unable to execute command");
            child.wait().unwrap();
    }
}
```

The code shown is essentially the same as the previous snippet, except for the three additional lines added, which are annotated with numbers. The annotations are described as follows:

1. Take the user input, split it by whitespace, and store the result in Vec.

2. The first element of the Vec corresponds to the command. Create a child process to execute this command.

3. Pass the list of Vec elements, starting from the second element, as a list of arguments to the child process.

4. Run the program with the following line:

    ```
    cargo run --bin iter2
    ```

5. Enter a command and pass arguments to it before hitting the *Enter* key. For example, you can type one of the following commands:

    ```
    ls -lah
    ps -ef
    cat a.txt
    ```

Note that in the last command, a.txt is an existing file holding some contents and located in the project root folder.

You will see the command outputs successfully displayed on the terminal. The shell works so far as we intended. Let's extend it now a little further in the next iteration.

Iteration 3 – Supporting natural-language commands

Since this is our own shell, let's implement a user-friendly alias for a shell command in this iteration (*why not?*). Instead of typing ls, what if a user could type a command in natural language, as follows:

```
show files
```

This is what we'll code next. The following snippet shows the code. Let's look at the module imports first:

```
use std::io::Write;
use std::io::{stdin, stdout};
use std::io::{Error, ErrorKind};
use std::process::Command;
```

Modules from `std::io` are imported for writing to the terminal, reading from the terminal, and for error handling. We already know the purpose of importing the `process` module.

Let's now look at the `main()` program in parts. We won't cover the code already seen in previous iterations. The complete code for the `main()` function can be found in the GitHub repo in the `src/iter3.rs` file:

1. After displaying the $ prompt, check whether the user has entered any command. If the user presses just the *Enter* key at the prompt, ignore and redisplay the $ prompt. The following code checks whether at least one command has been entered by the user, then processes the user input:

    ```
    if command_args.len() > 0 {..}
    ```

2. If the command entered is `show files`, execute the `ls` command in a child process. If the command is `show process`, execute the `ps` command. If `show` is entered without a parameter, or if the `show` command is followed by an invalid word, throw an error:

    ```
    let child = match command_args[0] {
            "show" if command_args.len() > 1 => match
            command_args[1] {
            "files" => Command::new("ls").
                    args(&command_args[2..]).spawn(),

            "process" => Command::new("ps").args
                    (&command_args[2..]).spawn(),

            _ => Err(Error::new(
                    ErrorKind::InvalidInput,
                    "please enter valid command",
            )),
    ```

```
        },
        "show" if command_args.len() == 1 =>
            Err(Error::new(
            ErrorKind::InvalidInput,
            "please enter valid command",
        )),
        "quit" => std::process::exit(0),
        _ => Command::new(command_args[0])
            .args(&command_args[1..])
            .spawn(),
    };
```

3. Wait for the child process to complete. If the child process fails to execute successfully, or if the user input is invalid, throw an error:

```
match child {
    Ok(mut child) => {
        if child.wait().unwrap().success() {
        } else {
            println!("\n{}", "Child process
                failed")
        }
    }
    Err(e) => match e.kind() {
        ErrorKind::InvalidInput => eprintln!(
            "Sorry, show command only
            supports following options: files
            , process "
        ),
        _ => eprintln!("Please enter a
            valid command"),
    },
}
```

4. Run the program with `cargo run --bin iter3` and try the following commands at the $ prompt to test:

```
show files
show process
du
```

You'll see the commands successfully execute, with a statement printed out indicating success.

You would have noticed that we've added some error handling in the code. Let's look at what error conditions we've addressed:

- If the user presses *Enter* without entering a command
- If the user enters the `show` command without a parameter (either a file or process)
- If the user enters the `show` command with an invalid parameter
- If the user enters a valid Unix command, but one that is not supported by our program (for example, `pipes` or `redirection`)

Let's try the following invalid inputs:

```
show memory
show
invalid-command
```

You'll see that an error message is printed to the terminal.

Try also hitting the *Enter* key without command. You will see that this is not processed.

In error-handling code, note use of `ErrorKind` enum, which is a set of pre-defined error types defined in the Rust standard library. The list of predefined error types can be found at `https://doc.rust-lang.org/std/io/enum.ErrorKind.html`.

Congratulations! You have implemented a basic shell program that can recognize natural-language commands for non-technical users. You've also implemented some error handling so that the program is reasonably robust and doesn't crash on invalid inputs.

As an exercise, you can do the following to enhance this shell program:

- Add support for pipe-operator-separated command chains such as `ps | grep sys`.

- Add support for redirections such as the > operator to divert the output of a process execution to a file.

- Move the logic of command-line parsing into a separate tokenizer module.

In this section, we've written a shell program that has a subset of the features of a real-world shell program such as `zsh` or `bash`. To be clear, a real-world shell program has a lot more complex features, but we have covered the fundamental concepts behind creating a shell program here. Also importantly, we've learned how to handle errors in case of invalid user inputs or if a child process fails. To internalize your learning, it is recommended to write some code for the suggested exercises.

This concludes the section on writing a shell program in Rust.

Summary

In this chapter, we reviewed the basics of processes in Unix-like operating systems. We learned how to spawn a child process, interact with its standard input and standard output, and execute a command with its arguments. We also saw how to set and clear environment variables. We looked at the various ways to terminate a process on error conditions, and how to detect and handle external signals. We finally wrote a shell program in Rust that can execute the standard Unix commands, but also accept a couple of commands in a natural-language format. We also handled a set of errors to make the program more robust.

Continuing on the topic of managing system resources, in the next chapter, we will learn how to manage threads of a process and build concurrent systems programs in Rust.

9
Managing Concurrency

Concurrent systems are all around us. When you download a file, listen to streaming music, initiate a text chat with a friend, and print something in the background on your computer, *all at the same time*, you are experiencing the magic of concurrency in action. The operating system manages all these for you in the background, scheduling tasks across available processors (CPUs).

But do you know how to write a program that can do multiple things at the same time? More importantly, do you know how to do it in a way that is both memory- and thread-safe, while ensuring optimal use of system resources? Concurrent programming is one way to achieve this. But concurrent programming is considered to be a difficult topic in most programming languages due to challenges in *synchronizing tasks* and *sharing data safely across multiple threads of execution*. In this chapter, you'll learn about the basics of concurrency in Rust and how Rust makes it easier to prevent common pitfalls and enables us to write concurrent programs in a safe manner. This chapter is structured as shown here:

- Reviewing concurrency basics
- Spawning and configuring threads
- Error handling in threads
- Message passing between threads
- Achieving concurrency with shared state
- Pausing thread execution with timers

By the end of this chapter, you'll have learned how to write concurrent programs in Rust by spawning new threads, handling thread errors, transferring and sharing data safely across threads to synchronize tasks, understanding the basics of thread-safe data types, and pausing the execution of current threads for synchronization.

Technical requirements

Verify that `rustup`, `rustc`, and `cargo` have been installed correctly with the following commands:

```
rustup --version
rustc --version
cargo --version
```

The Git repo for the code in this chapter can be found at: `https://github.com/PacktPublishing/Practical-System-Programming-for-Rust-Developers/tree/master/Chapter09`.

Let's get started with some basic concepts of concurrency.

Reviewing concurrency basics

In this section, we'll cover the basics of **multi-threading** and clarify the terminology around **concurrency** and **parallelism**.

To appreciate the value of concurrent programming, we have to understand the need of today's programs to make decisions quickly or process a large amount of data in a short period of time. Several use cases become impossible to achieve if we strictly rely on sequential execution. Let's consider a few examples of systems that must perform multiple things simultaneously.

An autonomous car needs to perform many tasks at the same time, such as processing inputs from a wide array of sensors (to construct an internal map of its surroundings), plotting the path of the vehicle, and sending instructions to the vehicle's actuators (to control the brakes, acceleration, and steering). It needs to process continually arriving input events, and respond in tenths of a second.

There are also other, more mundane examples. A web browser handles user inputs while simultaneously rendering a web page incrementally, as new data is received. A website handles requests from multiple simultaneous users. A web crawler has to access many thousands of sites simultaneously to gather information about the websites and their contents. It is impractical to do all these things sequentially.

We've so far seen a few use cases that require multiple tasks to be performed simultaneously. But there is also a technical reason that is driving concurrency in programming, which is that CPU clock speeds on a single core are hitting upper practical limits. So, it is becoming necessary to add more CPU cores, and more processors on a single machine. This is in turn driving the need for software that can efficiently utilize the additional CPU cores. To achieve this, portions of a program should be executable concurrently on different CPU cores, rather than being constrained by the sequential execution of instructions on a single CPU core.

These factors have resulted in the increased use of multi-threading concepts in programming. Here, there are two related terms that need to be understood – *concurrency* and *parallelism*. Let's take a closer look at this.

Concurrency versus parallelism

In this section, we'll review the fundamentals of multi-threading and understand the differences between *concurrent* and *parallel* execution models of a program.

Concurrency basics

Sequential execution

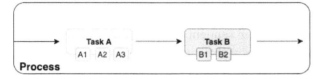

Concurrent execution

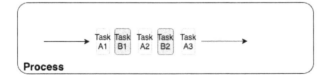

Parallel execution

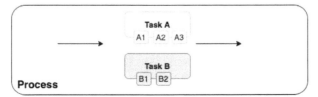

Figure 9.1 – Concurrency basics

Figure 9.1 shows three different computation scenarios within a Unix/Linux process:

- **Sequential execution**: Let's assume that a process has two tasks **A** and **B**. **Task A** has three subtasks **A1**, **A2**, and **A3**, which are executed sequentially. Likewise, **Task B** has two tasks, **B1** and **B2**, that are executed one after the other. Overall, the process executes all tasks of process *A* before taking on process *B* tasks. There is a challenge in this model. Assume the case where task **A2** involves waiting for an external network or user input, or for a system resource to become available. Here, all tasks lined up after task **A2** will be blocked until **A2** completes. This is not an efficient use of the CPU and causes a delay in the completion of all the scheduled tasks that belong to the process.

- **Concurrent execution**: Sequential programs are limited as they do not have the ability to deal with multiple simultaneous inputs. This is the reason many modern applications are *concurrent* where there are multiple threads of execution running concurrently.

  In the concurrent model, the process interleaves the tasks, that is, alternates between the execution of **Task A** and **Task B**, until both of them are complete. Here, even if **A2** is blocked, it allows progress with the other sub-tasks. Each sub-task, **A1**, **A2**, **A3**, **B1**, and **B2**, can be scheduled on separate execution threads. These threads could run either on a single processor or scheduled across multiple processor cores. One thing to bear in mind is that concurrency is about *order-independent* computations as opposed to sequential execution, which relies on steps executed in a specific order to arrive at the correct program outcome. Writing programs to accommodate *order-independent* computations is more challenging than writing sequential programs.

- **Parallel execution**: This is a variant of the *concurrent execution* model. In this model, the process executes **Task A** and **Task B** truly in parallel, on separate CPU processors or cores. This assumes, of course, that the software is written in a way that such parallel execution is possible, and there are no dependencies between **Task A** and **Task B** that could stall the execution or corrupt the data.

  Parallel computing is a broad term. *Parallelism* can be achieved either within a single machine by having **multi-cores** or **multi-processors** or there can be clusters of different computers that can cooperatively perform a set of tasks.

When to use concurrent versus parallel execution?

A program or a function is *compute-intensive* when it involves a lot of computations such as in graphics, meteorological, or genome processing. Such programs spend the bulk of their time using CPU cycles and will benefit from having better and faster CPUs.

A program is *I/O-intensive* when a bulk of the processing involves communicating with input/output devices such as network sockets, filesystems, and other devices. Such programs benefit from having faster I/O subsystems, such as for disk or network access.

Broadly, *parallel execution* (true parallelism) is more relevant for increasing the throughput of programs in *compute-intensive* use cases, while *concurrent processing* (or pseudo-parallelism) can be suitable for increasing throughput and reducing latency in *I/O-intensive* use cases.

In this section, we've seen two ways to write concurrent programs – *concurrency* and *parallelism*, and how these differ from sequential models of execution. Both these models use *multi-threading* as the foundational concept. Let's talk more about this in the next section.

Concepts of multi-threading

In this section, we'll deep-dive into how multi-threading is implemented in Unix.

Unix supports threads as a mechanism for a process to perform multiple tasks concurrently. A Unix process starts up with a single thread, which is the main thread of execution. But additional threads can be spawned, that can *execute concurrently in a single-processor system*, or *execute in parallel in a multi-processor system*.

Each thread has access to its own *stack* for storing its own *local variables* and *function parameters*. Threads also maintain their own register state including the *stack pointer* and *program counter*. All the threads in a process share the same memory address space, which means that they share access to the *data* segments (*initialized data*, *uninitialized data*, and the *heap*). Threads also share the same *program code* (process instructions).

In a multi-threaded process, multiple threads concurrently execute the same program. They may be executing different parts of a program (such as different functions) or they may be invoking the same function in different threads (working with a different set of data for processing). But note that for a function to be invoked by multiple threads at the same time, it needs to be *thread-safe*. Some ways to make a function thread-safe are to avoid the usage of *global* or *static* variables in the function, using a *mutex* to restrict usage of a function to just one thread at a time, or using *mutex* to synchronize usage of a piece of shared data.

But it is a design choice to model a concurrent program either as a group of processes or as a group of threads within the same process. Let's compare the two approaches, for a Unix-like system.

It is much easier to share data across threads as they are in the same process space. Threads also share common resources of a process such as *file descriptors* and *user/group IDs*. Thread creation is faster than process creation. Context switching between threads is also faster for the CPU due to their sharing the same memory space. But threads bring their own share of complexities.

As discussed earlier, shared functions must be thread-safe and access to shared global data should be carefully synchronized. Also, a critical defect in one of the threads can affect other threads or even bring the entire process down. Additionally, there is no guarantee about the order in which different parts of code in different threads will run, which can lead to data races, deadlocks, or hard-to-reproduce bugs. Bugs related to concurrency are difficult to debug since factors such as CPU speed, the number of threads, and the set of running applications at a point in time, can alter the outcome of a concurrent program. In spite of these drawbacks, if one decides to proceed with the thread-based concurrency model, aspects such as code structure, the use of global variables, and thread synchronization should be carefully designed.

Figure 9.2 shows the memory layout of threads within a process:

Process memory layout with threads

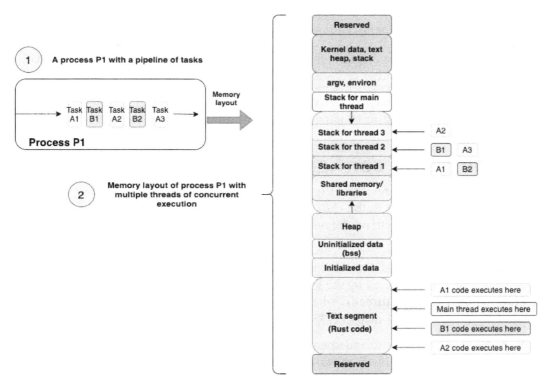

Figure 9.2 – Memory layout of threads in a process

The figure shows how a set of tasks in process P1 are represented in memory when they are executed in a multi-threaded model. We've seen in detail the memory layout of a process, in *Chapter 5, Memory Management in Rust. Figure 9.2* extends the process memory layout with details of how memory is allocated for individual threads within a process.

As discussed earlier, all threads are allocated memory within the process memory space. By default, the main thread is created with its own stack. Additional threads are also assigned their own stack as and when they are created. The shared model of concurrency, which we discussed earlier in the chapter, is possible because global and static variables of a process are accessible by all threads, and each thread also can pass around pointers to memory created on the heap to other threads.

The program code, however, is common for the threads. Each thread can execute a different section of the code from the program text segment, and store the local variables and function parameters within their respective thread stack. When it is the turn of a thread to execute, its program counter (containing the address of the instruction to execute) is loaded for the CPU to execute the set of instructions for a given thread.

In the example shown in the diagram, if task *A2* is blocked waiting for I/O, then the CPU will switch execution to another task such as *B1* or *A1*.

With this, we conclude the section on concurrency and multi-threading basics. We are now ready to get started with writing concurrent programs using the Rust Standard Library.

Spawning and configuring threads

In the previous section, we reviewed the fundamentals of multi-threading that apply broadly to all user processes in the Unix environment. There is, however, another aspect of threading that is dependent on the programming language for implementation – this is the *threading model*.

Rust implements a *1:1 model* of threading where each operating system thread maps to one user-level thread created by the Rust Standard Library. The alternative model is *M:N* (also known as **green threads**) where there are *M green threads* (user-level threads managed by a runtime) that map to *N kernel-level threads*.

In this section, we'll cover the fundamentals of creating *1:1* operating system threads using the Rust Standard Library. The Rust Standard Library module for thread-related functions is std::thread.

There are two ways to create a new thread using the Rust Standard Library. The first method uses the thread::spawn function, and the second method uses the builder pattern using the thread::Builder struct. Let's look at an example of the thread::spawn function first:

```
use std::thread;
fn main() {
    for _ in 1..5 {
        thread::spawn(|| {
            println!("Hi from thread id {:?}",
                thread::current().id());
        });
    }
}
```

The std::thread module is used in this program. thread::spawn() is the function used to spawn a new thread. In the program shown, we're spawning four new child threads in the main function (which runs in the main thread in the process). Run this program with cargo run. Run it a few more times. What did you expect to see, and what did you actually see?

You would have expected to see four lines printed to the terminal listing the *thread IDs*. But you would have noticed that the results vary each time. Sometimes you see one line printed, sometimes you see more, and sometimes none. Why is this?

The reason for this inconsistency is that there is no guarantee of the order in which the threads are executed. Further, if the main() function completes before the child threads are executed, you won't see the expected output in your terminal.

To fix this, what we need to do is to join the *child threads* that are created to the *main thread*. Then the main() thread waits until all the child threads have been executed. To see this in action, let's alter the program as shown:

```
use std::thread;
fn main() {
    let mut child_threads = Vec::new();
    for _ in 1..5 {
        let handle = thread::spawn(|| {
            println!("Hi from thread id {:?}",
                thread::current().id());
        });
        child_threads.push(handle);
    }
    for i in child_threads {
        i.join().unwrap();
    }
}
```

The changes from the previous program are highlighted. thread::spawn() returns a thread handle that we're storing in a Vec collection data type. Before the end of the main() function, we join each child thread to the main thread. This ensures that the main() function waits until the completion of all the child threads before it exits.

Let's run the program again. You'll notice four lines printed, one for each thread. Run the program a few more times. You'll see four lines printed every time. This is progress. It shows that joining the child threads to the main threads is helping. However, the order of thread execution (as seen by the order of print outputs on the terminal) varies with each run. This is because, when we span multiple child threads, there is no guarantee of the order in which the threads are executed. This is a feature of multi-threading (as discussed earlier), not a bug. But this is also one of the challenges of working with threads, as this brings difficulties in synchronizing activities across threads. We'll learn how to address this a little later in the chapter.

We've so far seen how to use the `thread::spawn()` function to create a new thread. Let's now see the second way to create a new thread.

The `thread::spawn()` function uses default parameters for thread name and stack size. If you'd like to set them explicitly, you can use `thread:Builder`. This is a *thread factory* that uses the `Builder` pattern to configure the properties of a new thread. The previous example has been rewritten here using the `Builder` pattern:

```rust
use std::thread;
fn main() {
    let mut child_threads = Vec::new();
    for i in 1..5 {
        let builder = thread::Builder::new().name(format!(
            "mythread{}", i));
        let handle = builder
            .spawn(|| {
                println!("Hi from thread id {:?}", thread::
                    current().name().unwrap());
            })
            .unwrap();
        child_threads.push(handle);
    }

    for i in child_threads {
        i.join().unwrap();
    }
}
```

The changes are highlighted in the code. We are creating a new `builder` object by using the `new()` function, and then configuring the name of the thread using the `name()` method. We're then using the `spawn()` method on an instance of the `Builder` pattern. Note that the `spawn()` method returns a `JoinHandle` type wrapped in `io::Result<JoinHandle<T>>`, so we have to unwrap the return value of the method to retrieve the child process handle.

Run the code and you'll see the four thread names printed to your terminal.

We've so far seen how to spawn new threads. Let's now take a look at error handling while working with threads.

Error handling in threads

The Rust Standard Library contains the `std::thread::Result` type, which is a specialized `Result` type for threads. An example of how to use this is shown in the following code:

```rust
use std::fs;
use std::thread;
fn copy_file() -> thread::Result<()> {
    thread::spawn(|| {
        fs::copy("a.txt", "b.txt").expect("Error
            occurred");
    })
    .join()
}
fn main() {
    match copy_file() {
        Ok(_) => println!("Ok. copied"),
        Err(_) => println!("Error in copying file"),
    }
}
```

We have a function, `copy_file()`, that copies a source file to a destination file. This function returns a `thread::Result<()>` type, which we are unwrapping using a `match` statement in the `main()` function. If the `copy_file()` function returns a `Result::Err` variant, we handle it by printing an error message.

Run the program with `cargo run` with an invalid source filename. You will see the error message: **Error in copying file** printed to the terminal. If you run the program with a valid source filename, it will match the `Ok()` branch of the `match` clause, and the success message will be printed.

This example shows us how to handle errors propagated by a thread in the calling function. What if we want a way to recognize that the current thread is panicking, even before it is propagated to the calling function. The Rust Standard Library has a function, `thread::panicking()`, available in the `std::thread` module for this. Let's learn how to use it by modifying the previous example:

```rust
use std::fs;
use std::thread;
struct Filenames {
    source: String,
    destination: String,
}
impl Drop for Filenames {
    fn drop(&mut self) {
        if thread::panicking() {
            println!("dropped due to  panic");
        } else {
            println!("dropped without panic");
        }
    }
}
fn copy_file(file_struct: Filenames) -> thread::Result<()> {
    thread::spawn(move || {
        fs::copy(&file_struct.source,
            &file_struct.destination).expect(
            "Error occurred");
    })
    .join()
}
fn main() {
    let foo = Filenames {
        source: "a1.txt".into(),
        destination: "b.txt".into(),
```

```
    };
    match copy_file(foo) {
        Ok(_) => println!("Ok. copied"),
        Err(_) => println!("Error in copying file"),
    }
}
```

We've created a struct, `Filenames`, which contains the source and destination filenames to copy. We're initializing the source filename with an invalid value. We're also implementing the `Drop` trait for the `Filenames` struct, which gets called when an instance of the struct goes out of scope. In this `Drop` trait implementation, we are using the `thread::panicking()` function to check if the current thread is panicking, and are handling it by printing out an error message. The error is then propagated to the main function, which also handles the thread error and prints out another error message.

Run the program with `cargo run` and an invalid source filename, and you will see the following messages printed to your terminal:

```
dropped due to  panic
Error in copying file
```

Also, note the use of the `move` keyword in the `closure` supplied to the `spawn()` function. This is needed for the thread to transfer ownership of the `file_struct` data structure from the `main` thread to the newly spawned thread.

We've seen how to handle thread panic in the calling function and also how to detect if the current thread is panicking. Handling errors in child threads is very important to ensure that the error is isolated and does not bring the whole process down. Hence special attention is needed to design error handling for multi-threaded programs.

Next, we'll move on to the topic of how to synchronize computations across threads, which is an important aspect of writing concurrent programs.

Message passing between threads

Concurrency is a powerful feature that enables the writing of new kinds of applications. However, the execution and debugging of concurrent programs are difficult because their execution is non-deterministic. We saw this through examples in the previous section where the order of print statements varied for each run of the program. The order in which the threads will be executed is not known ahead of time. A concurrent program developer must make sure that the program will execute correctly overall, regardless of the order in which the individual threads are executed.

One way to ensure program correctness in the face of the unpredictable ordering of thread execution is to introduce mechanisms for synchronizing activities across threads. One such model for concurrent programming is *message-passing concurrency*. It is a way to structure the components of a concurrent program. In our case, concurrent components are *threads* (but they can also be processes). The Rust Standard Library has implemented a *message-passing concurrency* solution called **channels**. A *channel* is basically like a pipe, with two parts – a *producer* and a *consumer*. The *producer* puts a message into a *channel*, and a *consumer* reads from the *channel*.

Many programming languages implement the concept of channels for inter-thread communications. But Rust's implementation of *channels* has a special property – *multiple producer single consumer* (mpsc). This means, there can be multiple sending ends but only one consuming end. Translate this to the world of threads: we can have multiple threads that send values into a channel, but there can be only one thread that can receive and consume these values. Let's see how this works with an example that we'll build out step by step. The complete code listing is also provided in the Git repo for the chapter under src/message-passing.rs:

1. Let's first declare the module imports – the mpsc and thread modules from the standard library:

    ```
    use std::sync::mpsc;
    use std::thread;
    ```

2. Within the main() function, create a new mpsc channel:

    ```
    let (transmitter1, receiver) = mpsc::channel();
    ```

3. Clone the channel so we can have two transmitting threads:

    ```
    let transmitter2 = mpsc::Sender::clone(&transmitter1);
    ```

4. Note that we now have two transmission handles – transmitter1 and transmitter2, and one receiving handle – receiver.

5. Spawn a new thread moving the transmission handle transmitter1 into the thread closure. Inside this thread, send a bunch of values into the channel using the transmission handle:

    ```
    thread::spawn(move || {
        let num_vec: Vec<String> = vec!["One".into(),
            "two".into(), "three".into(),
    ```

```
            "four".into()];
        for num in num_vec {
            transmitter1.send(num).unwrap();
        }
    });
```

6. Spawn a second thread moving the transmission handle `transmitter2` into the thread closure. Inside this thread, send another bunch of values into the channel using the transmission handle:

```
    thread::spawn(move || {
        let num_vec: Vec<String> =
            vec!["Five".into(), "Six".into(),
                "Seven".into(), "eight".into()];
        for num in num_vec {
            transmitter2.send(num).unwrap();
        }
    });
```

7. In the main thread of the program, use the receiving handle of the channel to consume the values being written into the channel by the two child threads:

```
    for received_val in receiver {
        println!("Received from thread: {}",
            received_val);
    }
```

The complete code listing is shown:

```
use std::sync::mpsc;
use std::thread;
fn main() {
    let (transmitter1, receiver) = mpsc::channel();
    let transmitter2 = mpsc::Sender::clone(
        &transmitter1);
    thread::spawn(move || {
        let num_vec: Vec<String> = vec!["One".into(),
            "two".into(), "three".into(),
```

```
            "four".into()];
        for num in num_vec {
            transmitter1.send(num).unwrap();
        }
    });
    thread::spawn(move || {
        let num_vec: Vec<String> =
            vec!["Five".into(), "Six".into(),
                "Seven".into(), "eight".into()];
        for num in num_vec {
            transmitter2.send(num).unwrap();
        }
    });
    for received_val in receiver {
        println!("Received from thread: {}",
            received_val);
    }
}
```

8. Run the program with cargo run. (*Note:* If you are running code from the Packt Git repo, use cargo run --bin message-passing). You'll see the values printed out in the main program thread, which are sent from the two child threads. Each time you run the program, you may get a different order in which the values are received, as the order of thread execution is *non-deterministic*.

The mpsc channel offers a lightweight inter-thread synchronization mechanism that can be used for message-based communications across threads. This type of concurrent programming model is useful when you want to spawn out multiple threads for different types of computations and want to have the main thread aggregate the results.

One aspect to note in mpsc is that once a value is sent down a channel, the sending thread no longer has ownership of it. If you want to retain ownership or continue to use a value, but still need a way to share the value with other threads, there is another concurrency model that Rust supports called **shared-state concurrency**. We'll look at that next.

Achieving concurrency with shared state

In this section, we'll discuss the second model of concurrent programming supported in the Rust Standard Library – the *shared-state* or *shared-memory* model of concurrency. Recall that all threads in a process share the same process memory space, so why not use that as a way to communicate between threads, rather than message-passing? We'll look at how to achieve this using Rust.

A combination of `Mutex` and `Arc` constitutes the primary way to implement *shared-state concurrency*. `Mutex` (mutual exclusion lock) is a mechanism that allows only one thread to access a piece of data at one time. First, a data value is wrapped in a `Mutex` type, which acts as a lock. You can visualize `Mutex` like a box with an external lock, protecting something valuable inside. To access what's in the box, first of all, we have to ask someone to open the lock and hand over the box. Once we're done, we hand over the box back and someone else asks to take charge of it.

Similarly, to access or mutate a value protected by a `Mutex`, we must acquire the lock first. Asking for a lock on a `Mutex` object returns a `MutexGuard` type, which lets us access the inner value. During this time, no other thread can access this value protected by the `MutexGuard`. Once we're done using it, we have to release the `MutexGuard` (which Rust does for us automatically as the `MutexGuard` goes out of scope, without us having to call a separate `unlock()` method).

But there is another issue to resolve. Protecting a value with a lock is just one part of the solution. We also have to give ownership of a value to multiple threads. To support multiple ownership of a value, Rust uses *reference-counted smart pointers* – `Rc` and `Arc`. `Rc` allows multiple owners for a value through its `clone()` method. But `Rc` is not safe to use across threads, and `Arc` (which stands for Atomically Reference Counted) is the thread-safe equivalent of `Rc`. So, we need to wrap the `Mutex` with an `Arc` reference-counted smart-pointer, and transfer ownership of the value across threads. Once the ownership of the Arc-protected Mutex is transferred to another thread, the receiving thread can call `lock()` on the Mutex to get exclusive access to the inner value. The Rust ownership model helps in enforcing the rules around this model.

The way the `Arc<T>` type works is that it provides the shared ownership of a value of type `T`, allocated in the heap. By calling the associated function `clone()` on an `Arc` instance, a new instance of the `Arc` reference-counted pointer is created, which points to the same allocation on the heap as the source `Arc`, while increasing a reference count. With each `clone()`, the reference count is increased by the `Arc` smart pointer. When each `cloned()` pointer goes out of scope, the reference counter is decremented. When the last of the clones go out of scope, both the `Arc` pointer and the value it points to (in the heap) are destroyed.

To summarize, `Mutex` ensures that at most one thread is able to access some data at one time, while `Arc` enables shared ownership of some data and prolongs its lifetime until all the threads have finished using it.

Let's see the usage of `Mutex` with `Arc` to demonstrate shared-state concurrency with a step-by-step example. This time, we'll write a more complex example than just incrementing a shared counter value across threads. We'll take the example we wrote in *Chapter 6, Working with Files and Directories in Rust*, to compute source file stats for all Rust files in a directory tree, and modify it to make it a concurrent program. We'll define the structure of the program in the next section. The complete code for this section can be found in the Git repo under `src/shared-state.rs`.

Defining the program structure

What we'd like to do is to take a list of directories as input to our program, compute source file statistics for each file within each of these directories, and print out a consolidated set of source code stats.

Let's first create a `dirnames.txt` file in the root folder of the cargo project, containing a list of directories with a full path, one per line. We'll read each entry from this file and spawn a separate thread to compute the source file stats for the Rust files within that directory tree. So, if there are five directory-name entries in the file, there will be five threads created from the main program, each of which will recursively walk through the directory structure of the entry, and compute the consolidated Rust source file stats. Each thread will increment the computed value in a shared data structure. We'll use `Mutex` and `Arc` to protect access and update the shared data safely across threads.

Let's start writing the code:

1. We'll start with the module imports for this program:

    ```
    use std::ffi::OsStr;
    use std::fs;
    use std::fs::File;
    use std::io::{BufRead, BufReader};
    use std::path::PathBuf;
    use std::sync::{Arc, Mutex};
    use std::thread;
    ```

2. Define a struct to store the source file stats:

```
#[derive(Debug)]
pub struct SrcStats {
    pub number_of_files: u32,
    pub loc: u32,
    pub comments: u32,
    pub blanks: u32,
}
```

3. Within the main() function, create a new instance of SrcStats, protect it with a Mutex lock, and then wrap it inside an Arc type:

```
let src_stats = SrcStats {
    number_of_files: 0,
    loc: 0,
    comments: 0,
    blanks: 0,
};
let stats_counter = Arc::new(
    Mutex::new(src_stats));
```

4. Read the dirnames.txt file, and store the individual entries in a vector:

```
let mut dir_list = File::open(
    "./dirnames.txt").unwrap();
let reader = BufReader::new(&mut dir_list);
let dir_lines: Vec<_> = reader.lines().collect();
```

5. Iterate through the dir_lines vector, and for each entry, spawn a new thread to perform the following two steps:

a) Accumulate the list of files from each subdirectory in the tree.

b) Then open each file and compute the stats. Update the stats in the shared-memory struct protected by Mutex and Arc.

The overall skeletal structure of the code for this step looks like this:

```
let mut child_handles = vec![];
for dir in dir_lines {
    let dir = dir.unwrap();
    let src_stats = Arc::clone(&stats_counter);

    let handle = thread::spawn(move || {
    // Do processing: A)
    // Do processing: B)
    });
    child_handles.push(handle);
}
```

In this section, we read the list of directory entries for computing source file statistics from a file. We then iterated through the list to spawn a thread to process each entry. In the next section, we'll define the processing to be done in each thread.

Aggregating source file statistics in shared state

In this section, we'll write the code for computing source file statistics in each thread and aggregate the results in shared state. We'll look at the code in two parts – *sub-steps A* and *B*:

1. In *sub-step A*, let's read through each subdirectory under the directory entry, and accumulate the consolidated list of all Rust source files in the `file_entries` vector. The code for *sub-step A* is shown. Here, we are first creating two vectors to hold the directory and filenames respectively. Then we are iterating through the directory entries of each item from the `dirnames.txt` file, and accumulating the entry names into the `dir_entries` or `file_entries` vector depending upon whether it is a directory or an individual file:

```
let mut dir_entries = vec![PathBuf::
        from(dir)];
let mut file_entries = vec![];
while let Some(entry) = dir_entries.pop()
    {
        for inner_entry in fs::read_dir(
            &entry).unwrap() {
```

```
if let Ok(entry) = inner_entry {
    if entry.path().is_dir() {
        dir_entries.push(
            entry.path());
    } else {
        if entry.path()
            .extension()
            == Some(OsStr::
                new("rs"))
        {
            println!("File name
                processed is
                {:?}",entry);

            file_entries.push(
                entry);

        }
    }
}
}
}
```

At the end of *sub-step A*, all individual filenames are stored in the `file_entries` vector, which we will use in *sub-step B* for further processing.

2. In *sub-step B*, we'll read each file from the `file_entries` vector, compute the source stats for each file, and save the values in the shared memory struct. Here is the code snippet for *sub-step B*:

```
for file in file_entries {
    let file_contents =
        fs::read_to_string(
        &file.path()).unwrap();

    let mut stats_pointer =
```

```
                    src_stats.lock().unwrap();
            for line in file_contents.lines() {
                if line.len() == 0 {
                    stats_pointer.blanks += 1;
                } else if line.starts_with("//") {
                    stats_pointer.comments += 1;
                } else {
                    stats_pointer.loc += 1;
                }
            }

            stats_pointer.number_of_files += 1;
        }
```

3. Let's again review the skeletal structure of the program shown next. We've so far seen the code to be executed within the thread, which includes processing for steps A and B:

```
    let mut child_handles = vec![];
    for dir in dir_lines {
        let dir = dir.unwrap();
        let src_stats = Arc::clone(&stats_counter);

        let handle = thread::spawn(move || {
        // Do processing: step A)
        // Do processing: step B)
        });
            child_handles.push(handle);
    }
```

Note that at the end of the thread-related code, we are accumulating the thread handle in the child_handles vector.

4. Let's look at the last part of the code now. As discussed earlier, in order to ensure that the main thread does not complete before the child threads are completed, we have to join the child thread handles with the main threads. Also, let's print out the final value of the thread-safe `stats_counter` struct, which contains aggregated source stats from all the Rust source files under the directory (updated by the individual threads):

```
for handle in child_handles {
    handle.join().unwrap();
}
println!(
    "Source stats: {:?}",
    stats_counter.lock().unwrap()
);
```

The complete code listing can be found in the Git repo for the chapter in `src/shared-state.rs`.

Before running this program, ensure to create a file, `dirnames.txt`, in the root folder of the cargo project, containing a list of directory entries with a full path, each on a separate line.

5. Run the project with `cargo run`. (*Note*: If you are running code from the Packt Git repo, use `cargo run --bin shared-state`.) You will see the consolidated source stats printed out. Note that we have now implemented a multi-threaded version of the project we wrote in *Chapter 6, Working with Files and Directories in Rust*. As an exercise, alter this example to implement the same project with the *message-passing concurrency* model.

In this section, we've seen how multiple threads can safely write to a shared value (wrapped in `Mutex` and `Arc`) that is stored in process heap memory, in a thread-safe manner. In the next section, we will review one more mechanism available to control thread execution, which is to selectively pause the processing of the current thread.

Send and Sync traits

We saw earlier how a data type can be shared across threads, and how messages can be passed between threads. There is another aspect of concurrency in Rust though. Rust defines data types as thread-safe or not.

From a concurrency perspective, there are two categories of data types in Rust: those that are Send (that is, implement the Send trait), which means they are safe to be transferred from one thread to another. And the rest are *thread-unsafe* types. A related concept is Sync, which is associated with references of types. A type is considered to be Sync if its reference can be passed to another thread safely. So, Send means it is safe to transfer ownership of a type from one thread to another, while Sync means the data type can be shared (using references) safely by multiple threads at the same time. Note though that in Send, after a value has been transferred from the sending to the receiving thread, the sending thread can no longer use that value.

Send and Sync are also automatically derived traits. This means that if a type consists of members that implement Send or Sync types, the type itself automatically becomes Send or Sync. The Rust primitives (almost all of them) implement Send and Sync, which means if you create a custom type from Rust primitives, your custom type also becomes Send or Sync. We've seen an example of this in the previous section, where the SrcStats (source stats) struct was transferred across the boundaries of threads without us having to explicitly implement Send or Sync on the struct.

However, if there is a need to implement Send or Sync traits for a data type manually, it would have to be done in unsafe Rust.

To summarize, in Rust, every data type is classified as either *thread-safe* or *thread-unsafe*, and the Rust compiler enforces the safe transfer or sharing of thread-safe types across threads.

Pausing thread execution with timers

Sometimes, during the processing of a thread, there may be a need to pause execution either to wait for another event or to synchronize execution with other threads. Rust provides support for this using the std::thread::sleep function. This function takes a time duration of type time::Duration and pauses execution of the thread for the specified time. During this time, the processor time can be made available to other threads or applications running on the computer system. Let's see an example of the usage of thread::sleep:

```rust
use std::thread;
use std::time::Duration;
```

```
fn main() {
    let duration = Duration::new(1,0);
    println!("Going to sleep");
    thread::sleep(duration);
    println!("Woke up");
}
```

Using the `sleep()` function is fairly straightforward, but this blocks the current thread and it is important to make judicious use of this in a multi-threaded program. An alternative to using `sleep()` would be to use an async programming model to implement threads with non-blocking I/O.

Async I/O in Rust

In the multi-threaded model, if there is a blocking I/O call in any thread, it blocks the program workflow. The *async* model relies on non-blocking system calls for I/O, for example, to access the filesystem or network. In the example of a web server with multiple simultaneous incoming connections, instead of spawning a separate thread to handle each connection in a blocking manner, *async* I/O relies on a runtime that does not block the current thread but instead schedules other tasks while waiting on I/O.

While Rust has built-in `Async/Await` syntax, which makes it easier to write *async* code, it does not provide any asynchronous system call support. For this, we need to rely on external libraries such as `Tokio`, which provide both the *async runtime* (executor) and the *async* versions of the I/O functions that are present in the Rust Standard Library.

So, when would one use *async* versus the *multi-threaded* approach to concurrency? The broad thumb-rule is that the *async* model is suited to programs that perform a lot of I/O, whereas, for computation-intensive (CPU-bound) tasks, *multi-threaded concurrency* is a better approach. Keep in mind though that it is not a binary choice, as in practice it is not uncommon to see *async* programs that also utilize *multi-threading* in a hybrid model.

For more information on async in Rust, refer to the following link: `https://rust-lang.github.io/async-book/`.

Summary

In this chapter, we covered the basics of concurrency and multi-threaded programming in Rust. We started by reviewing the need for concurrent programming models. We understood the differences between the concurrent and parallel execution of programs. We learned how to spawn new threads using two different methods. We handled errors using a special `Result` type in the thread module and also learned how to check whether the current thread is panicking. We looked at how threads are laid out in process memory. We discussed two techniques for synchronizing processing across threads – *message-passing concurrency* and *shared-state concurrency*, with practical examples. As a part of this, we learned about channels, `Mutex` and `Arc` in Rust, and the role they play in writing concurrent programs. We then discussed how Rust classifies data types as *thread-safe* or not, and saw how to pause the execution of the current thread.

This concludes the chapter on managing concurrency in Rust. This also concludes *Section 2* of this book, which is on managing and controlling system resources in Rust.

We will now move on to the last part of the book – *Section 3* covering *advanced topics*. In the next chapter, we will cover how to perform *device I/O* in Rust, and internalize learning through an example project.

Section 3: Advanced Topics

This section covers advanced topics, including working with peripheral devices, network primitives and TCP/UDP communications, unsafe Rust, and interacting with other programming languages. Example projects include writing a program to detect details of connected USB devices, writing a TCP reverse proxy with an origin server, and an example of FFI.

This section comprises the following chapters:

- *Chapter 10, Working with Device I/O*
- *Chapter 11, Learning Network Programming*
- *Chapter 12, Writing Unsafe Rust and FFI*

10
Working with Device I/O

In *Chapter 6*, *Working with Files and Directories in Rust*, we covered the details of how to perform file I/O operations (such as reading and writing to files) using the Rust Standard Library. In Unix-like operating systems, a file is an abstraction that is used to work not only with regular disk files (which are used to store data) but also with several types of devices that are connected to a machine. In this chapter, we will look at the features of the Rust Standard Library that enable us to perform reads and writes to any type of device (also called device I/O) in Rust. Device I/O is an essential aspect of system programming to monitor and control various types of devices attached to a computer, such as keyboards, USB cameras, printers, and sound cards. You may be curious to know what support Rust provides to a system programmer to handle all these different types of devices. We'll answer this question as we go through the chapter.

In this chapter, we will review the basics of I/O management in Unix/Linux using the Rust Standard Library, including handling errors, and then write a program to detect and print details of connected USB devices.

We will cover these topics in the following order:

- Understanding device I/O fundamentals in Linux
- Doing buffered reads and writes
- Working with standard input and output
- Chaining and iterators over I/O
- Handling errors and returning values
- Getting details of connected USB devices (project)

By the end of this chapter, you will have learned how to work with standard readers and writers, which constitute the foundation of any I/O operation. You'll also learn how to optimize system calls through the use of buffered reads and writes. We'll cover reading and writing to standard I/O streams of a process and handling errors from I/O operations, as well as learning ways to iterate over I/O. These concepts will be reinforced through an example project.

Technical requirements

Verify that `rustup`, `rustc`, and `cargo` have been installed correctly with the following command:

```
rustup --version
rustc --version
cargo --version
```

The Git repo for the code in this chapter can be found at `https://github.com/PacktPublishing/Practical-System-Programming-for-Rust-Developers/tree/master/Chapter10/usb`.

For running and testing the project in this book, you must have the native libusb library installed where it can be found by `pkg-config`.

The project in this book has been tested on macOS Catalina 10.15.6.

For instructions on building and testing on Windows, refer: `https://github.com/dcuddeback/libusb-rs/issues/20`

For general instructions on environmental setup of `libusb` crate, refer to: `https://github.com/dcuddeback/libusb-rs`

Understanding device I/O fundamentals in Linux

In previous chapters, we saw how to schedule work on CPUs using **processes and threads**, and how to manage **memory** by controlling the memory layout of a program. In addition to the CPU and memory, the operating system also manages the system's hardware devices. Examples of hardware devices include keyboards, mice, hard disks, video adapters, audio cards, network adapters, scanners, cameras, and other USB devices. But the peculiarities of these physical hardware devices are hidden from the user programs by the operating system, using software modules called **device drivers**. Device drivers are indispensable software components for doing device I/O. Let's take a closer look at them.

What are device drivers?

Device drivers are shared libraries loaded into the kernel that contain functions to perform low-level hardware control. They communicate with the devices through the computer bus or communication subsystem to which the device is connected. They are specific to each device type (for example, a mouse or network adaptor) or class of devices (for example, IDE or SCSI disk controllers). They are also specific to an operating system (for example, a device driver for Windows doesn't work on Linux even for the same device type).

Device drivers handle the peculiarities of the devices (or device classes) for which they are written. For example, a device driver to control a hard disk receives requests to read or write some file data identified by a **block number**. The device driver translates the block number into track, sector, and cylinder numbers on the disk. It also initializes the device, checks whether the device is in use, validates input parameters to its function calls, determines the commands to be issued, and issues them to the device. It handles the interrupts from the device and communicates them back to the calling program. The device driver further implements the specific hardware protocols that the device supports, such as **SCSI/ATA/SATA** for disk access or **UART** for serial port communications. Device drivers thus abstract away a lot of the hardware-specific details of controlling devices.

The operating system (specifically the kernel) accepts system calls from the user programs for device access and control, and then uses the respective device driver to physically access and control the device. *Figure 10.1* illustrates how user space programs (for example, Rust programs that use the standard library to talk to the operating system kernel) use system calls to manage and control various types of devices:

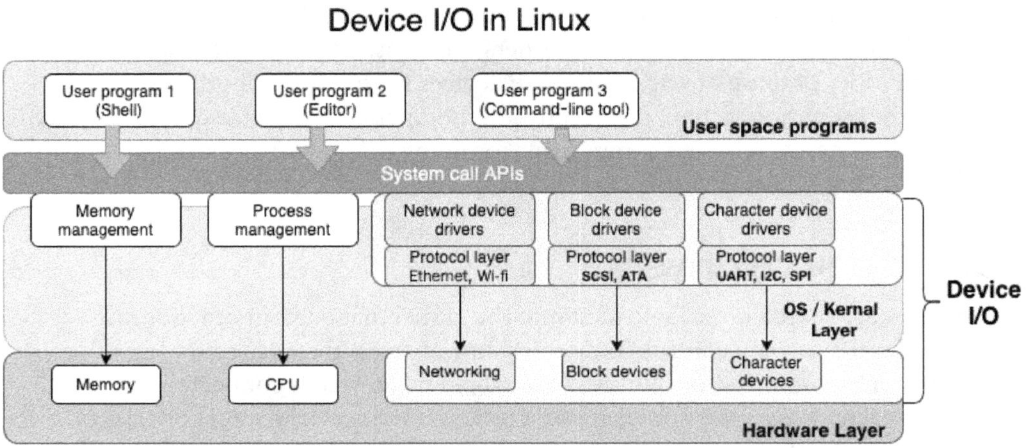

Device I/O in Linux

Figure 10.1 – Device I/O in Linux

In *Chapter 6, Working with Files and Directories in Rust*, we saw that Linux/Unix has the philosophy that *everything is a file*, characterized by the universality of I/O. The same system calls, such as open(), close(), read(), and write(), can be applied to all types of I/O whether it's a regular file (used to store text or binary data), a directory, device files, or network connections. What this means is that programmers of user space programs can write code to communicate with and control devices without worrying about the protocol and hardware specifics of the devices, thanks to the abstraction layers provided by the kernel (system calls) and device drivers. Furthermore, the Rust Standard Library adds another layer of abstraction to provide a device-independent software layer, which Rust programs can use for device I/O. This is the primary focus of this chapter.

Types of devices

In Unix/Linux, devices are broadly classified into three types:

- **Character devices** send or receive data as a serial stream of bytes. Examples are terminals, keyboards, mice, printers, and sound cards. Unlike regular files, data cannot be accessed at random but only sequentially.

- **Block devices** store information in fixed-size blocks and allow random access to these blocks. Filesystems, hard disks, tape drives, and USB cameras are examples of block devices. A filesystem is mounted on a block device.

- **Network devices** are similar to character devices as data is read serially, but there are some differences. Data is sent in variable-length packets using a network protocol, which the operating system and the user program have to deal with. A network adaptor is usually a hardware device (with some exceptions, such as the loopback interface, which is a software interface) that interfaces to a network (such as **Ethernet** or **Wi-Fi**).

A hardware device is identified by its *type* (block or character) and a *device number*. The device number in turn is split into a major and minor device number.

When a new hardware is connected, the kernel needs a device driver that is compatible with the device and can operate the device controller hardware. A device driver, as discussed earlier, is essentially a shared library of low-level, hardware-handling functions that can operate in a privileged manner as part of the kernel. Without device drivers, the kernel does not know how to operate the device. When a program attempts to connect to a device, the kernel looks up associated information in its tables and transfers control to the device driver. There are separate tables for *block* and *character* devices. The device driver performs the required task on the device and returns control back to the operating system kernel.

As an example, let's look at a web server sending a page to a web browser. The data is structured as an **HTTP response message** with the **web page (HTML)** sent as part of its **data payload**. The data itself is stored in the kernel in a buffer (data structure), which is then passed to the **TCP layer**, then to the **IP layer**, on to the **Ethernet device driver**, then to the **Ethernet adaptor**, and onward to the **network**. The Ethernet device driver does not know anything about connections and only handles data packets. Similarly, when data needs to be stored to a file on the disk, the data is stored in a buffer, which is passed on to the **filesystem device driver** and then onward to the **disk controller**, which then saves it to the disk (for example, hard disk, SSD, and so on). Essentially, the *kernel* relies on a *device driver* to interface with the device.

Device drivers are usually part of the kernel (**kernel device driver**), but there are also **user space device drivers**, which abstract out the details of kernel access. Later in this chapter, we will be using one such user space device driver to detect USB devices.

We've discussed the basics of device I/O, including device drivers and types of devices in Unix-like systems, in this section. Starting from the next section, we'll focus on how to do device-independent I/O using features from the Rust Standard Library.

Doing buffered reads and writes

Reads and writes are the fundamental operations performed on I/O types such as files and streams and are very crucial for working with many types of system resources. In this section, we'll discuss different ways to do *reads* and *writes* to I/O in Rust. We'll first cover the core traits – Read and Write – which allow Rust programs to perform read and write operations on objects that implement these traits (which are also called **readers** and **writers**). Then, we'll see how to do *buffered reads* and *buffered writes*, which are more efficient for certain types of read and write operations.

Let's start with the basic Read and Write traits.

In line with the *everything-is-a-file* philosophy, the Rust Standard Library provides two traits – Read and Write – which provide a general interface for reading and writing inputs and outputs. This trait is implemented for different types of I/O, such as files, TcpStream, standard input, and standard output streams of processes.

An example of using the Read trait is shown in the following code. Here, we are opening a records.txt file with the open() function in the std::fs::File module (which we learned earlier). We're then bringing the Read trait from the std::io module into scope, and using the read() method of this trait to read bytes from a file. The same read() method can also be used to read from any other entity implementing the Read trait, such as a **network socket** or a **standard input** stream:

```
use std::fs::File;
use std::io::Read;
fn main() {
    // Open a file
    let mut f = File::open("records.txt").unwrap();
    //Create a memory buffer to read from file
    let mut buffer = [0; 1024];
    // read from file into buffer
    let _ = f.read(&mut buffer[..]).unwrap();
}
```

Create a file called records.txt in the project root and run the program with cargo run. You can optionally print out the value of the buffer, which will display the raw bytes.

Read and `Write` are byte-based interfaces, which can get inefficient as they involve continual system calls to the operating system. To overcome this, Rust also provides two structs to enable doing buffered reads and writes – `BufReader` and `BufWriter`, which have a built-in buffer and reduce the number of calls to the operating system.

The previous example can be rewritten as shown here, to use `BufReader`:

```rust
use std::fs::File;
use std::io::{BufRead, BufReader};
fn main() {
    // Open a file
    let f = File::open("records.txt").unwrap();
    // Create a BufReader, passing in the file handle
    let mut buf_reader = BufReader::new(f);
    //Create a memory buffer to read from file
    let mut buffer = String::new();
    // read a line into the buffer
    buf_reader.read_line(&mut buffer).unwrap();
    println!("Read the following: {}", buffer);
}
```

The code changes (from the previous version) have been highlighted. `BufReader` uses the `BufRead` trait, which is brought into scope. Instead of reading directly from the file handle, we create a `BufReader` instance and read a line into this struct. The `BufReader` methods internally optimize calls to the operating system. Run the program and verify that the value from the file is printed correctly.

`BufWriter` similarly buffers writes to the disk, thus minimizing system calls. It can be used in a similar manner as shown in the following code:

```rust
use std::fs::File;
use std::io::{BufWriter, Write};
fn main() {
    // Create a file
    let f = File::create("file.txt").unwrap();
    // Create a BufWriter, passing in the file handle
    let mut buf_writer = BufWriter::new(f);
    //Create a memory buffer
    let buffer = String::from("Hello, testing");
```

```
    // write into the buffer
    buf_writer.write(buffer.as_bytes()).unwrap();
    println!("wrote the following: {}", buffer);
}
```

In the code shown, we're creating a new file to write into, and are also creating a new `BufWriter` instance. We then write a value from the buffer into the `BufWriter` instance. Run the program and verify that the specified string value has been written to a file with the name `file.txt` in the project root directory. Note that here, in addition to `BufWriter`, we also have to bring the `Write` trait into scope as this contains the `write()` method.

Note when to use and when not to use `BufReader` and `BufWriter`:

- `BufReader` and `BufWriter` speed up programs that make small and frequent reads or writes to a disk. If the reads or writes only occasionally involve large-sized data, they do not offer any benefit.

- `BufReader` and `BufWriter` do not help while reading from or writing to in-memory data structures.

In this section, we saw how to do both unbuffered and buffered reads and writes. In the next section, we'll learn how to work with standard inputs and outputs of a process.

Working with standard input and output

In Linux/Unix, **streams** are communication channels between a process and its environment. By default, three standard streams are created for every running process: **standard input**, **standard output**, and **standard error**. A stream is a communication channel that has two ends. One end is connected to the process and the other end to another system resource. For example, a standard input can be used by a process to read characters or text from a keyboard or another process. Similarly, a standard output stream can be used by a process to send some characters to the terminal or to a file. In many modern programs, the standard error of a process is connected to a log file, which makes analyzing and debugging errors easier.

The Rust Standard Library provides methods to interact with standard input and output streams. The `Stdin` struct in the `std::io` module represents the handle to the input stream of a process. This handle implements the `Read` trait, which we covered in the previous section.

The code example here shows how to interact with the standard input and standard output streams of a process. In the code shown, we are reading a line from the standard input into a buffer. We're then writing back the contents of the buffer to the standard output of the process. Note that here, the word *process* refers to the running program that you have written. You are essentially *reading from* and *writing to* the *standard input* and *standard output*, respectively, of the running program:

```
use std::io::{self, Write};
fn main() {
    //Create a memory buffer to read from file
    let mut buffer = String::new();
    // read a line into the buffer
    let _ = io::stdin().read_line(&mut buffer).unwrap();
    // Write the buffer to standard output
    io::stdout().write(&mut buffer.as_bytes()).unwrap();
}
```

Run the program with cargo run, enter some text, and hit the *Enter* key. You'll see the text echoed back on the terminal.

Stdin, which is a handle to the input stream of a process, is a shared reference to a global buffer of input data. Likewise, Stdout, which is the output stream of a process, is a shared reference to a global data buffer. Since Stdin and Stdout are references to shared data, to ensure exclusive use of these data buffers, the handles can be locked. For example, the StdinLock struct in the std::io module represents a locked reference to the Stdin handle. Likewise, the StdoutLock struct in the std::io module represents a locked reference to the Stdout handle. Examples of how to use the locked reference are shown in the code example here:

```
use std::io::{Read, Write};
fn main() {
    //Create a memory buffer
    let mut buffer = [8; 1024];
    // Get handle to input stream
    let stdin_handle = std::io::stdin();
    // Lock the handle to input stream
    let mut locked_stdin_handle = stdin_handle.lock();
    // read a line into the buffer
    locked_stdin_handle.read(&mut buffer).unwrap();
```

```
    // Get handle to output stream
    let stdout_handle = std::io::stdout();
    // Lock the handle to output stream
    let mut locked_stdout_handle = stdout_handle.lock();
    // Write the buffer to standard output
    locked_stdout_handle.write(&mut buffer).unwrap();
}
```

In the code shown, the standard input and output stream handles are locked before reading and writing to them.

We can similarly write to the *standard error* stream. A code example is shown here:

```
use std::io::Write;
fn main() {
    //Create a memory buffer
    let buffer = b"Hello, this is error message from
        standard
        error stream\n";
    // Get handle to output error stream
    let stderr_handle = std::io::stderr();
    // Lock the handle to output error stream
    let mut locked_stderr_handle = stderr_handle.lock();
    // write into error stream from buffer
    locked_stderr_handle.write(buffer).unwrap();
}
```

In the code shown, we're constructing a handle to the standard error stream using the stderr() function. Then, we're locking this handle and then writing some text to it.

In this section, we've seen how to interact with the standard input, standard output, and standard error streams of a process using the Rust Standard Library. Recall that in the previous chapter on managing concurrency, we saw how, from a parent process, we can read from and write to the standard input and output streams of the child process.

In the next section, let's look at a couple of functional programming constructs that can be used for I/O in Rust.

Chaining and iterators over I/O

In this section, we'll look at how to use iterators and chaining with the `std::io` module.

Many of the data structures provided by the `std::io` module have built-in **iterators**. Iterators let you process a series of items, such as lines in a file or incoming network connections on a port. They provide a nicer mechanism compared to `while` and `for` loops. Here is an example of using the `lines()` iterator with the `BufReader` struct, which is a part of the `std::io` module. This program reads lines from the *standard input* stream in a loop:

```rust
use std::io::{BufRead, BufReader};
fn main() {
    // Create handle to standard input
    let s = std::io::stdin();
    //Create a BufReader instance to optimize sys calls
    let file_reader = BufReader::new(s);
    // Read from standard input line-by-line
    for single_line in file_reader.lines() {
        println!("You typed:{}", single_line.unwrap());
    }
}
```

In the code shown, we have created a handle to the standard input stream and passed it to a `BufReader` struct. This struct implements the `BufRead` trait, which has a `lines()` method that returns an *iterator* over the lines of the reader. This helps us to type inputs on the terminal *line by line* and have it read by our running program. The text entered on the terminal is echoed back to the terminal. Execute `cargo run`, and type some text, and then hit the *Enter* key. Repeat this step as many times as you'd like. Exit from the program with *Ctrl + C*.

Likewise, the iterator can be used to read line by line from a *file* (instead of from standard input, which we saw in the previous example). A code snippet is shown here:

```rust
use std::fs::File;
use std::io::{BufRead, BufReader};

fn main() {
    // Open a file for reading
    let f = File::open("file.txt").unwrap();
    //Create a BufReader instance to optimize sys calls
```

```
    let file_reader = BufReader::new(f);
    // Read from standard input line-by-line
    for single_line in file_reader.lines() {
        println!("Line read from file :{}",
            single_line.unwrap());
    }
}
```

Create a file called `file.txt` in the project root directory. Enter a few lines of text in this file. Then, run the program using `cargo run`. You'll see the file contents printed out to the terminal.

We've so far seen how to use iterators from the `std::io` module. Let's now look at another concept: **chaining**.

The `Read` trait in the `std::io` module has a `chain()` method, which allows us to chain multiple `BufReader` together into one handle. Here is an example of how to create a single **chained handle** combining two files, and how to read from this handle:

```
use std::fs::File;
use std::io::Read;
fn main() {
    // Open two file handles for reading
    let f1 = File::open("file1.txt").unwrap();
    let f2 = File::open("file2.txt").unwrap();
    //Chain the two file handles
    let mut chained_handle = f1.chain(f2);
    // Create a buffer to read into
    let mut buffer = String::new();
    // Read from chained handle into buffer
    chained_handle.read_to_string(&mut buffer).unwrap();
    // Print out the value read into the buffer
    println!("Read from chained handle:\n{}", buffer);
}
```

The statement using the `chain()` method has been highlighted in the code. The rest of the code is fairly self-explanatory, as it is similar to what we've seen in previous examples. Ensure to create two files, `file1.txt` and `file2.txt`, under the project root folder and enter a few lines of text in each. Run the program with `cargo run`. You'll see the data from both files printed out line by line.

In this section, we've seen how to use iterators and how to chain readers together. In the next section, let's take a look at error handling for I/O operations.

Handling errors and returning values

In this section, we'll learn about the built-in error handling support in the `std::io` module. Handling recoverable errors in an appropriate manner makes Rust programs more robust.

In the code examples we've seen so far, we've used the `unwrap()` function to extract the return value from the `std::io` module methods and associated functions, such as `Read`, `Write`, `BufReader`, and `BufWriter`. However, this is not the correct way to handle errors. The `std::io` module has a specialized `Result` type that is returned from any function or method in this module that may produce an error.

Let's rewrite the previous example (of chaining readers) using the `io::Result` type as the return value from the function. This allows us to use the `?` operator to directly pass errors back from the `main()` function, instead of using the `unwrap()` function:

```rust
use std::fs::File;
use std::io::Read;
fn main() -> std::io::Result<()> {
    // Open two file handles for reading
    let f1 = File::open("file1.txt")?;
    let f2 = File::open("file3.txt")?;
    //Chain the two file handles
    let mut chained_handle = f1.chain(f2);
    // Create a buffer to read into
    let mut buffer = String::new();
    // Read from chained handle into buffer
    chained_handle.read_to_string(&mut buffer)?;
    println!("Read from chained handle: {}", buffer);
    Ok(())
}
```

Code related to error handling has been highlighted. Run the program with `cargo run`, this time making sure that neither `file1.txt` nor `file3.txt` exists in the project root folder.

You'll see the error message printed to the terminal.

In the code we've just seen, we're just propagating the error received from the operating system while making the calls. Let's now try to handle the errors in a more active manner. The code example here shows custom error handling for the same code:

```rust
use std::fs::File;
use std::io::Read;
fn read_files(handle: &mut impl Read) ->
std::io::Result<String> {
    // Create a buffer to read into
    let mut buffer = String::new();
    // Read from chained handle into buffer
    handle.read_to_string(&mut buffer)?;
    Ok(buffer)
}
fn main() {
    let mut chained_handle;
    // Open two file handles for reading
    let file1 = "file1.txt";
    let file2 = "file3.txt";
    if let Ok(f1) = File::open(file1) {
        if let Ok(f2) = File::open(file2) {
            //Chain the two file handles
            chained_handle = f1.chain(f2);
            let content = read_files(&mut chained_handle);
            match content {
                Ok(text) => println!("Read from chained
                    handle:\n{}", text),
                Err(e) => println!("Error occurred in
                    reading files: {}", e),
            }
        } else {
            println!("Unable to read {}", file2);
        }
    } else {
        println!("Unable to read {}", file1);
    }
}
```

You'll notice that we've created a new function that returns `std::io::Result` to the `main()` function. We're handling errors in various operations, such as reading from a file and reading from the chained readers.

First, run the program with `cargo run`, ensuring that both `file1.txt` and `file2.txt` exist. You'll see the contents from both files printed to the terminal. Rerun the program by removing one of these files. You should see the custom error message from our code.

With this, we conclude the section on handling errors. Let's now move on to the last section of the chapter, where we will go through a project to detect and display details of USB devices connected to a computer.

Getting details of connected USB devices (project)

In this section, we will demonstrate an example of working with devices in Rust. The example chosen is to display details of all connected USB devices of a computer. We'll be using `libusb`, a C library that helps to interact with USB devices. The `libusb` crate in Rust is a safe wrapper around the C `libusb` library. Let's first look at the design.

Designing the project

Here is how this would work:

- When a USB device is plugged into a computer, the electrical signals on the computer bus trigger the **USB controller** (hardware device) on the computer.

- The USB controller raises an interrupt on the CPU, which then executes the interrupt handler registered for that interrupt in the kernel.

- When a call is made from the Rust program through the Rust `libusb` wrapper crate, the call is routed to the `libusb` C library, which in turn makes a system call on the kernel to read the device file corresponding to the USB device. We've seen earlier in this chapter how Unix/Linux enables standard **syscalls**, such as `read()` and `write()`, for I/O.

- When the system call returns from the kernel, the `libusb` library returns the value from the syscall to our Rust program.

We're using the `libusb` library because writing a USB device driver from scratch requires implementing the USB protocol specifications, and writing device drivers is the subject of a separate book in itself. Let's look at the design of our program:

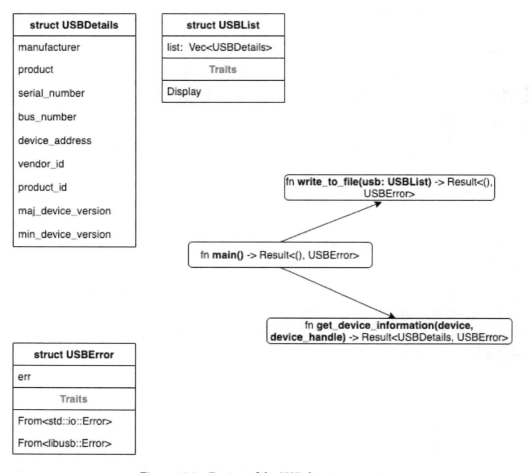

Figure 10.2 – Design of the USB detector project

Figure 10.2 shows the structs and functions in the program. Here is a description of the data structures:

- `USBList`: List of USB devices detected.
- `USBDetails`: This contains the list of USB details that we want to retrieve through this program for each USB device.
- `USBError`: Custom error handling.

These are the functions that we will write:

- `get_device_information()`: Function to retrieve the required device details given a device reference and device handle.
- `write_to_file()`: Function to write device details to an output file.
- `main()`: This is the entry point to the program. It instantiates a new `libusb::Context`, retrieves a list of attached devices, and iterates through the list to call `get_device_information()` for each device. The retrieved details are printed to the terminal and also written to the file using the `write_to_file()` function.

We can now begin to write the code.

Writing data structures and utility functions

In this section, we'll write the data structures for storing the USB device list and USB details and for custom error handling. We'll also write a few utility functions:

1. Let's begin by creating a new project:

   ```
   cargo new usb && cd usb
   ```

2. Let's add the `libusb` crate to `Cargo.toml`:

   ```
   [dependencies]
   libusb = "0.3.0"
   ```

3. We'll now look at the code in parts. Add all the code for this project in `usb/src/main.rs`.

Here are the module imports:

```
use libusb::{Context, Device, DeviceHandle};
use std::fs::File;
use std::io::Write;
use std::time::Duration;
use std::fmt;
```

We're importing the libusb modules and a few modules from the Rust Standard Library. fs::File and io::Write are for writing to an output file, result::Result is the return value from the functions, and time::Duration is for working with the libusb library.

4. Let's look at the data structures now:

```
#[derive(Debug)]
struct USBError {
    err: String,
}

struct USBList {
    list: Vec<USBDetails>,
}
#[derive(Debug)]
struct USBDetails {
    manufacturer: String,
    product: String,
    serial_number: String,
    bus_number: u8,
    device_address: u8,
    vendor_id: u16,
    product_id: u16,
    maj_device_version: u8,
    min_device_version: u8,
}
```

USBError is for custom error handling, USBList is to store a list of the USB devices detected, and USBDetails is to capture the list of details for each USB device.

5. Let's implement the `Display` trait for the `USBList` struct so that custom formatting can be done to print the contents of the struct:

```
impl fmt::Display for USBList {
    fn fmt(&self, f: &mut fmt::Formatter<'_>) ->
        fmt::Result {
        Ok(for usb in &self.list {
            writeln!(f, "\nUSB Device details")?;
            writeln!(f, "Manufacturer: {}",
                usb.manufacturer)?;
            writeln!(f, "Product: {}", usb.product)?;
            writeln!(f, "Serial number: {}",
                usb.serial_number)?;
            writeln!(f, "Bus number: {}",
                usb.bus_number)?;
            writeln!(f, "Device address: {}",
                usb.device_address)?;
            writeln!(f, "Vendor Id: {}",
                usb.vendor_id)?;
            writeln!(f, "Product Id: {}",
                usb.product_id)?;
            writeln!(f, "Major device version: {}",
                usb.maj_device_version)?;
            writeln!(f, "Minor device version: {}",
                usb.min_device_version)?;
        })
    }
}
```

6. Next, we'll implement `From` traits for the `USBError` struct so that errors from the `libusb` crate and from the Rust Standard Library are automatically converted into the `USBError` type when we use the ? operator:

```
impl From<libusb::Error> for USBError {
    fn from(_e: libusb::Error) -> Self {
        USBError {
            err: "Error in accessing USB
```

```
                    device".to_string(),
            }
        }
    }
    impl From<std::io::Error> for USBError {
        fn from(e: std::io::Error) -> Self {
            USBError { err: e.to_string() }
        }
    }
```

7. Let's next look at the function to write the details retrieved for all the attached devices to an output file:

```
//Function to write details to output file
fn write_to_file(usb: USBList) -> Result<(), USBError> {
    let mut file_handle = File::create
        ("usb_details.txt")?;
    write!(file_handle, "{}\n", usb)?;
    Ok(())
}
```

We can now move on to the main() function.

Writing the main() function

In this section, we'll write the main() function, which sets up the device context, gets a list of connected USB devices, and then iterates through the list of devices to retrieve the details of each device. We'll also write a function to print out the device details:

1. We'll start with the main() function:

```
fn main() -> Result<(), USBError> {
    // Get libusb context
    let context = Context::new()?;

    //Get list of devices
    let mut device_list = USBList { list: vec![] };
    for device in context.devices()?.iter() {
        let device_desc = device.device_descriptor()?;
```

```
        let device_handle = context
            .open_device_with_vid_pid(
                device_desc.vendor_id(),
                device_desc.product_id())
            .unwrap();

        // For each USB device, get the information
        let usb_details = get_device_information(
            device, &device_handle)?;
        device_list.list.push(usb_details);
    }
    println!("\n{}", device_list);
    write_to_file(device_list)?;
    Ok(())
}
```

In the `main()` function, we're first creating a new `libusb` `Context` that can return the list of connected devices. We are then iterating through the device list obtained from the `Context` struct, and calling the `get_device_information()` function for each USB device. The details are finally also printed out to an output file by calling the `write_to_file()` function that we saw earlier.

2. To wrap up the code, let's write the function to get the device details:

```
// Function to print device information
fn get_device_information(device: Device, handle:
    &DeviceHandle) -> Result<USBDetails, USBError> {
    let device_descriptor =
        device.device_descriptor()?;
    let timeout = Duration::from_secs(1);
    let languages = handle.read_languages(timeout)?;
    let language = languages[0];
    // Get device manufacturer name
    let manufacturer =
        handle.read_manufacturer_string(
            language, &device_descriptor, timeout)?;
    // Get device USB product name
```

```
let product = handle.read_product_string(
    language, &device_descriptor, timeout)?;
//Get product serial number
let product_serial_number =
    match handle.read_serial_number_string(
        language, &device_descriptor, timeout) {
        Ok(s) => s,
        Err(_) => "Not available".into(),
    };
// Populate the USBDetails struct
Ok(USBDetails {
    manufacturer,
    product,
    serial_number: product_serial_number,
    bus_number: device.bus_number(),
    device_address: device.address(),
    vendor_id: device_descriptor.vendor_id(),
    product_id: device_descriptor.product_id(),
    maj_device_version:
        device_descriptor.device_version().0,
    min_device_version:
        device_descriptor.device_version().1,
})
}
```

This concludes the code. Make sure to plug in a USB device (such as a thumb drive) to the computer. Run the code with cargo run. You should see the list of attached USB devices printed to the terminal, and also written to the output usb_details.txt file.

Note that in this example, we have demonstrated how to do file I/O using both an external crate (for retrieving USB device details) and the standard library (for writing to an output file). We've unified error handling using a common error handling struct, and automated conversions of error types to this custom error type.

The Rust crates ecosystem (crates.io) has similar crates to interact with other types of devices and filesystems. You can experiment with them.

This concludes the section on writing a program to retrieve USB details.

Summary

In this chapter, we reviewed the foundational concepts of device management in Unix/Linux. We looked at how to do buffered reads and writes using the `std::io` module. We then learned how to interact with the standard input, standard output, and standard error streams of a process. We also saw how to chain readers together and use iterators for reading from devices. We then looked at the error handling features with the `std::io` module. We concluded with a project to detect the list of connected USB devices and printed out the details of each USB device both to the terminal and to an output file.

The Rust Standard Library provides a clean layer of abstraction for doing I/O operations on any type of device. This encourages the Rust ecosystem to implement these standard interfaces for any type of device, enabling Rust system programmers to interact with different devices in a uniform manner. Continuing on the topic of I/O, in the next chapter, we will learn how to do network I/O operations using the Rust Standard Library.

11
Learning Network Programming

In the previous chapter, we learned how to communicate with peripheral devices from Rust programs. In this chapter, we will switch our focus to another important system programming topic – networking.

Most modern operating systems, including Unix/Linux and Windows variants, have native support for networking using TCP/IP. Do you know how you can use TCP/IP to send byte streams or messages from one computer to another? Do you want to know what kind of language support Rust provides for synchronous network communications between two processes running on different machines? Are you interested in learning the basics of configuring TCP and UDP sockets, and working with network addresses and listeners in Rust? Then, read on.

We will cover these topics in the following order:

- Reviewing networking basics in Linux
- Understanding networking primitives in the Rust standard library
- Programming with TCP and UDP in Rust
- Writing a TCP reverse proxy (project)

By the end of this chapter, you will have learned how to work with network addresses, determine address types, and do address conversions. You will also learn how to create and configure sockets and query on them. You will work with TCP listeners, create a TCP socket server, and receive data. Lastly, you'll put these concepts into practice through an example project.

It is important to learn these topics because sockets-based programming using TCP or UDP forms the basis for writing distributed programs. Sockets help two processes on different (or even the same) machines to establish communication with each other and exchange information. They form the foundation for practically all web and distributed applications on the internet, including how an internet browser accesses a web page and how a mobile application retrieves data from an API server. In this chapter, you will learn what kind of support is provided by the Rust standard library for *socket-based* network communications.

Technical requirements

Verify that `rustup`, `rustc`, and `cargo` have been installed correctly with the following command:

```
rustup --version
rustc --version
cargo --version
```

The Git repo for the code in this chapter can be found at `https://github.com/PacktPublishing/Practical-System-Programming-for-Rust-Developers/tree/master/Chapter11`.

Reviewing networking basics in Linux

The internet connects several different networks across the globe, enabling machines across networks to communicate with each other in different ways, including the **request-response** model (synchronous), **asynchronous messaging**, and **publish-subscribe**-style notifications. *Figure 11.1* shows an example of a connection between two networks:

Internet router connecting two networks

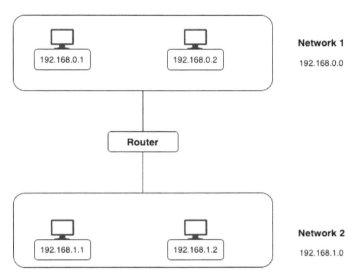

Figure 11.1 – Internet router connecting two networks

The internet also provides abstractions in the form of **networking protocols and standards** to make it easy for hosts on different networks to communicate with each other.

Examples of standards include a common *host addressing format*, a combination of host address and port to define a *network endpoint*. The IP address of a host is a *32-bit* number for IPv4 addresses and a *128-bit* number for IPv6 addresses.

Examples of network protocols include for web browsers to retrieve documents from web servers, **domain name system** (**DNS**) to map domain names to host addresses, the IP protocol to package and route packets of data across the internet, and TCP to add reliability and error handling for IP data packets.

In particular, *networking protocols* are very important in defining how information is transmitted and interpreted by programs running in different host computers across different networks. The **TCP/IP protocol suite** is the foundation of how the internet, which we use on a daily basis, enables our digital world of information, transactions, and entertainment.

Figure 11.2 shows the layered TCP/IP protocol suite:

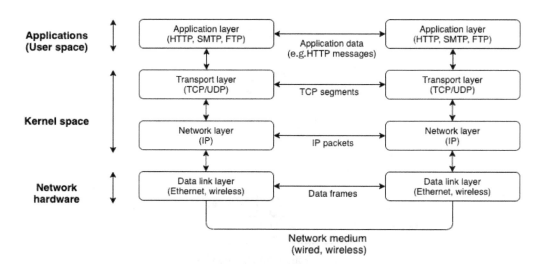

Figure 11.2 – Internet router connecting two networks

In the previous chapter, we discussed device drivers. In *Figure 11.2*, the lowest layer of the *TCP/IP protocol suite* shown – the **data link layer** – comprises the **device driver** and **network interface card** corresponding to the network medium used for communication between the hosts (for example, coax cable, fiber, or wireless). The data link layer assembles data packets received from the higher network (IP) layer into **data frames**, and transmits them over the physical link.

The next layer up in the TCP/IP protocol suite is the **IP layer**, which is the most important layer in the TCP/IP stack. It assembles data into packets and sends them to the data link layer. The IP layer is also responsible for routing data across the internet. This is achieved by adding a header for each datagram (packet) transmitted, which includes the address of the remote host to which the packet should be transmitted. Two packets sent from host A to host B can take different routes through the internet. IP is a connectionless protocol, which means there is no communication channel created between two hosts to have multi-step communication. This layer just sends a data packet from one host IP address to another host IP address without any guarantees.

The next layer up in the TCP/IP protocol suite is the **transport layer**. Here, there are two popular protocols used on the internet – TCP and UDP. **TCP** stands for **transmission control protocol** and **UDP** is **user datagram protocol**. While the network (IP) layer is concerned with sending data packets between two hosts, the transport layer (TCP and UDP) is concerned with sending data streams between two processes (applications or programs) running on the same host or different hosts.

If there are two applications running on a single host IP address, the way to uniquely identify each application is by using a *port number*. Each application that is involved in network communications listens on a specific port, which is a 16-bit number.

Examples of popular ports are 80 for the *HTTP* protocol, 443 for the *HTTPS* protocol, and 22 for the *SSH* protocol. The combination of an IP address and a port number is called a **socket**. We'll see in this chapter how to work with sockets using the Rust standard library. UDP, like IP, is connectionless and does not incorporate any reliability mechanisms. But it is fast and has a low overhead compared to TCP. It is used in higher-level services, such as DNS, to get host IP addresses corresponding to a domain name.

Compared to UDP, TCP provides a connection-oriented, reliable communication channel between two endpoints (application/user space programs) over which byte streams can be exchanged while preserving the sequence of data. It incorporates features such as **retransmission** in the case of errors, **acknowledgments** of packets received, and **timeouts**. We'll discuss TCP-based communication in detail in this chapter and later build a reverse proxy using TCP socket-based communications.

The uppermost layer in the TCP/IP protocol suite is the **application layer**. While the TCP layer is connection-oriented and works with byte streams, it has no knowledge of the semantics of a message transmitted. This is provided by the application layer. For example, HTTP, which is the most popular application protocol on the internet, uses HTTP request and response messages to communicate between **HTTP clients** (for example, internet browsers) and **HTTP servers** (for example, web servers). The application layer reads the byte streams received from the TCP layer and interprets them into HTTP messages, which are then processed by the application program that we write in Rust or other languages. There are several libraries (or crates) available in the Rust ecosystem that implement the HTTP protocol, so Rust programs can leverage them (or write their own) to send and receive HTTP messages. In the example project for this chapter, we will write some code to interpret an incoming HTTP request message and send back an HTTP response message.

The primary Rust Standard Library module for networking communications is `std::net`. This focuses on writing code for communicating using TCP and UDP. The Rust `std::net` module does not deal directly with the data link layer or application layer of the TCP/IP protocol suite. With this background, we are ready to understand the networking primitives provided in the Rust standard library for TCP and UDP communications.

Understanding networking primitives in the Rust standard library

In this section, we'll discuss the foundational data structures in the Rust standard library for networking. *Figure 11.3* lists the commonly used data structures:

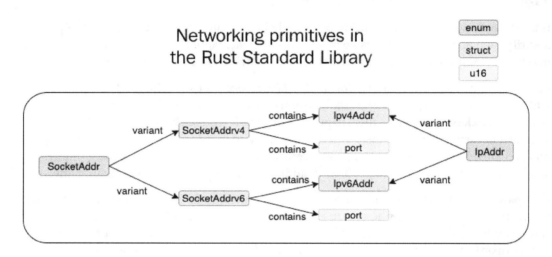

Figure 11.3 – Networking primitives in the Rust standard library

Let's look at the data structures one by one:

- `Ipv4Addr`: This is a struct that stores a 32-bit integer representing an IPv4 address, and provides associated functions and methods to set and query address values.

- `Ipv6Add`: This is a struct that stores a 128-bit integer representing an IPv6 address, and provides associated functions and methods to query and set address values.

- `SocketAddrv4`: This is a struct representing an internet domain socket. It stores an IPv4 address and a 16-bit port number and provides associated functions and methods to set and query socket values.

- `SocketAddrv6`: This is a struct representing an internet domain socket. It stores an IPv6 address and a 16-bit port number and provides associated functions and methods to set and query socket values.

- `IpAddr`: This is an enum with two variants – `V4 (Ipv4Addr)` and `V6 (Ipv6Addr)`. This means that it can hold either an IPv4 host address or an IPv6 host address.

- SocketAddr: This is an enum with two variants – V4 (SocketAddrV4) and V6 (SocketAddrV6). This means that it can hold either an IPv4 socket address or an IPv6 socket address.

> **Note**
>
> The size of an *Ipv6* address might vary, depending on the target operating system architecture.

Let's now see a few examples of how to use them. We'll start by creating IPv4 and IPv6 addresses.

In the example shown next, we're creating IPv4 and IPv6 addresses using the std::net module and using built-in methods to query on the created addresses. The is_loopback() method confirms whether the address corresponds to localhost, and the segments() method returns the various segments of the IP address. Note also that the std::net module provides a special constant, Ipv4Addr::LOCALHOST, which can be used to initialize the IP address with the localhost (loopback) address:

```
use std::net::{Ipv4Addr, Ipv6Addr};

fn main() {
    // Create a new IPv4 address with four 8-bit integers
    let ip_v4_addr1 = Ipv4Addr::new(106, 201, 34, 209);
    // Use the built-in constant to create a new loopback
    // (localhost) address
    let ip_v4_addr2 = Ipv4Addr::LOCALHOST;
    println!(
        "Is ip_v4_addr1 a loopback address? {}",
        ip_v4_addr1.is_loopback()
    );
    println!(
        "Is ip_v4_addr2 a loopback address? {}",
        ip_v4_addr2.is_loopback()
    );
    //Create a new IPv6 address with eight 16-bit
    // integers, represented in hex
    let ip_v6_addr = Ipv6Addr::new(2001, 0000, 3238,
        0xDFE1, 0063, 0000, 0000, 0xFEFB);
```

```
        println!("IPV6 segments {:?}", ip_v6_addr.segments());
}
```

The following example shows how to use the `IpAddr` enum. In this example, usage of the `IpAddr` enum is shown to create IPv4 and IPv6 addresses. The `IpAddr` enum helps us to define IP addresses in a more generic way in our program data structures and gives us the flexibility to work with both IPv4 and IPv6 addresses in our programs:

```
use std::net::{IpAddr, Ipv4Addr, Ipv6Addr};

fn main() {
    // Create an ipv4 address
    let ip_v4_addr = IpAddr::V4(Ipv4Addr::new(106, 201, 34,
        209));
    // check if an address is ipv4 or ipv6 address
    println!("Is ip_v4_addr an ipv4 address? {}",
        ip_v4_addr.is_ipv4());
    println!("Is ip_v4_addr an ipv6 address? {}",
        ip_v4_addr.is_ipv6());

    // Create an ipv6 address
    let ip_v6_addr = IpAddr::V6(Ipv6Addr::new(0, 0, 0, 0,
        0, 0, 0, 1));
    println!("Is ip_v6_addr an ipv6 address? {}",
        ip_v6_addr.is_ipv6());
}
```

Let's now turn our attention to sockets. As discussed earlier, sockets comprise an IP address and a port. Rust has separate data structures for both IPv4 and IPv6 sockets. Let's see an example next. Here, we're creating a new IPv4 socket, and querying for the IP address and port numbers from the constructed socket, using the `ip()` and `port()` methods, respectively:

```
use std::net::{IpAddr, Ipv4Addr, SocketAddr};
fn main() {
    // Create an ipv4 socket
    let socket = SocketAddr::new(IpAddr::V4(
        Ipv4Addr::new(127,0,0,1)),8000);
    println!("Socket address is {}, port is {}",
```

```
            socket.ip(), socket.port());
    println!("Is this IPv6 socket?{}",socket.is_ipv6());
}
```

IP addresses and sockets represent the foundational data structures for network programming using the Rust standard library. In the next section, we'll see how to write programs in Rust that can communicate over TCP and UDP protocols.

Programming with TCP and UDP in Rust

As discussed earlier, TCP and UDP are the fundamental transport layer network protocols for the internet. In this section, let's first write a UDP server and client. Then we'll look at doing the same using TCP.

Create a new project called tcpudp where we will write the TCP and UDP servers and clients:

```
cargo new tcpudp && cd tcpudp
```

Let's first look at network communication using UDP.

Writing a UDP server and client

In this section, we'll learn how to configure UDP sockets, and how to send and receive data. We'll write both a UDP server and a UDP client.

Starting with the UDP server

In the example shown, we're creating a UDP server by binding to a local socket using UdpSocket::bind. We're then creating a fixed-size buffer, and listening for incoming data streams in a loop. If data is received, we are spawning a new thread to process the data by echoing it back to the sender. As we already covered how to spawn new threads in *Chapter 9, Managing Concurrency*, it shouldn't need explanation again here:

tcpudp/src/bin/udp-server.rs

```
use std::str;
use std::thread;

fn main() {
    let socket = UdpSocket::bind("127.0.0.1:3000").expect(
```

```rust
            "Unable to bind to port");
    let mut buffer = [0; 1024];
    loop {
        let socket_new = socket.try_clone().expect(
            "Unable to clone socket");
        match socket_new.recv_from(&mut buffer) {
            Ok((num_bytes, src_addr)) => {
                thread::spawn(move || {
                    let send_buffer = &mut
                        buffer[..num_bytes];
                    println!(
                        "Received from client:{}",
                        str::from_utf8(
                            send_buffer).unwrap()
                    );
                    let response_string =
                        format!("Received this: {}",
                            String::from_utf8_lossy(
                            send_buffer));
                    socket_new
                        .send_to(&response_string
                            .as_bytes(), &src_addr)
                        .expect("error in sending datagram
                            to remote socket");
                });
            }
            Err(err) => {
                println!("Error in receiving datagrams over
                    UDP: {}", err);
            }
        }
    }
}
```

Writing a UDP client to send data packets to the server

In the code shown, we're first asking the standard library to bind to a local port (by providing an address port combination of 0.0.0.0:0, which allows the operating system to pick a transient IP address/port to send the datagram from). Then, we are trying to connect to the remote socket where the server is running, and displaying an error in the case of failure to connect. In the case of a successful connection, we are printing out the socket address of the peer using the peer_addr() method. Lastly, we are using the send() method to send a message to the remote socket (server):

tcpudp/src/bin/udp-client.rs

```
use std::net::UdpSocket;
fn main() {
    // Create a local UDP socket
    let socket = UdpSocket::bind("0.0.0.0:0").expect(
        "Unable to bind to socket");
    // Connect the socket to a remote socket
    socket
        .connect("127.0.0.1:3000")
        .expect("Could not connect to UDP server");
    println!("socket peer addr is {:?}",
        socket.peer_addr());
    // Send a datagram to the remote socket
    socket
        .send("Hello: sent using send() call".as_bytes())
        .expect("Unable to send bytes");
}
```

Run the UDP server with the following:

```
cargo run --bin udp-server
```

From a separate terminal, run the UDP client with the following:

```
cargo run --bin udp-client
```

You'll see the message received at the server, which was sent from the client.

We've seen so far how to write programs in Rust to do communications over UDP. Let's now look at how TCP communications are done.

Writing a TCP server and client

In this section, we'll learn how to configure TCP listeners, create a TCP socket server, and send and receive data over TCP. We'll write both a TCP server and a TCP client.

We'll start with the TCP server. In the code shown next, we're using `TcpListener::bind` to create a TCP server listening on a socket. Then, we use the `incoming()` method, which returns an iterator of incoming connections. Each connection returns a TCP stream that can be read from using the `stream.read()` method. We're reading the data and printing out the values. Also, we're echoing back the received data over the connection using the `stream.write()` method:

tcpudp/src/bin/`tcp-server.rs`

```
use std::io::{Read, Write};
use std::net::TcpListener;
fn main() {
    let connection_listener = TcpListener::bind(
        "127.0.0.1:3000").unwrap();
    println!("Running on port 3000");
    for stream in connection_listener.incoming() {
        let mut stream = stream.unwrap();
        println!("Connection established");
        let mut buffer = [0; 100];
        stream.read(&mut buffer).unwrap();
        println!("Received from client: {}",
            String::from_utf8_lossy(&buffer));
        stream.write(&mut buffer).unwrap();
    }
}
```

This concludes the code for the TCP server. Let's now write a TCP client to send some data to the TCP server.

In the TCP client code shown next, we're using the `TcpStream::connect` function to connect to a **remote socket** where the server is listening. This function returns a **TCP stream**, which can be *read from* and *written to* (as we saw in the previous example). Here, we're first going to write some data to the TCP stream, and then read back the response received from the server:

tcpudp/src/bin/tcp-client.rs

```rust
use std::io::{Read, Write};
use std::net::TcpStream;
use std::str;
fn main() {
    let mut stream = TcpStream::connect(
        "localhost:3000").unwrap();
    let msg_to_send = "Hello from TCP client";
    stream.write(msg_to_send.as_bytes()).unwrap();
    let mut buffer = [0; 200];
    stream.read(&mut buffer).unwrap();
    println!(
        "Got echo back from server:{:?}",
        str::from_utf8(&buffer)
            .unwrap()
            .trim_end_matches(char::from(0))
    );
}
```

Run the TCP server with the following:

```
cargo run --bin  tcp-server
```

From a separate terminal, run the TCP client with the following:

```
cargo run --bin  tcp-client
```

You'll see the message that was sent from the client being received at the server and echoed back.

This concludes this section on performing TCP and UDP communications using the Rust standard library. In the next section, let's use the concepts learned so far to build a TCP reverse proxy.

Writing a TCP reverse proxy (project)

In this section, we will demonstrate the basic functionality of a **TCP reverse proxy** using just the Rust standard library, without the use of any external libraries or frameworks.

A proxy server is an intermediary software service that is used while navigating across multiple networks on the internet. There are two types of proxy servers – a **forward proxy** and a **reverse proxy**. A forward proxy acts as an intermediary for clients making requests out to the internet, and a reverse proxy acts as an intermediary for servers. *Figure 11.4* illustrates the usage of forward and reverse proxy servers:

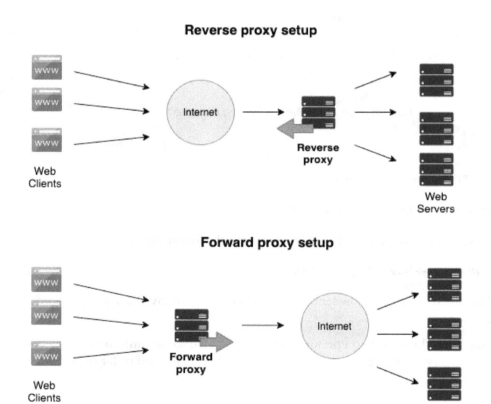

Figure 11.4 – Types of proxy servers

Forward proxies act as gateways to the internet for a group of client machines. They help individual client machines to hide their IP addresses while browsing the internet. They also help to enforce organizational policies for machines within a network to access the internet, such as restricting websites to visit.

While a forward proxy acts on behalf of clients, a reverse proxy acts on behalf of hosts (for example, web servers). They hide the identity of the backend servers from the clients. The clients only make a request to the reverse proxy server address/domain, and the reverse proxy server, in turn, knows how to route that request to the backend server (also sometimes called the **origin server**), and returns the response received from the origin server to the requesting client. A reverse proxy can also be used to perform other functions, such as load balancing, caching, and compression. We will, however, just focus on demonstrating the core concept of a reverse proxy by directing requests received from clients to the backend origin servers and routing responses back to the requesting client.

To demonstrate a working *reverse proxy*, we will build two servers:

- **Origin server**: TCP server (which understands limited HTTP semantics).

- **Reverse proxy server**: Client requests coming to this server will be directed to the *origin server*, and responses from the origin server will be routed back to the client.

Create a new project to write the origin and proxy servers:

```
cargo new tcpproxy && cd tcpproxy
```

Create two files: `tcpproxy/src/bin/origin.rs` and `tcpproxy/src/bin/proxy.rs`.

Let's start with the code for the origin server. This server will do the following:

- Receive an incoming HTTP request.

- Extract the first line of the request (called the **HTTP request line**).

- Accept a `GET HTTP` request on a specific route (for example, `/order/status/1`).

- Return the status of the order. We will demonstrate parsing of the HTTP request line to retrieve the order number and just send back a response stating **Order status for order number 1 is: Shipped**.

Let's see the code now for the origin server.

Writing the origin server – structs and methods

We'll first see the code for module imports, struct definitions and methods. Then, we'll see the code for the main() function. All the code for the origin server can be found in tcpproxy/src/bin/origin.rs.

The module imports are shown first in the code snippet. We're importing various modules from the standard library here. The std::io module will be used to read and write to the TCP stream, and the std::net module provides the primitives for the TCP listener, sockets, and addresses. The string modules (std::str and std::String) are used for string manipulations and handling string parsing errors:

tcpproxy/src/bin/origin.rs

```
use std::io::{Read, Write};
use std::net::TcpListener;
use std::net::{IpAddr, Ipv4Addr, SocketAddr};
use std::str;
use std::str::FromStr;
use std::string::ParseError;
```

Next, let's declare a struct to hold the incoming HTTP request line (the first line of the multi-line HTTP request message). We'll also write some helper methods for this struct.

In the code shown next, we'll declare a RequestLine struct consisting of three fields – the HTTP method, the path of the resource requested, and the HTTP protocol version supported by the internet browser or another HTTP client sending the request. We'll also write some methods to return the values of the struct members. Custom logic will be implemented for the get_order_number() method. If we get a request for a resource with the /order/status/1 path, we will split this string by /, and return the last part of the string, which is order number 1:

tcpproxy/src/bin/origin.rs

```
#[derive(Debug)]
struct RequestLine {
    method: Option<String>,
    path: Option<String>,
    protocol: Option<String>,
}
```

```rust
impl RequestLine {
    fn method(&self) -> String {
        if let Some(method) = &self.method {
            method.to_string()
        } else {
            String::from("")
        }
    }
    fn path(&self) -> String {
        if let Some(path) = &self.path {
            path.to_string()
        } else {
            String::from("")
        }
    }
    fn get_order_number(&self) -> String {
        let path = self.path();
        let path_tokens: Vec<String> = path.split("/").map(
            |s| s.parse().unwrap()).collect();
        path_tokens[path_tokens.len() - 1].clone()
    }
}
```

Let's also implement the `FromStr` trait for the `RequestLine` struct so that we can convert the incoming HTTP request line (string) into our internal Rust data structure – `RequestLine`. The structure of the HTTP request line is shown here:

```
<HTTP-method> <path> <protocol>
```

These three values are separated by white spaces and are all present in the first line of an HTTP request message. In the program shown, we're going to parse these three values and load them into the `RequestLine` struct. Later, we will further parse the path member and extract the order number from it, for processing:

tcpproxy/src/bin/`origin.rs`

```rust
impl FromStr for RequestLine {
    type Err = ParseError;
```

```
fn from_str(msg: &str) -> Result<Self, Self::Err> {
    let mut msg_tokens = msg.split_ascii_whitespace();
    let method = match msg_tokens.next() {
        Some(token) => Some(String::from(token)),
        None => None,
    };
    let path = match msg_tokens.next() {
        Some(token) => Some(String::from(token)),
        None => None,
    };
    let protocol = match msg_tokens.next() {
        Some(token) => Some(String::from(token)),
        None => None,
    };

    Ok(Self {
        method: method,
        path: path,
        protocol: protocol,
    })
}
}
```

We've so far seen the module imports, struct definition, and methods for the RequestLine struct. Let's now write the main() function.

Writing the origin server – the main() function

In the main function of the origin server, we are going to do the following:

1. Start the TCP server.

2. Listen for incoming connections.

For each incoming connection, we will then perform the following:

1. Read the first line of the incoming HTTP request message and convert it into a `RequestLine` struct.

2. Construct the HTTP response message and write it to the TCP stream.

Let's now see the code for the main function in two parts – starting the TCP server and listening for connections, and processing incoming HTTP requests.

Starting the TCP server and listening for connections

To start the TCP server, we will construct a socket address, and bind to a socket using `TcpStream::bind`:

tcpproxy/src/bin/`origin.rs`

```
// Start the origin server
let port = 3000;
let socket_addr = SocketAddr::new(IpAddr::V4(
    Ipv4Addr::new(127, 0, 0, 1)), port);
let connection_listener = TcpListener::bind(
    socket_addr).unwrap();


println!("Running on port: {}", port);
```

Then, we'll listen for incoming connections, and read from the stream for each connection:

tcpproxy/src/bin/`origin.rs`

```
for stream in connection_listener.incoming() {
    //processing of incoming HTTP requests
}
```

Let's now see the processing of the incoming request.

Processing incoming HTTP requests

For processing incoming requests, the first step is to retrieve the first line of the request message and convert it into a RequestLine struct. In the code shown next, we're using the lines() method to return an iterator of lines. We're then retrieving the first line of the HTTP request using lines().next(). We are converting this into a RequestLine struct using RequestLine::from_str(). This is possible only because we have implemented the FromStr trait for the RequestLine struct:

tcpproxy/src/bin/origin.rs

```rust
        // Read the first line of incoming HTTP request
        // and convert it into RequestLine struct
        let mut stream = stream.unwrap();
        let mut buffer = [0; 200];
        stream.read(&mut buffer).unwrap();
        let req_line = "";
        let string_request_line =
            if let Some(line) = str::from_utf8(
                &buffer).unwrap().lines().next() {
                line
            } else {
                println!("Invalid request line received");
                req_line
            };
        let req_line = RequestLine::from_str(
            string_request_line).unwrap();
```

Now that we have parsed the required data into the RequestLine struct, we can process it and send the HTTP response back. Let's see the code. If the message received is not a GET request, if the path in the request message does not start with /order/status, or if the order number is not provided, construct an HTTP response message with the 404 Not found HTTP status code:

tcpproxy/src/bin/origin.rs

```rust
        // Construct the HTTP response string
        let html_response_string;
        let order_status;
```

```
        println!("len is {}", req_line.get_order_number()
            .len());

        if req_line.method() != "GET"
            || !req_line.path().starts_with(
                "/order/status")
            || req_line.get_order_number().len() == 0
        {
            if req_line.get_order_number().len() == 0 {
                order_status = format!("Please provide
                    valid order number");
            } else {
                order_status = format!("Sorry,this page is
                    not found");
            }

            html_response_string = format!(
                "HTTP/1.1 404 Not Found\nContent-Type:
                    text/html\nContent-Length:{}\n\n{}",
                order_status.len(),
                order_status
            );
    }
```

If the request is correctly formatted to retrieve the order status for an order number, we should construct an HTML response message with the 200 OK HTTP status code for sending the response back to the client:

tcpproxy/src/bin/origin.rs

```
        else {
            order_status = format!(
                "Order status for order number {} is:
                    Shipped\n",
                req_line.get_order_number()
            );
            html_response_string = format!(
```

```
            "HTTP/1.1 200 OK\nContent-Type:
                text/html\nContent-Length:{}\n\n{}",
            order_status.len(),
            order_status
        );
    }
```

Lastly, let's write the constructed HTTP response message to the TCP stream:

tcpproxy/src/bin/origin.rs

```
stream.write(html_response_string.as_bytes()).unwrap();
```

This concludes the code for the origin server. The complete code can be found in the Packt GitHub repo for `Chapter12` at `tcpproxy/src/bin/origin.rs`.

Run the program with the following:

```
cargo run --bin origin
```

You should see the server start with the following message:

Running on port: 3000

In a browser window, enter the following URL:

```
localhost:3000/order/status/2
```

You should see the following response displayed on the browser screen:

Order status for order number 2 is: Shipped

Try entering a URL with an invalid path, such as the following:

```
localhost:3000/invalid/path
```

You should see the following message displayed:

Sorry, this page is not found

Further, you can provide a valid path but without an order number, such as the following:

```
localhost:3000/order/status/
```

You'll see the following error message displayed:

Please provide valid order number

With this, we conclude the section on the origin server. Let's now write the code for the *reverse proxy*.

Writing the reverse proxy server

Let's dive into the code for the reverse proxy, starting with the module imports. All of the code for this reverse proxy server can be found in `tcpproxy/src/bin/proxy.rs`.

Let's first look at the module imports.

The `std::env` module is used to read command-line parameters. `std::io` is used to read and write to TCP streams. `std::net` is the main module for communications, as we have seen. `std::process` is used to exit the program in case of unrecoverable errors. `std::thread` is used to spawn a new thread for processing incoming requests:

tcpproxy/src/bin/`proxy.rs`

```
use std::env;
use std::io::{Read, Write};
use std::net::{TcpListener, TcpStream};
use std::process::exit;
use std::thread;
```

Let's write the `main()` function next. When we start the reverse proxy server, let's accept two command-line parameters, corresponding to socket addresses of the *reverse proxy* and *origin server*, respectively. If two command-line parameters are not provided by the user, then print out an error message and exit the program. Then, let's parse the command-line inputs and start the server using `TcpListener::bind`. After binding to the local port, we connect to the origin server and print out an error message in the case of failure to connect.

Place the following code within the `main()` function block:

tcpproxy/src/bin/`proxy.rs`

```
    // Accept command-line parameters for proxy_stream and
    // origin_stream
    let args: Vec<_> = env::args().collect();
```

```
    if args.len() < 3 {
        eprintln!("Please provide proxy-from and proxy-to
            addresses");
        exit(2);
    }
    let proxy_server = &args[1];
    let origin_server = &args[2];
    // Start a socket server on proxy_stream
    let proxy_listener;
    if let Ok(proxy) = TcpListener::bind(proxy_server) {
        proxy_listener = proxy;
        let addr = proxy_listener.local_addr()
            .unwrap().ip();
        let port = proxy_listener.local_addr().unwrap()
            .port();
        if let Err(_err) = TcpStream::connect(
            origin_server) {
            println!("Please re-start the origin server");
            exit(1);
        }
        println!("Running on Addr:{}, Port:{}\n", addr,
            port);
    } else {
        eprintln!("Unable to bind to specified proxy
            port");
        exit(1);
    }
```

After starting the server, we must listen for incoming connections. For every connection, spawn a separate thread to handle the connection. The thread in turn calls the handle_connection() function, which we will describe shortly. Then, join the child thread handles with the main thread to make sure that the main() function does not *exit* before the child threads are completed:

tcpproxy/src/bin/`proxy.rs`

```
// Listen for incoming connections from proxy_server
// and read byte stream
let mut thread_handles = Vec::new();
for proxy_stream in proxy_listener.incoming() {
    let mut proxy_stream = proxy_stream.expect("Error
        in incoming TCP connection");
    // Establish a new TCP connection to origin_stream
    let mut origin_stream =
        TcpStream::connect(origin_server).expect(
            "Please re-start the origin server");
    let handle =
        thread::spawn(move || handle_connection(&mut
            proxy_stream, &mut origin_stream));
    thread_handles.push(handle);
}
for handle in thread_handles {
    handle.join().expect("Unable to join child
        thread");
}
```

This concludes the `main()` function. Let's now write the code for `handle_function()`. This contains the core logic for proxying to the origin server:

tcpproxy/src/bin/`proxy.rs`

```
fn handle_connection(proxy_stream: &mut TcpStream,
    origin_stream: &mut TcpStream) {
    let mut in_buffer: Vec<u8> = vec![0; 200];
    let mut out_buffer: Vec<u8> = vec![0; 200];
    // Read incoming request to proxy_stream
    if let Err(err) = proxy_stream.read(&mut in_buffer) {
        println!("Error in reading from incoming proxy
            stream: {}", err);
    } else {
        println!(
```

```
            "1: Incoming client request: {}",
            String::from_utf8_lossy(&in_buffer)
    );
}
// Write the byte stream to origin_stream
let _ = origin_stream.write(&mut in_buffer).unwrap();
println!("2: Forwarding request to origin server\n");
// Read response from the backend server
let _ = origin_stream.read(&mut out_buffer).unwrap();
println!(
    "3: Received response from origin server: {}",
    String::from_utf8_lossy(&out_buffer)
);
// Write response back to the proxy client
let _ = proxy_stream.write(&mut out_buffer).unwrap();
println!("4: Forwarding response back to client");
}
```

For ease of debugging, the four key steps involved in the proxy functionality are marked in the code and also printed out to the console:

1. In the first step, we read the incoming data from the incoming *client connection.*

2. In the second step, we open a new TCP stream with the *origin server,* and send the data we received from the *client* to the origin server.

3. In the third step, we are reading the response we received from the origin server and store the data in a buffer.

4. In the final step, we are using the data received in the previous step to write to the TCP stream corresponding to the client that sent the original request.

This concludes the code for reverse proxy. We've kept the functionality simple and handled only the base case. As an extra exercise, you can add edge cases to make the server more robust, and also add additional functionality such as load-balancing and caching.

This concludes the code for the origin server. The complete code can be found in the Packt GitHub repo for Chapter12 at tcpproxy/src/bin/proxy.rs.

First, start the origin server with the following:

```
cargo run --bin origin
```

Then, run the proxy server with the following:

```
cargo run --bin proxy localhost:3001 localhost:3000
```

The first command-line parameter that we pass is used by the *reverse proxy* server to bind to the specified socket address. The second command-line parameter corresponds to the socket address at which the *origin server* is running. This is the address to which we have to proxy the incoming requests.

Let's now run the same tests from a browser that we did for the origin server, only this time we'll send the request to port 3001, where the reverse proxy server is running. You'll notice that you will get similar response messages. This demonstrates that the requests sent by the internet browser client are being proxied by the reverse proxy server to the backend origin server, and the response received from the origin server is being routed back to the browser client.

You should see the server start with the following message:

Running on Addr:127.0.0.1, Port:3001

In a browser window, enter the following URL:

```
localhost:3001/order/status/2
```

You should see the following response displayed on the browser screen:

Order status for order number 2 is: Shipped

Try entering a URL with an invalid path, such as the following:

```
localhost:3001/invalid/path
```

You should see the following message displayed:

Sorry, this page is not found

Further, you can provide a valid path but without an order number, such as the following:

```
localhost:3001/order/status/
```

You'll see the following error message displayed:

Please provide valid order number

This concludes this example project, where we wrote two servers – a TCP origin server and a simple TCP reverse proxy server.

Summary

In this chapter, we reviewed the basics of networking in Linux/Unix. We learned about the networking primitives in the Rust standard library, including data structures for IPv4 and IPv6 addresses, IPv4 and IPv6 sockets, and associated methods. We learned how to create addresses, as well as create sockets and query them.

We then learned how to use UDP sockets and wrote a UDP client and server. We also reviewed the TCP communication basics, including how to configure TCP listeners, how to create a TCP socket server, and how to send and receive data. Lastly, we wrote a project consisting of two servers – an *origin server* and a *reverse proxy server* that routes requests to the origin server.

In the next and final chapter of the book, we'll cover another important topic for system programming – **unsafe Rust and FFI**.

12
Writing Unsafe Rust and FFI

In the previous chapter, we learned about the network primitives built into the Rust Standard Library and saw how to write programs that communicate over TCP and UDP. In this chapter, we will conclude the book by covering a few advanced topics related to **unsafe Rust** and **foreign function interfaces** (FFIs).

We have seen how the Rust compiler enforces rules of ownership for memory and thread safety. While this is a blessing most of the time, there may be situations when you want to implement a new low-level data structure or call out to external programs written in other languages. Or, you may want to perform other operations prohibited by the Rust compiler, such as dereferencing raw pointers, mutating static variables, or dealing with uninitialized memory. Have you wondered how the Rust Standard Library itself makes system calls to manage resources, when system calls involve dealing with raw pointers? The answer lies in understanding unsafe Rust and FFIs.

In this chapter, we'll first look at why and how Rust code bases use unsafe Rust code. Then, we'll cover the basics of FFIs and talk about special considerations while working with them. We'll also write Rust code that calls a C function, and a C program that calls a Rust function.

We will cover these topics in the following order:

- Introducing unsafe Rust

- Introducing FFIs

- Reviewing guidelines for safe FFIs

- Calling Rust from C (project)

- Understanding the ABI

By the end of this chapter, you will have learned when and how to use unsafe Rust. You will learn how to interface Rust to other programming languages, through FFIs, and learn how to work with them. You'll also get an overview of a few advanced topics, such as **application binary interfaces (ABIs)**, conditional compilation, data layout conventions, and providing instructions to the linker. Understanding these will be helpful when building Rust binaries for different target platforms, and for linking Rust code with code written in other programming languages.

Technical requirements

Verify that `rustup`, `rustc`, and `cargo` have been installed correctly with the following command:

```
rustup --version
rustc --version
cargo --version
```

Since this chapter involves compiling C code and generating a binary, you will need to set up the C development environment on your development machine. After setup, run the following command to verify that the installation is successful:

```
gcc --version
```

If this command does not execute successfully, please revisit your installation.

> **Note**
>
> It is recommended that those developing on a Windows platform use a Linux virtual machine to try out the code in this chapter.
>
> The code in this section has been tested on Ubuntu 20.04 (LTS) x64 and should work on any other Linux variant.

The Git repo for the code in this chapter can be found at `https://github.com/PacktPublishing/Practical-System-Programming-for-Rust-Developers/tree/master/Chapter12`.

Introducing unsafe Rust

So far in this book, we've seen and used Rust language that enforces memory and type safety at compilation time and prevents various kinds of undefined behavior, such as memory overflows, null or invalid pointer constructions, and data races. This is *safe* Rust. In fact, the Rust Standard Library gives us good tools and utilities to write safe, idiomatic Rust, and helps to keep the program safe (and you sane!).

But in some situations, the compiler can *get in the way*. The Rust compiler performs static analysis of code that is conservative (meaning the Rust compiler does not mind generating a few false positives and rejecting valid code, as long as it does not let bad code get through). You, as a programmer, know that a piece of code is safe, but the compiler thinks it is risky, so it rejects this code. This includes operations such as system calls, type coercions, and direct manipulations of memory pointers, which are used in the development of several categories of system software.

Another example is in embedded systems where registers are accessed through a fixed memory address and require the dereferencing of pointers. So, to enable such actions, the Rust language provides the `unsafe` keyword. For Rust as a system programming language, it is essential to enable the programmer to have the means to write low-level code to interface directly with the operating system, bypassing the Rust Standard Library if needed. *This is unsafe Rust*. This is the part of the Rust language that does not adhere to the rules of the borrow checker.

Unsafe Rust can be thought of as a superset of safe Rust. It is a superset because it allows you to do all the things you can do in standard Rust, but you can do more things that are otherwise prohibited by the Rust compiler. In fact, Rust's own compiler, and the standard library, include unsafe Rust code that is carefully written.

How do you distinguish between safe and unsafe Rust code?

Rust provides a convenient and intuitive mechanism where a block of code can be enclosed within an unsafe block using the `unsafe` keyword. Try the following code:

```
fn main() {
    let num = 23;
```

```
    let borrowed_num = &num; // immutable reference to num
    let raw_ptr = borrowed_num as *const i32; // cast the
    // reference borrowed_num to raw pointer
    assert!(*raw_ptr == 23);
}
```

Compile this code with `cargo check` (or run it from Rust playground IDE). You'll see the following error message:

```
error[E0133]: dereference of raw pointer is unsafe and requires
unsafe function or block
```

Let's now modify the code by enclosing the dereferencing of the raw pointer within an unsafe block:

```
fn main() {
    let num = 23;
    let borrowed_num = &num; // immutable reference to num
    let raw_ptr = borrowed_num as *const i32; // cast
    // reference borrowed_num to raw pointer
    unsafe {
        assert!(*raw_ptr == 23);
    }
}
```

You will see that the compilation is successful now, even though this code can potentially cause undefined behavior. This is because, once you enclose some code within an unsafe block, the compiler expects the programmer to ensure the safety of unsafe code.

Let's now look at the kind of operations unsafe Rust enables.

Operations in unsafe Rust

There are really only five key operations in the *unsafe* category – dereferencing a raw pointer, working with mutable static variables, implementing unsafe traits, calling an external function through an FFI interface, and sharing union structs across FFI boundaries.

We'll look at the first three in this section and the last two in the next section:

- **You can dereference a raw pointer**: Unsafe Rust has two new types called **raw pointers** – `*const` T is a pointer type that corresponds to `&T` (immutable reference type) in safe Rust, and `*mut` T is a pointer type that corresponds to `&mut` T (mutable reference type in safe Rust). Unlike Rust reference types, these raw pointers can have both immutable and mutable pointers to a value at the same time or have multiple pointers simultaneously to the same value in memory. There is no automatic cleanup of memory when these pointers go out of scope, and these pointers can be null or refer to invalid memory locations too. The guarantees provided by Rust for memory safety do not apply to these pointer types. Examples of how to define and access pointers in an unsafe block are shown next:

```
fn main() {
    let mut a_number = 5;
    // Create an immutable pointer to the value 5
    let raw_ptr1 = &a_number as *const i32;
    // Create a mutable pointer to the value 5
    let raw_ptr2 = &mut a_number as *mut i32;

    unsafe {
        println!("raw_ptr1 is: {}", *raw_ptr1);
        println!("raw_ptr2 is: {}", *raw_ptr2);
    }
}
```

You'll note from this code that we've simultaneously created both an immutable reference and a mutable reference to the same value, by casting from the corresponding immutable and mutable reference types. Note that to create the raw pointers, we do not need an `unsafe` block, but only for dereferencing them. This is because dereferencing a raw pointer may result in unpredictable behavior as the borrow checker does not take responsibility for verifying its validity or lifetime.

- **Accessing or modifying a mutable static variable**: Static variables have a fixed memory address and they can be marked as mutable. But if a static variable is marked as mutable, accessing and modifying it is an unsafe operation, and has to be enclosed in an `unsafe` block. In the example shown next, we are declaring a mutable static variable that is initialized with a default value for the number of threads to be spawned. Then, in the `main()` function, we are checking for an environment variable, which if specified will override the default. This override of the value in the static variable must be enclosed in an *unsafe* block:

```rust
static mut THREAD_COUNT: u32 = 4;
use std::env::var;
fn change_thread_count(count: u32) {
    unsafe {
        THREAD_COUNT = count;
    }
}
fn main() {
    if let Some(thread_count) =
        var("THREAD_COUNT").ok() {
        change_thread_count(thread_count.parse::
            <u32>()
            .unwrap());
    };
    unsafe {
        println!("Thread count is: {}", THREAD_COUNT);
    }
}
```

This code snippet shows the declaration of a mutable static variable, THREAD_COUNT, initialized to 4. When the `main()` function executes, it looks for an environmental variable with the name THREAD_COUNT. If the `env` variable is found, it calls the `change_thread_count()` function, which mutates the value of the static variable in an `unsafe` block. The `main()` function then prints out the value in an `unsafe` block.

- **Implementing an unsafe trait**: Let's try to understand this with an example. Let's say we have a custom struct containing a raw pointer that we want to *send* or *share* across threads. Recall from *Chapter 9*, *Managing Concurrency*, that for a type to be sent or shared across threads, it needs to implement the `Send` or `Sync` traits. To implement these two traits for the raw pointer, we have to use unsafe Rust, as shown:

```
struct MyStruct(*mut u16);
unsafe impl Send for MyStruct {}
unsafe impl Sync for MyStruct {}
```

The reason for the `unsafe` keyword is because raw pointers have untracked ownership, which then becomes the responsibility of the programmer to track and manage.

There are two more features of unsafe Rust that are related to interfacing with other programming languages, which we will discuss in the next section on FFIs.

Introducing FFIs

In this section, we'll understand what FFI is, and then see the two unsafe Rust features related to FFI.

To understand FFI, let's look at the following two examples:

- There is a blazing-fast machine learning algorithm written in Rust for linear regression. A Java or Python developer wants to use this Rust library. How can this be done?

- You want to make Linux **syscalls** without using the Rust Standard Library (which essentially means you want to either implement a feature that's not available in the standard library or want to improve an existing feature). How would you do it?

While there may be other ways to solve this problem, one popular method is to use FFI.

In the first example, you can wrap the Rust library with an FFI defined in Java or Python. In the second example, Rust has a keyword, `extern`, with which an FFI to a C function can be set up and called. Let's see an example of the second case next:

```
use std::ffi::{CStr, CString};
use std::os::raw::c_char;
extern "C" {
    fn getenv(s: *const c_char) -> *mut c_char;
}
```

```
fn main() {
    let c1 = CString::new("MY_VAR").expect("Error");
    unsafe {
        println!("env got is {:?}", CStr::from_ptr(getenv(
            c1.as_ptr())));
    }
}
```

Here, in the `main()` function, we are invoking the `getenv()` external C function (instead of directly using the Rust Standard Library) to retrieve the value of the `MY_VAR` environment variable. The `getenv()` function accepts a `*const c_char` type parameter as input. To create this type, we are first instantiating the `CString` type, passing in the name of the environment variable, and then converting it into the required function input parameter type using the `as_ptr()` method. The `getenv()` function returns a `*mut c_char` type. To convert this into a Rust-compatible type, we are using the `CStr::from_ptr()` function.

Note the two main considerations here:

- We are specifying the call to the C function within an `extern "C"` block. This block contains the signature of the function that we want to call. Note that the data types in the function are not Rust data types, but those that belong to C.
- We are importing a couple of modules – `std::ffi` and `std::os::raw` – from the Rust Standard Library. The `ffi` module provides utility functions and data structures related to FFI bindings, which makes it easier to do data mapping across non-Rust interfaces. We are using the `CString` and `CStr` types from the `ffi` module, to transfer UTF-8 strings to and from C. The `os::raw` module contains platform-specific types that map to the C data types so that the Rust code that interacts with C will refer to the correct types.

Now, let's run the program using the following:

```
MY_VAR="My custom value" cargo -v run --bin ffi
```

You'll see the value of `MY_VAR` printed out to the console. With this, we have successfully retrieved the value of an environment variable using a call to an external C function.

Recall that we learned how to get and set environment variables in previous chapters using the Rust Standard Library. Now we have done something similar, but this time using the Rust FFI interface to invoke a C library function. Note that the call to the C function is enclosed in an `unsafe` block.

So far, we've seen how to invoke a C function from Rust. Later, in the *Calling Rust from C (project)* section, we'll see how to do it the other way around, that is, invoke a Rust function from C.

Let's now take a look at another feature of unsafe Rust, which is to define and access fields of a union struct, for communicating with a C function across an FFI interface.

Unions are data structures used in C, and are not memory-safe. This is because in a union type, you can set the instance of a `union` to one of the invariants and access it as another invariant. Rust does not directly provide `union` as a type in safe Rust. Rust, however, has a type of union called a **tagged union**, which is implemented as the `enum` data type in safe Rust. Let's see an example of `union`:

```
#[repr(C)]
union MyUnion {
    f1: u32,
    f2: f32,
}
fn main() {
    let float_num = MyUnion {f2: 2.0};
    let f = unsafe { float_num.f2 };
    println!("f is {:.3}",f);
}
```

In the code shown, we are first using a `repr(C)` annotation, which tells the compiler that the order, size, and alignment of fields in the `MyUnion` union is what you would expect in the C language (we'll discuss more about `repr(C)` in the *Understanding the ABI* section). We're then defining two invariants of the union: one is an integer of type `u32` and the other is a float of type `f32`. For any given instance of this union, only one of these invariants is valid. In the code, we're creating an instance of this union, initializing it with a `float` invariant, and then accessing its value from the `unsafe` block.

Run the program with the following:

```
cargo run
```

You'll see the value `f is 2.000` printed to your terminal. So far, it looks right. Now, let's try to access the union as an integer, instead of a float type. To do this, just alter one line of code. Locate the following line:

```
let f = unsafe { float_num.f2 };
```

Change it to the following:

```
let f = unsafe { float_num.f1 };
```

Run the program again. This time, you won't get an error but you'll see an invalid value printed like this. The reason is that the value in the memory location pointed to is now being interpreted as an integer even though we had stored a float value:

```
f is 1073741824
```

Using unions in C is dangerous unless it is done with the utmost care, and Rust provides the ability to work with unions as part of unsafe Rust.

So far, you've seen what unsafe Rust and FFI are. You've also seen examples of calling unsafe and external functions. In the next section, we'll discuss guidelines for creating safe FFI interfaces.

Reviewing guidelines for safe FFIs

In this section, we'll look at a few guidelines to keep in mind while interfacing with other languages using FFI in Rust:

- **The extern keyword**: Any foreign function defined with an `extern` keyword in Rust is inherently unsafe, and such calls must be done from an `unsafe` block.

- **Data layout**: Rust does not provide guarantees on how data is laid out in memory, because it takes charge of allocations, reallocations, and deallocations. But when working with other (foreign) languages, explicit use of a C-compatible layout (using the `#repr(C)` annotation) is important to maintain memory safety. We've seen an example earlier of how to use this. Another thing to note is that only C-compatible types should be used as parameters or return values for external functions. Examples of C-compatible types in Rust include integers, floats, `repr(C)`-annotated structs, and pointers. Examples of Rust types incompatible with C include trait objects, dynamically sized types, and enums with fields. There are tools available such as `rust-bindgen` and `cbindgen` that can help in generating types that are compatible between Rust and C (with some caveats).

- **Platform-dependent types**: C has many platform-dependent types, such as `int` and `long`, which means the exact length of these types vary based on the platform architecture. When interacting with C functions that use these types, the Rust Standard Library `std::raw` module can be used, which offers type aliases that are portable across platforms. `c_char` and `c_uint` are two examples of raw types we used in an example earlier. In addition to the standard library, the `libc` crate also provides such portable type aliases for these data types.

- **References and pointers**: Due to differences between C's pointer types and Rust's reference types, Rust code should not use reference types but rather pointer types while working across FFI boundaries. Any Rust code that dereferences a pointer type must make null checks before use.

- **Memory management**: Each programming language has its own way of doing memory management. When transmitting data between language boundaries, it is important to be clear about which language has the responsibility to release memory, to avoid *double-free* or *use-after-free* issues. It is recommended practice for Rust code to not implement the `Drop` trait for any type that is transmitted directly to foreign code. It is even safer to use only `Copy` types for use across FFI boundaries.

- **Panic**: When calling Rust from other language code, it must be ensured that the Rust code does not panic, or it should use a panic-handling mechanism such as `std::panic::catch_unwind` or `#[panic_handler]` (which we saw in *Chapter 9*, *Managing Concurrency*). This will ensure that the Rust code will not abort or return in an unstable state.

- **Exposing a Rust library to a foreign language**: Exposing a Rust library and its functions to a foreign language (such as Java, Python, or Ruby) should only be done through a C-compatible API.

This concludes the section on writing safe FFI interfaces. In the next section, we'll see an example of using a Rust library from C code.

Calling Rust from C (project)

In this section, we will demonstrate the setup needed to build a Rust shared library (with a `.so` extension on Linux) incorporating an FFI interface and invoke it from a C program. The C program would be a simple program that just prints out a greeting message. The example is deliberately kept simple to enable you (as you're not expected to be familiar with complex C syntax) to focus on the steps involved, and for easy verification of this first FFI program in a variety of operating system environments.

Here are the steps that we will go through to develop and test a working example of a C program that calls a function from a Rust library using the FFI interface:

1. Create a new Cargo lib project.

2. Modify `Cargo.toml` to specify that we want a shared library to be built.

3. Write an FFI in Rust (in the form of a C-compatible API).

4. Build the Rust shared library.

5. Verify whether the Rust shared library has been built correctly.

6. Create a C program that invokes a function from the Rust shared library.

7. Build the C program specifying the path of the Rust shared library.

8. Set `LD_LIBRARY_PATH`.

9. Run the C program.

Let's get going and execute the aforementioned steps:

1. Create a new cargo project:

   ```
   cargo new --lib ffi && cd ffi
   ```

2. Add the following to `Cargo.toml`:

   ```
   [lib]
   name = "ffitest"
   crate-type = ["dylib"]
   ```

3. Write an FFI in Rust in `src/lib.rs`:

   ```
   #[no_mangle]
   pub extern "C" fn see_ffi_in_action() {
       println!("Congrats! You have successfully invoked
           Rust shared library from a C program");
   }
   ```

The `#[no_mangle]` annotation tells the Rust compiler that the `see_ffi_in_action()` function should be accessible to external programs with the same name. Otherwise, by default, the Rust compiler alters it.

The function uses the extern "C" keyword. As discussed earlier, the Rust compiler makes any functions marked with extern compatible with C code. The "C" keyword in extern "C" indicates the standard C calling convention on the target platform. In this function, we are simply printing out a greeting.

4. Build the Rust shared library from the ffi folder with the following command:

```
cargo build --release
```

If the build completes successfully, you'll see a shared library with the name libffitest.so, created in the target/release directory.

5. Verify whether the shared library has been built correctly:

```
nm -D target/release/libffitest.so | grep see_ffi_in_
action
```

The nm command-line utility is used to examine binary files (including libraries and executables) and view the symbols in these object files. Here, we are checking whether the function that we have written is included in the shared library. You should see a result similar to this:

```
000000000005df30 T see_ffi_in_action
```

If you don't see something similar, the shared library may not have been built correctly. Please revisit the previous steps. (Note that the shared library is created with a .dylib extension on the Mac platform.)

6. Let's create a C program that invokes the function from the Rust shared library that we have built. Create a rustffi.c file in the root of the ffi project folder and add the following code:

```
#include "rustffi.h"
int main(void) {
        see_ffi_in_action();
}
```

This is a simple C program that includes a header file and has a main() function that in turn invokes a see_ffi_in_action() function. At this point, the C program does not know where this function is located. We'll provide this information to the C compiler when we build the binary. Let's now write the header file that's referred to in this program. Create a rustffi.h file in the same folder as the C source file, and include the following:

```
void see_ffi_in_action();
```

This header file declares the function signature, which denotes that this function does not return any value or take any input parameter.

7. Build the C binary with the following command, from the root folder of the project:

```
gcc rustffi.c -Ltarget/release -lffitest -o ffitest
```

Let's break up the command for better understanding:

gcc: Invokes the GCC compiler.

-Ltarget/release: The -L flag specifies to the compiler to look for the shared library in the folder target/release.

-lffitest: The -l flag tells the compiler that the name of the shared library is ffitest. Note that the actual library built is called libffitest.so, but the compiler knows that the lib prefix and .so suffix are part of the standard shared library name, so it is sufficient to specify ffitest for the -l flag.

rustffi.c: This is the source file to be compiled.

-o ffitest: Tells the compiler to generate the output executable with the name ffitest.

8. Set the LD_LIBRARY_PATH environment variable, which in Linux specifies the paths in which the libraries will be searched:

```
export LD_LIBRARY_PATH=$(rustc --print sysroot)/
lib:target/release:$LD_ LIBRARY_PATH
```

9. Run the executable with the following:

```
./ffitest
```

You should see the following message displayed on your terminal:

```
Congrats! You have successfully invoked Rust shared library
from a C program
```

If you have reached this far, congratulations!

You have written a shared library in Rust that contains a function with a C-compatible API. You have then invoked this Rust library from a C program. This is FFI in action.

Understanding the ABI

This section provides a brief introduction to the ABI and a few related (advanced) features of Rust that deal with conditional compilation options, data layout conventions, and link options.

The **ABI** is a set of conventions and standards that compilers and linkers adhere to, for function-calling conventions, and for specifying data layouts (type, alignment, offset).

To understand the significance of the ABI, let's draw an analogy with APIs, which are a well-known concept in application programming. When a program wants to access an external component or library at the source-code level, it looks for the definition of the API exposed by that external component. The external component can be a library or an external service accessible over the network. The API specifies the name of the functions that can be called, the parameters (along with their names and data types) that need to be passed to invoke the function, and the type of value returned from the function.

An ABI can be seen as the equivalent of an API but at the binary level. The compiler and linker need a way to specify how a calling program can locate the called function within a binary object file, and how to deal with the arguments and return values (types and order of arguments and return type). But unlike source code, in the case of the binaries produced, details such as the length of integers, padding rules, and whether the function parameters are stored on the stack or registers vary by platform architecture (for example, x86, x64, AArch32) and operating system (for example, Linux and Windows). A 64-bit operating system can have different ABIs for executing 32-bit and 64-bit binaries. A Windows-based program will not know how to access a library built on Linux, as they use different ABIs.

While the study of ABIs is a specialized topic in itself, it is sufficient to understand the significance of ABIs and see what features Rust provides to specify ABI-related parameters while writing code. We'll cover the following – *conditional compilation options*, *data layout conventions*, and *link options*:

- **Conditional compilation options**: Rust allows specifying conditional compilation options using the `cfg` macro. The following are examples of `cfg` options:

  ```
  #[cfg(target_arch = "x86_64")]
  #[cfg(target_os = "linux")]
  #[cfg(target_family = "windows")]
  #[cfg(target_env = "gnu")]
  #[cfg(target_pointer_width = "32")]
  ```

These annotations are attached to a function declaration as shown in this example:

```
// Only if target OS is Linux and architecture is x86,
// include this function in build
#[cfg(all(target_os = "linux", target_arch = "x86"))]
// all conditions must be true
fn do_something() { // ... }
```

More details about the various conditional compilation options can be found at https://doc.rust-lang.org/reference/conditional-compilation.html.

• **Data layout conventions**: Apart from the platform and operating system considerations, data layout is another aspect that is important to understand, especially while transferring data across FFI boundaries.

In Rust, as in other languages, type, alignment, and offsets are associated with its data elements. For example, say you declare a struct of the following type:

```
struct MyStruct {
    member1: u16,
    member2: u8,
    member3: u32,
}
```

It may be represented internally, as shown, on a processor with 32-bit (4-byte) word size:

```
struct Mystruct {
    member1: u16,
    _padding1: [u8; 2], // to make overall size
                        // multiple of 4
    member2: u8,
    _padding2: [u8; 3], // to align `member2`
    member3: u32,
}
```

This is done in order to reconcile the differences in the integer sizes with the processor word size. The idea is that the whole struct will have a size that's a multiple of 32 bits, and there may be multiple layout options to achieve this. This internal layout for Rust data structures can also be annotated as #[repr(Rust)]. But if there is data that needs to pass through an FFI boundary, the accepted standard is to use the data layout of C (annotated as #[repr(C)]). In this layout, the order, size, and alignment of fields are as it is done in C programs. This is important to ensure the compatibility of data across the FFI boundary.

Rust guarantees that if the #[repr(C)] attribute is applied to a struct, the layout of the struct will be compatible with the platform's representation in C. There are automated tools, such as cbindgen, that can help generate the C data layout from Rust programs.

- **Link options**: The third aspect we will cover regarding calling functions from other binaries is the link annotation. Take the following example:

```
#[link(name = "my_library")]
extern {
    static a_c_function() -> c_int;
}
```

The #[link(...)] attribute is used to instruct the linker to link against my_ library in order to resolve the symbols. It instructs the Rust compiler how to link to native libraries. This annotation can also be used to specify the kind of library to link to (*static* or *dynamic*). The following annotation tells rustc to link to a *static* library with the name my_other_library:

```
#[link(name = "my_other_library", kind = "static")]
```

In this section, we've seen what an ABI is and its significance. We've also looked at how to specify instructions to the compiler and linker through various annotations in code, for aspects such as the target platform, operating system, data layout, and link instructions.

This concludes this section. The intent of this section was only to introduce a few advanced topics related to the ABI, FFI, and associated instructions to the compiler and linker. For more details, refer to the following link: https://doc.rust-lang.org/ nomicon/.

Summary

In this chapter, we reviewed the basics of unsafe Rust and understood the key differences between safe and unsafe Rust. We saw how unsafe Rust enables us to perform operations that would not be allowed in safe Rust, such as dereferencing raw pointers, accessing or mutating static variables, working with unions, implementing unsafe traits, and calling external functions. We also looked at what a foreign function interface is, and how to write one in Rust. We wrote an example of invoking a C function from Rust. Also, in the example project, we wrote a Rust shared library and invoked it from a C program. We saw guidelines for how to write safe FFIs in Rust. We took a look at the ABI and annotations that can be used to specify conditional compilation, data layout, and link options.

With this, we conclude this chapter, and also this book.

I thank you for joining me on this journey into the world of system programming with Rust, and wish you the very best with exploring the topic further.

Other Books You May Enjoy

If you enjoyed this book, you may be interested in these other books by Packt:

Creative Projects for Rust Programmers

Carlo Milanesi

ISBN: 978-1-78934-622-0

- Access TOML, JSON, and XML files and SQLite, PostgreSQL, and Redis databases
- Develop a RESTful web service using JSON payloads
- Create a web application using HTML templates and JavaScript and a frontend web application or web game using WebAssembly
- Build desktop 2D games
- Develop an interpreter and a compiler for a programming language
- Create a machine language emulator
- Extend the Linux Kernel with loadable modules

Rust Programming Cookbook

Claus Matzinger

ISBN: 978-1-78953-066-7

- Understand how Rust provides unique solutions to solve system programming language problems
- Grasp the core concepts of Rust to develop fast and safe applications
- Explore the possibility of integrating Rust units into existing applications for improved efficiency
- Discover how to achieve better parallelism and security with Rust
- Write Python extensions in Rust
- Compile external assembly files and use the Foreign Function Interface (FFI)
- Build web applications and services using Rust for high performance

Leave a review - let other readers know what you think

Please share your thoughts on this book with others by leaving a review on the site that you bought it from. If you purchased the book from Amazon, please leave us an honest review on this book's Amazon page. This is vital so that other potential readers can see and use your unbiased opinion to make purchasing decisions, we can understand what our customers think about our products, and our authors can see your feedback on the title that they have worked with Packt to create. It will only take a few minutes of your time, but is valuable to other potential customers, our authors, and Packt. Thank you!

Index

Symbols

A

B

C

S

www.ingramcontent.com/pod-product-compliance
Lightning Source LLC
Chambersburg PA
CBHW060922060326
40690CB00041B/2987